WHY WE ARE COMING

Yasin Kakande

D1524087

WHY WE ARE COMING

Yasin Kakande

Dedicated to the memory of my parents
Hajjati Hadija Nakkazi and Mr. Edirisa Kalule

CONTENTS

INTRODUCTION

I began work on this book in the winter of 2017, having arrived in the U.S. and applied for asylum only a few months after the election that sent Donald Trump to the White House. The electorate—enough of it at least—had bought into his monochrome narrative of blunt jingoism and simple solutions and lifted him to office. His was a pantomime politics with a cast of American heroes and migrant villains; that framed any newcomer to the States as at worst a dangerous criminal and at best a societal parasite feeding on tax-funded public assistance programs. True to at least part of its word the Administration ratcheted up already rigorous and restrictive policies towards migrants. My timing could have not been less auspicious.

The U.S. was not my first destination. For more than a decade I worked in the Middle East as a migrant journalist and my exit from both the countries to which I had migrated, was ugly[i]. Furthermore, I tried my best to stay in my homeland Uganda, but the economic, social, and political conditions made life as I envisaged it, impossible. The concept of economic inequality does not characterize adequately the circumstances in Uganda, where everyone struggles to earn a sustainable income and the country's most valuable resources have been stripped by foreign interests.

I offer the concerned reader an explanation for the migrant crisis, one that is delivered in the first person singular because I have lived it. I am not a freeloader. Indeed, I am just like you but come from a world that you can't imagine. I am going to help you to see and understand that world in order that you can empathize with those who leave it in order to come to yours. I answer the question: why we are coming? First, I frame this as a moral question in an historical context. Migration is driven by the human desire to escape

---

i   I worked in the United Arab Emirates reporting for local newspapers for ten years. I published my first book *The Ambitious Struggle: An African Journalist's Journey to Hope and Identity in a Land of Migrants*. My second book *Slave States: The practice of Kafala in the Gulf Arab Countries* was published while I was working in Qatar.

poverty, corruption, and tyranny in the undeveloped and underdeveloped world. These circumstances are the legacy of the West's interaction with that world: colonialism, slavery, neo-colonialism, dictatorship by proxy, and corporate adventurism. That legacy is deeply enmeshed not only with the society of my homeland but also with that of nearly every country in Africa. So, this story elucidates a complex picture and traces a long, historical arc to explain why migrants flee their homelands rather than staying to resist, in the hopes of achieving true political and economic reform.

Into the fabric of my historical material is woven a moral thread. The single most important unifying strand of every major moral philosophical ideal in human civilization is the recognition that every human is of equal moral value. Many migrants see their homeland inundated with long-term seemingly insoluble problems. They see the West as a lifeboat transporting individuals to a harbor that opens up to a landscape of progress and development. Migrants will take on any risk to get aboard the lifeboat because the only alternative is to drown. The only sensible question is why are the people in treacherous water not as important as the people in the boat.

That moral question is central to both the issue and the experience of migration but, putting it aside, we can see both in purely material—economic and political—terms. The U.S. in particular benefits enormously from the huge inflow of migrants—both documented and undocumented—who provide cheap labor in virtually every sector of the economy, and particularly in those in which Americans would prefer not to work: the 3Ds of dirty, dangerous, and demeaning. However, few Americans understand and still less acknowledge that significance. Migrants work in agriculture and hospitality, but we will focus here on a sector that is as important as it is neglected: caregiving. As the American population continues to age, the demand for caregivers—mostly immigrants—will continue to rise.

Despite the inflammatory rhetoric of both the Nativist politicians, there are many Americans who do not see migrants as dangerous intruders. Likewise, the American media have investigated and reported stories that contradict and challenge the political rhetoric. As Americans prepare for the next presidential election, they understand that some politicians have projected disparaging portrayals of migrants to foment anger, resentment, and fear that have led voters to cast ballots without stopping to think about the multidimensional moral, economic, and political consequences of their decision.

The book's overall objective is simple. Migrants are asking only that the truth is acknowledged and that they are allowed to live and work here legally. Like any American, they aspire to become productive and grateful contributors in a land where hard work and commitment are rewarded.

SECTION I: SLAVERY

Chapter 1: How it all started

"Whenever I hear anyone arguing for slavery, I feel a strong impulse to see it tried on him personally." President Abraham Lincoln

In late 2017, the U.S. media outlet Cable News Network (CNN) aired reports of West African migrants in the latter stages of their journey to Europe, who had been sold openly in slave markets in Libya. The reports generated widespread condemnation as audiences watched footage of Arab slave traders selling individual people—who were to be used as farm workers—for as little as $400.[1]

Libyan officials refuted the original CNN report by echoing the *fake news* mantra that President Donald Trump has made so familiar, especially when dismissing this particular network.[2] The story received a brief flurry of attention in the established media, the story would have faded into the background but for the efforts a number of Hip Hop stars—Cardi B, T. I., Nas, Diddy, Common, Pharrell, Azealia Banks and Fat Joe—who brought sustained interest to bear on the issues raised by the report by mobilizing their followers on social media.[ii]

But, for many Africans, the risk of being captured and sold into slavery remains acutely familiar. The CNN revelations suggested that some Africans were so desperate for freedom that they knowingly accepted the risks of entering slavery. Unlike his aforementioned peers in the music industry, American rapper Kanye West publicly speculated that the ancient practice of slavery always was predicated as a choice.

That people would submit to slavery—would willingly give up what little freedom they have in Africa in exchange for nothing

ii   Cardi B in particular made an Instagram video that went viral cursing the United Nations for letting the situation in Libya deteriorate so much to the extent of selling people. See https://www.youtube.com/watch?v=9rbgvPElcuk.

more than the hope of freedom in Europe—is emblematic both of the depth of their despair and the intensity of their aspiration. But the defining characteristic of the migrant crisis is not this scale. Never in the history of the African continent has such desperation about the distant realms of freedom and economic independence pushed so many people to attempt this long and dangerous journey as in the 21st century. Yet, few are willing to confront a long yet still active record that contextualizes why slavery remains such an indelible stain on human history. Furthermore, the number of Africans who drown in stormy seas en route to Europe has not deterred their peers from trying their luck. In fact, if it is true as some critics say, that Europe's strategy to defend herself from migration is one of "letting people drown to deter others in desperate need,"[iii] then it is a mistaken one: the stream of migration grows continuously despite the present dangers.

No one has addressed adequately the root causes which would be required to find a meaningful solution. Leaders of many western governments seem to hope the refugee crisis will eventually exhaust itself completely. It is rare to find anyone willing to address the question with political courage: What leads millions of people to leave their homes? If it is wars, as some contend, then end them. If it is naked exploitation, then honestly find humane solutions.

Forced migration has always been at the center of slavery. It is what brought Africans to the American shores to keep and expand a growing agricultural economy in the nascent American colonies. Later, it would become the impetus for the Industrial Revolution and the development of mass manufacturing. To the observer, 21st century migration seems to be wholly different from the vast intercontinental

---

iii   In September 2018, Doctors Without Borders blamed Italy for refusing to dispatch a rescue ship to save migrants on a sinking boat, as a result 100 people drowned. Similarly, at least 20 people trying to reach Europe from Libya drowned in the Mediterranean on Nov. 6, 2017, not far from the raft was a ship belonging to Sea Watch, a German humanitarian organization. That ship had enough space on it for everyone who had been aboard the raft. It could have brought them all to the safety of Europe, Instead Sea-Watch's ship and rescue rafts did document the entire scene in video and audio on nine cameras.

displacements of the Age of Empire, because it is based on choice. That *choice*, the nature and quality of it lies at the heart both of the migrant experience and of this argument. I am a migrant. I know that it is not a choice in the positive sense of the word. It is an act of forced migration one takes but soon realizes that it really is slavery reengineered with nuances and subtleties that encumber a false set of promises that will never deliver the legal work protections and benefits advertised by those who seek and welcome migrants into their workplaces and countries.

Slavery and mass migration have always been at the center of African history. It is a story both of the people who are enslaved and of the communities from which they were taken. The transatlantic slave trade that consolidated the economies of the Americas as well as the nations in the southern Atlantic and Caribbean region, transported African slaves classified as cargo to the Americas as quickly and cheaply as possible. They would then be sold to work on coffee, tobacco, rice, cocoa, sugar, and cotton plantations; in gold and silver mines; in the construction industry, cutting timber for ships, for example, and then as skilled labor, and as domestic servants.[3] At the peak of the slave trade in the 18th century, more than 20 million young Africans were displaced.

But what of the various social, economic, and political institutions from which those millions had been removed? In many American cities, there are numerous discussions about the *brain drain*, in which young people leave their communities believing they no longer can sustain their career and economic aspirations. The timeframe is a few decades, or perhaps one or two generations. In Africa, the centuries-old practice of stealing the continent's most energetic and strong youth cemented a near-fatalistic prophecy of never being able to recover or sustain a thriving economy worthy of a legacy for young people. Nzinga Mbemba Affonzo, a prominent African King who ruled the kingdom now known as the present-day Congo in the early 16th century, was, unusual among his peers in being literate. Indeed, he had become well-versed in the European ways of communication and petitioned European leaders, including the King of Portugal and the

Pope, regarding the pernicious effects of the slave trade on his kingdom. The following is a transcript of one letter he exchanged with the King Joao III of Portugal in 1526:

> Each day the traders are kidnapping our people—
> children of this country, sons of our nobles and vas-
> sals, even people of our own family . . . This corrup-
> tion and depravity are so widespread that our land
> is entirely depopulated . . . We need in this kingdom
> only priests and schoolteachers, and no merchandise,
> unless it is wine and flour for Mass . . . It is our wish
> that this Kingdom not be a place for the trade or
> transport of slaves.[4]

In the same year he sent a follow-up communique:

> Many of our subjects eagerly lust after the Portu-
> guese merchandise that your subjects have brought
> into our domains. To satisfy this inordinate appetite,
> they seize many of our black free subjects . . . They
> sell them . . . after having taken these prisoners (to
> the coast) secretly or at night . . . As soon as the cap-
> tives are in the hands of white men they are branded
> with red hot iron.

King Joao replied,

> You . . . tell me that you want no slave trading in your
> domains, because this trade is depopulating your
> country . . . The Portuguese there, on the contrary,
> tell me how vast the Congo is, and how it is so thickly
> populated that it seems as if no slave has ever left.

Meanwhile, Zanzibar was once East Africa's main slave-trading port. Under the supervision of Omani Arabs in the 19th century, as many as 50,000 slaves were passed through the city each year. The famous missionary and explorer David Livingstone estimated that 80,000 Africans died each year before ever reaching the slave markets of Zanzibar.[5] No African ever returned from the Americas so if one was captured, one could only guess at the dire consequences awaiting them.

Some historians have investigated the dangers risked by Africans who tried to escape. The journey on the open waters was terrifying. For every 100 Africans captured, only 64 would reach the coast, and only about 50 would reach the New World.[6] Stephanie Smallwood in her book *Saltwater Slavery* references Equiano's account on board ships to describe the general thoughts going through the minds of most slaves. "What shocked Africans the most was how death was handled in the ships," Smallwood writes, adding the,

> traditions for handling and commemorating an African's death were delicate in its cultural traditions and was community based. On ships, bodies would be thrown into the open sea. Because the sea represented bad omens, bodies in the sea represented a form of purgatory and the ship, a form of hell. In the end, the Africans who made the journey would have survived disease, malnutrition, confined space, close death, and the trauma of the ship.

The irony came in the trauma for those who survived—a scar that has remained almost as painful to this day.

In the history of the continent, Affonzo is notable as an example of a conscientious and concerned leader—an enlightened exception to the rule of despotism—whose benevolent reign has garnered him enduring respect among Africans. By contrast, his contemporaries were cutting deals with European traders to exchange their citizens for textiles, just as today in a more formal way, the European Union is seeking to cut deals with African countries to prevent and discourage their citizens from migrating to Europe. This effort has focused on Niger, Libya, and Morocco, from where African migrants—usually those who have come from the western regions of the continent—have taken boats to Europe. The agreement offers aid for development in exchange for tighter borders and threatens economic consequences if there is a failure to cooperate.

Chapter 2: European Opulence

"This European Opulence is literally a scandal for it was built on the backs of slaves, it fed on the blood of slaves, and owes its very existence to the soil and subsoil of the underdeveloped." Frantz Fanon

Bridgetown, Barbados's capital, was the first stopover for slave ships traveling from Africa. It was the busiest port in the Americas with gun batteries guarding the harbor. Indeed, no detail was overlooked, and no expense spared in the effort to fortify and defend the best interests of the net beneficiaries of the Slave Trade.

That trade depended heavily on sugar, the most important commodity in the contemporary geopolitical arena and nearly matching the global economic status and talismanic significance of oil in today's marketplace. Some 60 percent of slaves that were brought to the Americas were bound for the Caribbean where they would cultivate and harvest sugar cane.

Just as global demand for the commodity shaped the economic machinery of Slavery so the physical requirements of its cultivation, harvesting and refinement, formed the daily lives of the slaves. It was brutal work. As a field hand, a slave planted cane shoots in holes or trenches dug by hand, often in marshlands where the humid air was dense with insects including the potentially deadly mosquito. At harvest time, the worker carried huge, heavy bundles of cane to the processing mill, where each bundle was fed twice through powerful vertical rollers that squeezed out juice that then flowed into large copper vats situated in a *boilinghouse*, where it simmered before being strained, filtered, and allowed to crystallize into sugar.[7]

The process—from planting to refinement—demanded both skilled and unskilled labor, and that division lay almost entirely on the lines of gender; a reality that carried enormous consequences for the average enslaved female. Nearly all of the skilled jobs—like maintaining mill equipment, building sugar barrels, or doing masonry—went to men, which meant that the majority of slaves in the sugar cane fields were women. The relentless hard labor required—in conjunction with a diet so poor it bordered on malnourishment—had a terrible impact on the women who were forced to endure these conditions. The physiological impact was measurable in the form of delayed menarche and shortened phases of fertility, which in turn meant women were no longer able to conceive or give birth by the time they reached their middle thirties. Indeed, in mid-18th century British West Indies, fully half of all women slaves who lived and worked on sugar plantations would never bear a child.

This personal human cost to the health of the individual female slaves concerned had consequences for the functionality of the institution of Slavery. The extraordinarily low birth rate, the working conditions of stoop labor that incapacitated many, the risk of early death from disease, combined to render so many of the female slaves infertile, ill, injured or dead, that the slave population could not regenerate; it was not sustainable. As a result, the Caribbean economy and the slave owners at its helm retained an insatiable appetite for fresh slaves from Africa.[8]

With its demand supply of slaves guaranteed, Barbados thrived on the world's demand for sugar. But the story of the success of England's first, experimental, tropical, agricultural export colony is somewhat more nuanced than this statement suggests. Barbados had for some time functioned as the de facto English capital of the Caribbean when, with the Crown's blessing, its settlement was realized in 1627. Market conditions for its first commercial crop, tobacco, enabled the accumulation of quick profits, which were later utilized to finance the shift to sugar production in the 1650s.[iv] This occurred after large-scale, high quality Virginian tobacco production caused a glut on the European market and commodity prices plummeted. By the late 17th century a contemporary writer proclaimed it the "richest spote of ground in the worlde."[9]

In just twenty years, the Sugar Revolution transformed the face of Barbados forever. The pristine tropical luxuries gave way to a carefully controlled garden-like appearance across the entire island, as a result of near total deforestation. The human environment

iv   This change occurred after large-scale, high quality Virginian tobacco production caused a glut on the European market and commodity prices plummeted.

too was radically re-modelled by Revolution; the demographic and economic change that came with it shaped a new society. The commodity demanded massive amounts of intense labor, the source of which poured into Barbados in increasingly large quantities on the form of African slaves. Sugar production made the island not only the most populated of England's overseas colonies, but also one of the most densely populated places in the world.[10]

Slavery as an institution was a vital component in the engine of the global economy. Here Herman Merivale an English historian of the 19th century writes of the centrality of both to the daily commercial experience of the ordinary trader or consumer:

> We speak of the blood cemented fabric of the prosperity of New Orleans or Havana; let us look at home. What raised Liverpool and Manchester from provincial towns to gigantic cities? What maintains now their ever active industry and their rapid accumulation of wealth? The exchange of their produce with that raised by the American slaves; and their present opulence is really owing to the toil and suffering of the negro, as if hands had excavated their docks and fabricated their steam engine. Every trader who carries on commerce with those countries, from the great house which lends its name and funds to support the credit of the American Bank, down to the Birmingham merchant who makes a shipment of shackles to Cuba or the coast of Africa, is in his own way an upholder of slavery; and I do not see how any consumer who drinks coffee or wears cotton can escape from the same sweeping charge.[11]

As a practice Slavery was endemic across the New World. An estimated 4.9 million slaves from Africa were brought to Brazil during the period of 1501 to 1866, which explains why Brazil, behind Nigeria, has the highest numbers of people with African heritage. Slave labor was the driving force in Brazil's sugar economy and sugar was the former Portuguese colony's primary export for the first half of the 17th century. Most slaves arriving in Brazil left from the port of Luanda in another of Portugal's colonies, Angola. And Brazil's demand for slaves, already vast, increased when gold and diamond deposits were discovered in Brazil in 1690.[12]

The primacy and success of slavery in Brazil during the 16th century emboldened other polities in Central America and the Caribbean—including Hispaniola[v], Cuba, Jamaica, Guatemala, Honduras, and the eventual United States to take up the slave trade. It is worth noting that slavery had been so integral to life in Brazil that the country Brazil was the last of the great imperial slave states, the last country in the Western world to abolish slavery—in 1888, almost a quarter of a century after the end of the American U.S. Civil War ended. Brazil's experience with slavery during the 16th century emboldened other American destinations including Hispaniola (present-day Haiti and Dominican Republic), Cuba, Jamaica, Guatemala, Honduras, and the eventual United States to take up the slave trade.

The American experience, however, was unlike that of Brazil. The developmental progress of the young American colonies in the 17th century was confounded by resolving their problems of scarcity of labor markets. Transatlantic migrants who had come to the colonies in search of hoping for more favorable terms and benefits of employment were painfully disappointed. In England, indentured servitude contracts for farm workers were short term—, no more than a year—but in America, they could expect such punitive arrangements to last for many years. However, in the American colonies, governors managed to stretch their contracts to seven years. In the words of Edmund Morgan, who wrote the acclaimed 1975 book *American Slavery, American Freedom: The Ordeal of Colonial Virginia*, chronicled the changes taking place in a booming colonial economy during the 17th century. He wrote,

> "We may also see Virginians beginning to move toward a system of labor that treated men as things. In order to make the most out of the high price of tobacco it was necessary to get hard work out of Englishmen who were not

---

v   The Caribbean island now shared by the sovereign states of Haiti and the Dominican Republic.

used to giving it. The boom produced, and in
some measure depended upon, a tightening of
labor discipline beyond what had been known
in England and probably beyond what had been
formerly known in Virginia."[13]

This rocky relationship between the demand and supply of labor;
between the frustrated ambition of Virginia's landowners, and the
blighted expectations of the aspirant migrant worker, proved fertile
ground for slavery. The preference of Virginia's landed gentry, already shifting from white indentured servants to enslaved Africans,
was firmly anchored to the latter by Bacon's Rebellion of 1676–1677.
A change that gave rise to the slave system that epitomized the Old
South of the new America. What had started as a fight with Doeg
Indians on the Potomac River expanded into a civil war between
Virginia's established elite and colonial newcomers.

By the end of the 17th century, British immigration had stalled
while the population of African slaves was growing substantially. In 1660, there were fewer than 1,000 slaves in the Chesapeake
Bay region, which included the established colonies of Virginia and
Maryland. Twenty years later, the numbers had tripled in less than
a decade, rising from approximately 4,500 to 12,000. In the early
18th century, there was an average of eight slaves on each Virginia
plantation. By the time of the outbreak of the U.S. Civil War some
150 years later, the slave population in the Tidewater and Piedmont
regions of Virginia constituted a majority.

The slave trade continued to expand during the industrialization
of the19th century. And although improvements in cotton agriculture and harvesting—most notably the Cotton Gin—helped to
transform the United States from a minor European trading partner
into a major global economy, the mainstay of that economy remained
slave labor; a fact largely ignored by the contemporary chroniclers of
the economic and social miracle of the USA.

The commodification and enslavement of Africans on plantations in the Americas is what made Europe and the United States
powerful and rich. It is no surprise that Frantz Fanon, an Algerian
activist and author, would characterize European wealth in his book

The Wretched of the Earth as, "this European Opulence is literally a scandal for it was built on the backs of slaves, it fed on the blood of slaves, and owes its very existence to the soil and sub soil of the under developed."[14]

And the tension between the manifest relationship between prosperity and slavery, and personal and public respectability in ostensibly Christian societies was a constant theme in literature and discourse of the age. John Gladstone for example, a member of parliament and the father of a future (deeply Christian) prime minister, owned Caribbean sugar and coffee estates which were worked by more than one thousand slaves. Likewise, the cathedral-like library of Oxford's All Souls College was financed by profits from a slave plantation in Barbados. Family slave estates in Jamaica paid for an elegant house on Wimpole Street. William Beckford, with a vast fortune based on slave-grown Jamaican sugar cane, hosted the most sumptuous banquets known since the time of Henry VIII. He hired Mozart to give his son piano lessons. Edward Colston, a member of parliament, was the best-known philanthropist in Bristol: vestryman of his church; lavish benefactor of schools, poorhouses, hospitals and retired seamen; creator of the endowment that paid for sermons on specified subjects to be preached annually at several churches and the city jail. Colston proudly declared that "every helpless widow is my wife and her distressed orphans my children." In 1998, a large bronze statue of him that overlooks Bristol's Colston Avenue was vandalized with the inscription: "SLAVE TRADER."[15]

Slavery—here understood as the socio-economic machinery that captured Africans, transported them to the Americas to be traded, imprisoned, raped, beaten, coerced, bred, and killed—is surely by any measure of scale or quality, the most heinous crime to be visited on the society of one continent by that of another. Perhaps even more daunting than the vast canvas of slavery; the innumerable acts of violence of all kinds visited upon countless people across generations and hemispheres, is the extent to which they were enacted from behind the arm of a detailed, codified, legal validation of the concept of Africans as objects. The barbarous treatment regularly meted out on slaves was done so without fear of consequence because the intellectual concept of the institution did not consider the African slave to be a human being but rather a commodity, reiterating Morgan's earlier words. The slave had no rights but instead plenty of duties and obligations, as evidenced by the increasingly hard, cold legal codes the colonial governments adopted. "Slavery was not born of racism: rather, racism was the consequence of slavery," writes Eric Williams, a pioneering historian and the first prime minister of independent Trinidad and Tobago, in his seminal analysis *Capitalism & Slavery*. While working on the plantations that brought a lot of wealth for Europe, the slaves were tied in heavy chains to prevent them from running away. They were beaten while working just because beating them brought pleasures to their masters. They were never given enough food but just small provisions to keep them barely alive and working. At night, large groups of men, chained in groups numbering ten to fifty, were led to sleep in dark, foul-smelling cells, infested with mice and insects. They were denied even the comfort of a spacious sleep area that would be enjoyed by cattle. Their masters had the legal right to beat, exploit, and even kill mercilessly any slave. There was no legal recourse for the slave, and few could even contemplate gaining a modicum of moral support from a white working class that now had been unified in purpose with the elite gentry that owned and ran the colonial plantations. A slave's life had no worth and with his murder, there was no retaliation.[16]

The parent concept that conceived of people as property spawned a large and close-knit family of laws and norms that heaved on the chains that bound the ordinary slave. They were not taught to read or write; not allowed to gamble with whites; not privileged to own property, and not allowed to leave the plantation without a pass. They could not possess alcohol without their white masters' permission. They could not trade, traffic, or barter without a permit. They were subjected to the most desperate circumstances and they had little recourse of action without risking torture, imprisonment, or death. Many committed suicide, or rendered themselves useless through physical mutilation. They could attempt escape, revolt or insurrection, which many did, but the consequences ranged from flogging to tortured execution. Most slaves chose to survive under unimaginable circumstances. In exchange for being allowed to live, slaves were forced to accept the terms and conditions of bondage, and they were often assaulted by constant, often brutal reminders of their subordinated status.[17] Solomon Northrup, whose memoirs were adapted to the critically acclaimed film *12 Years a Slave* in 2013, wrote in 1853,

> There have been hours in my unhappy life, many of them, when the contemplation of death as the end of earthly sorrow—of the grave as a resting place for the tired and worn out body—has been pleasant to dwell upon. But such contemplations vanish in the hour of peril. No man, in his full strength, can stand undismayed, in the presence of the "king of terrors." Life is dear to every living thing; the worm that crawls upon the ground will struggle for it. At that moment [while battling a white overseer in self-defense] it was dear to me, enslaved and treated as I was.

When crime is institutionally sanctioned by law, it's very difficult to get the legislative machinery of the country in question to change gear. In post-bellum U.S., especially in states such as Georgia which were part of the defeated Confederacy, newly emancipated African Americans found it difficult to escape poverty and white Republicans in the U.S. Congress refused requests to change laws that would have allowed freedmen to acquire homestead rights. Substantial numbers opted to return to Africa, often with the help of organizations, supporters, and community leaders who worked with the African American Emigration Movement in Georgia. The movement had endured for nearly 200 years—a fact suggesting "it is a clear and resounding example of black discontentment with their political and socioeconomic condition in American society and willingness to act in their own self-interest. For a movement to sustain itself as long as the African American Emigration Movement did, there must have been the continued existence of strong motivational factors that drove blacks towards fully embracing emigration as the only pathway towards freedom."[18]

Just as the relationship between the legislative machinery of slave states and the descendants of the slave population remained complex and difficult so too was that between slavery and economic prosperity. The latter formed neither an exponential nor a geometric line upwards. Long before the U.S. Civil War, towards the end of the 18th century, Europeans had experienced many economic difficulties in operating their American slave domains. The slaves had become more of an economic liability than an asset to their white masters who were compelled to spend far larger amounts of money on sustaining and supervising their slaves than the profits they recouped as a result of their toils. In addition, the use of slave labor forced non-slave workers and slave-free businesses into trouble or out of the market entirely, which had pernicious effects on the societies in question.

It is a widely held but somewhat simplistic view that the slave trade enabled the onset of the Industrial Revolution, based on the idea that profits from the slave trade opened opportunities for new capital investment. There is evidence to refute such a straightforward explanation. Indeed, if slave trade profits were the essential ingredient fueling the investment in technologies emerging from the Industrial Revolution, Portugal should have emerged as a leader in industrialization. But, the 19th century saw the Portuguese economic empire collapse, first in 1822 when the country lost its prized colony of Brazil and then by a six-year civil war that ended in 1834 with Portugal as a handicapped constitutional monarchy that was unable to implement economic reforms.[19] After centuries of economic domination, Portugal saw its GDP shrink to barely 40 percent of the Western Europe average by 1900: its society tottered near collapse; with nearly three out of every four Portuguese citizens classified as illiterate.[20]

Likewise, the birth of the Abolitionist Movement in Europe coincided with the waning economic influence of the slave trade. And, abolitionists were widely supported as their cause did little to interfere economically with the rapid advances of industrialization in Europe. Nonetheless, for these abolitionists, the challenge of ending slavery in a world that considered it normalized up until the middle of the 19th century was as daunting as it might seem today, given our own hesitating and paralyzing tendencies to confront directly the entrenched wrongs of our own age. But while the noble work of these decent activists should be commended, it is notable that abolition in Europe arose primarily as a purely economic response for purposes of profit and wealth maximization.

Put simply, liberating slaves made economic sense in Europe where the consequences of slavery were nonexistent. Britain always made it seem as if the motive for the abolition of slavery was its virtue, though it was merely a shift of interest from slaves to capturing and capitalizing upon resources in Africa. British ships had long dominated the slave trade not only in Africa but also in the West Indies. Thus, British anti-slavery zeal was more directed to the Arab slave traders, especially in the markets of Zanzibar, and not toward Portugal or Spain. It was about an uncivilized race enslaving another uncivilized race.[21][vi]

Most of Britain's slaves in the Caribbean region left bondage, just as their ancestors had entered it—with little more than the clothes they were wearing at the time. of their emancipation. The British government only compensated 20 million pounds for the benefit of white plantation owners or their creditors. In fact, the slave owners still owned the plantations and many blacks begged them for jobs because as soon as they were set free they also had become obligated to pay rent to landlords and taxes to the government. For decades, freed blacks continued to cut sugar cane in conditions not much better than slavery. Harsh labor legislation took the place of slavery in guaranteeing a compliant and inexpensive workforce. For example, in British Honduras, "insolence and disobedience" to an employer or being absent without leave from work, commonly drew a sentence of three months at hard labor.[22] Even after his liberation, the slave could not leave the soil for which, if he did, he then was declared a fugitive by law, bound in chains, cauterized with fire and returned to his master, to surrender his freedom and willingly prefer servitude to freedom.[23] In Maryland, for example, freed blacks could not sell corn, wheat, or tobacco without a license. Several states required freed blacks to have passes, while there also were laws against freed blacks leaving the state for any length of time. Virginia, for instance, barred freed blacks from entering the state. Indeed, the stubbornness of slavery's presence was cast in deeper historical roots that were tied to the world's largest faith communities.

---

vi   Britain made the international slave trade illegal in 1807, as did the U.S. in 1808.

Chapter 3: Slavery and Religion

"You are all sons of Adam and Adam was created from dust."
the Prophet Mohammed

It is certainly an unpleasant paradox that Africa—populated as it is by the Faithful—should be so closely associated with that most ir-religious institution: the Slave Trade. But all the great religions have co-existed with—if not actually benefitted from—the Trade. At one point or another in the record of human history, every single place of extraordinarily holy significance for the world's major religions experience times when slavery was condoned and practiced without hesitation or fear of conscience. Neither Christianity nor Islam advocated for the abolition of slavery even though it had been widely practiced.

In the Christian Roman Empire, slavery was a normal feature of the economy and society. Many centuries later, slaveholders in Europe and America—many of whom espoused to some Christian faith community—would cite passages in the Bible to support slavery as God's destined institution.

For example, in the book of Genesis, Noah condemns Canaan (Son of Ham) to perpetual servitude: "Cursed be Canaan! The lowest of slaves will he be to his brothers" (Genesis 9:25). T. David Curp, an Ohio University historian who has studied events of ethnic cleansing in Eastern Europe and the Balkan, notes that this scripture often has been used to justify slavery on race, since "Christians and even some Muslims eventually identified Ham's descendants as black Africans."[24]

The Bible contained numerous passages that served as conveniences of legitimizing the practice of slavery. They included the following oft-quoted examples. Abraham, the "father of faith," and all the patriarchs held slaves without God's disapproval (Genesis 21:9–10). The Ten Commandments mention slavery twice, showing God's implicit acceptance of it (Exodus 20:10, 17). The apostle

Paul specifically commanded slaves to obey their masters (Ephesians 6:5–8). Paul returned a runaway slave, Philemon, to his master (Philemon 12).

Today, nearly all Christians are united in condemning the modern practices of slavery and human trafficking, as wrong and contrary to God's will. The Church of England has since apologized for the "sinfulness of our predecessors," with the history of plantation estates highlighted as the example of the church's inconsistent approach to slavery; [25] an apology that came nearly 200 years after Britain ended the trade exchanges of slaves in their jurisdiction and also as the pre-eminent naval power policed the Atlantic for any violations. had ended the international trade exchange of slaves.

On the other hand, When the Prophet Mohammed arrived with the message of Islam in Mecca, many slaves were among the first converts. His message urged its followers not to look at slaves as commodity merchandise but as human beings with a soul similar to that of his master. "You are all sons of Adam and Adam was created from dust," the Prophet Mohammed commanded, and he also put in place laws that sought justice for a slave by proclaiming: "He who kills his slave, we shall kill him; who mutilates his nose, we shall cut his nose; and who gelds our slave, we shall get him gelded in return."

Among the earliest, most prominent slave converts to Islam included Billal bin Rabah, who was chosen as the first *muezzin* (caller for prayers) in Islam. Zayd bin Harith, a former slave of Prophet Mohammed, became the prophet's adopted son. At his last sermon of his farewell pilgrimage, Prophet Mohammed told his followers: "There is no superiority for an Arab, nor for a black man over a red one, nor for a red over a black man save due to piety."

Islam, in its early days, restricted and regulated slavery to remove some of its cruelties, but accepted its practice was legal. Upon Prophet Mohammed's death, the institution of slavery was still intact in Islamic communities of faith. Its refusal to abolish slavery would be vigorously criticized for many centuries. How can any system of moral philosophy based on the concept of the absolute and equal value of human lives condone the trade in them? Recognize slavery as a part of its social system and as such made laws for it?

While slavery was, in theory, greatly limited by Islamic law, in practice it persisted on a large scale in places where Islam was a main religion. In Islam's *Black Slaves, The Other Black Diaspora*, scholar Ronald Segal attempted to explain the paradox, starting with the premise that the ideals of Islamic society were informed by the presence of divine well, as articulated in the Quran, which dealt with the issue of slavery. "That pretensions to piety might coexist with disregard for the spirit and even the letter of such details did not preclude their overall influence. Slaves were to be regarded and treated as people, not simply as possessions." While noting that eunuchs and sexual concubines essentially were treated no better in Islam than in Christianity, Segal says Islam's treatment of slaves was "overall more benign, in part because the values and attitudes promoted by religion inhibited the very development of a Western-style capitalism, with its effective subjugation of people to the priority of profit."

On the other end of the spectrum, some Muslim philosophers such as the Tunisian Ibn Khaldun would write in his popular book *The Muqadimmah*, after visiting Mali, a country of Muslim black people, about why black nations were prone to slavery: He wrote unashamedly: "Because blacks have little that is human and possess attributes that are similar to those of dumb animals."[26]

Regardless of those who characterize the practice as more benign or those who see no reason to filter their own racist, bigoted beliefs, the nature of slavery was the same under Islamic countries, as elsewhere. It involved serious breaches of human rights and however well they were treated, the slaves still had restrictions placed on their freedom. And, when the law was not obeyed, their lives could be made very unpleasant.

Today the current plight of migrant workers in the Gulf Arab countries of Saudi Arabia, Dubai, and Qatar is evident of how cruel slavery was in those countries. African domestic workers fleeing abuses such as rape and constant mistreatment from their employers are returned to the abusers by the police because the mentality is the worker should surrender, her fate being similar to a slave. Many who were murdered by their employers never received justice. Instead state institutions join the murderers to cover up such crimes (murders) as suicides and unexplained falls from high-rise buildings (often deemed as accidental).

A recent example of how entrenched these disturbing values have always been in Arab society came from Sondos al-Qattan, a makeup consultant in Kuwait whose Instagram account has more than 2.3 million followers and who wears traditional Islamic clothing and head covering. She posted a video criticizing a new Kuwait law that would give migrant workers one day off per month and would discourage employers from seizing the passports of the workers. Qattan wrote: "The passport of any expat employee should be in the possession of the employer to protect the employer's interest." She added, "The servant (Housemaid) lives in the house just like the owners, he eats the same food, rests, and goes out shopping . . . this is a natural right. He's not like a waiter who works fixed hours, so we give him a weekly leave." While Qattan stood by her comments even after a public outcry led to her removing the controversial video and several international cosmetics brand lines dropping her, the incident highlighted the horrific abuses domestic workers suffer. The law was proposed after the government of the Philippines prohibited any further migrants from going to the Gulf Arab country, after a maid was murdered and her body was found in a freezer. The Kuwaiti government also expelled Filipino diplomats after a video surfaced showing the embassy staff rescuing migrant workers who had been abused by their employers.

Mohammed Qutb, a contemporary Islamic scholar, is among the few that have discussed Slavery in Islam. He explains that Islamic teachings were intended to lead communities to ending slavery in a gradual process by limiting opportunities to acquire new slaves and allowing existing slaves to become free. Taking up the question of why Islam did not abolish slavery outright, Qutb wrote that when Islam emerged, slavery was prevalent throughout the world as an acknowledged fact of socioeconomic existence. "There was hardly a man to be met with whom was repelled by it, or who felt any need for a change. As such the changing or the total discarding of it required a gradual process stretched over a long period of time." Qutb wrote at length:

That is why its abolition required a period of time far longer than the life of the Holy Prophet, the period which coincided with the period of Divine revelation through him. God, the Best Knower of all that He created, knew that the total prohibition of wine would be achieved after a few years by a mere commandment. So He did command its prohibition when such time came. Similarly, if the conditions of life had been such as a mere direction was to suffice to suppress the evil of slavery, God Almighty would have expressly forbidden it once for all without any further delay.[27]

By the 19th century, as the West and many predominantly Christian nations moved to abolish the Atlantic Slave Trade, the pernicious practices were expanding in the Islamic East. It was a sign that for some Africans the abolition of the Atlantic Trade would not lead to freedom but would merely change their destination of forced servitude.

Muslim countries were compelled to implement secular laws borrowed from the West and enlightened Christian nations to prohibit slavery. Several Muslim countries outlawed slavery only recently: Saudi Arabia in 1962, Qatar, 1952; and Yemen, 1962. Slaves were also kept in Africa and, in fact, African states were among the last ones to abolish slavery. Mauritania only abolished slavery in 2007.[28] Though it is estimated that up to 600,000 men, women and children, or 20 percent of the Mauritanian population, are still enslaved, many of them used as bonded labour.[29]

The *Middle East Quarterly* reported that slavery was still endemic in Sudan with estimates of about 200,000 people abducted—mostly women and children and enslaved during the Second Sudanese Civil War.[30] Also the Janjaweed Arab militias are reported to have kidnapped numerous people and sold them as agricultural labor, domestic servants and sex slaves, during the Darfur conflict that began in 2003.[31]

The long-running Darfur conflict, as unfortunate and as profoundly regrettable as it has become in its unchecked brutalities, also signifies the underlying factors of Islamic and Arab identities in the face of the slavery question. As Abdullahi El-Tom noted, "Darfur is 100 percent Muslim, a substantial proportion of the population has a credible claim to 'Arab ancestry,' and all Black Darfuris use Arabic as a mother tongue or as a lingua franca."[32] He explains that for many of the Black Darfuris, "Africanism has finally superseded language, Islam, and the influence of Arab culture as a determining factor of identity. For them, Africanism connotes both historic belonging to the land and pride in their darker colour but above all distinctiveness from their new Arab opponents."[33]

In the project of modernity, colonialism and imperialism ensured the social relations of pre-modernity remained the same. "The marginalized retain their marginality and the ruling elite . . . prevails with its power and privileges intact."[34]

SECTION II:
COLONIALISM AND IMPERIALISM

Chapter 4: Replacing Slavery with Colonialism

"Colonialism was not merely a system of exploitation, but one whose essential purpose was to repatriate the profits to the so-called 'mother country.' " Walter Rodney

Even as the West eventually moved toward abolishing slavery, Westerners were still not yet ready to let Africans be free in the pursuit of economic independence and enterprise. In the new wave of imperialism, the unconscionable theft of African labor was replaced by indiscriminate, full-throttle exploitation of Africa's natural and precious mineral resources. With industrialization, these resources were more important than the human labor and the race was on, especially at the end of the 18th century, to scramble for the conquest of Africa. New sectors of industries in Europe demanded raw materials like cotton, iron, palm oil, rubber, copper, and cocoa, all of which were unavailable in Europe. The West signaled that while Africans no longer had to be worried about forced servitude as unpaid slaves, they could be hired albeit at low wages to work on behalf of digging up the continent's resources.

In late 19th century, South Africa's gold mines recruited black workers from the rural hinterlands to handle miscellaneous unskilled tasks. As Michael Burawoy explained in a journal article in 1976, "Once cajoled into selling their labor power by expropriation of land, imposition of taxation, and similar nonmarket inducements, African workers became attracted to wage employment as a way of making up or supplementing their means of subsistence."[35] Surprising to some perhaps, mine owners were willing to advance Black African workers but the legal color bar of apartheid dictated that skilled areas of employment were off limits and were to be reserved only for whites. "Once the color bar was accepted as irrevocable, management sought to offset the costly protection of white labor by externalizing the costs of renewal of a black labor force. This process was made possible by the reproduction of the system of migrant labor."[36]

And to read these words from 1976 amplifies the contention even further today: "That blacks have had less political power than whites means that they are more vulnerable to excessive exploitation, but this has been only realized through specific modes of reproduction of labor power on the plantation and in the ghetto."[37] The structures of social relationships that were created and sustained in the practices of colonialism and imperialism undoubtedly mediated and shaped the connections between resource exploitation and profit. Ironically, the costs of sustaining that economic connection in post-colonial or post-imperial society have cut into profits, only because the exploiters must continuously reestablish their means of control and enforcement. The point then is that by reducing the emphasis on exploitation, there might be a better premise for mutually beneficial economic results that also include African workers. This is part of the emerging premise in those enterprises that seek to implement blockchain technology by way of improving land governance and assuring land titling for Africans.

Manufacturers, especially in the clothing industries, also have looked to Africa to dispose large volumes of surplus production, instigating a new subtle form of colonialism. Dubbed by one researcher as "waste couture," the practice involves "clothing that is not considered vintage or high-end is baled for export to developing nations."[38] For the 15-year period ending in 2003, the International Trade Commission reported that American exports of used clothing tripled in volume to more than seven billion pounds being sold in more than 100 countries. The 2007 article in the *Environmental Health Perspectives* journal highlighted Tanzania, "where used clothing is sold at the *mitumba* (Swahili for *second-hand*) markets that dot the country, [and] these items are the number one import from the U.S."[39]

While European colonists freely came to the "Dark Continent" in search of new markets, Africans historically have never had a realistic chance to reciprocate and gain even a modicum of presence in any European or American market. Yet, the steady stream of African migrants flowing into these countries has caused a lot of unease to the citizens who complain about competing with Africans immigrants for social welfare and jobs.

Industrialization spearheaded colonialism as it brought improvements in transportation and communication, starting with railways, steam navigation, and the telegraph. Many inventions tipped the hand more favorably toward the West on a continuous basis. One of the most notable was the Maxim gun, invented by American-born British inventor Hiram Stevens Maxim in 1884. It was the first recoil-operated machine gun that was mass produced. Likewise, medical advancements such as quinine, known as an effective treatment of malaria, led Europeans to venture into vast expanses of the tropics and Africa, which had been known previously as the "white man's grave." The Berlin Conference of 1884–1885 (also known as the Congo Conference) declared the whole continent as fair game. By the start of the 20th century, only two African countries were still free or uncolonized: Ethiopia and Liberia. As for Liberia, the republic originally began as a settlement coordinated by the American Colonization Society, which believed that freed blacks would do better economically in Africa than in the U.S. The country declared its independence in 1847 but the U.S. waited 15 years until it recognized the republic as free. Ethiopia nearly lost its independence after Italian armed forces invaded it in 1936.

Walter Rodney, the Guyanese historian and political activist who has written about colonialism in Africa noted: "Colonialism was not merely a system of exploitation, but one whose essential purpose was to repatriate the profits to the so-called 'mother country.' From an African viewpoint, that amounted to consistent expatriation of surplus produced by African labor out of African resources. It meant the development of Europe as part of the same dialectical process in which Africa was underdeveloped."[40]

Rodney explains that colonial governments maintained conditions most favorable for their respective private companies that had taken up the plunder of Africa. Among the tools they deployed was the imposition of taxes that provided requisite funds for administering the colony as a field of exploitation. Africans were required to pay taxes for their cattle, land, houses, and themselves. The colonizers ensured that Africans paid for the upkeep of the governors, police, and army who oppressed them while serving as watchdogs for their private companies. After setting up the police, army, civil service and judiciary on African soil, the colonizers were in the position to intervene much more directly in the economic life of Africans: they forced Africans to become laborers or cash crop farmers.

The exploitation of African resources and land was a predominant feature of colonialism. After seizing African land, the colonizers distributed it to white residents and private companies. So, the landless Africans ended up working on white farms not just to pay taxes but also to survive. In settled areas such as Kenya and Rhodesia, the colonial governments also prevented Africans from growing cash crops so that their labor would remain exclusively for the benefit of white settlers. In present-day Congo Brazzaville, the French colonialists banned Africans from hunting a main source of meat critical to their diet and forced them to engage solely in cotton cultivation. In other parts where land was still in African hands, colonial governments forced Africans to produce cash crops no matter how low the prices commanded in the market.

Forced labor was exacted to carry out projects labeled as "public works." Labor for a specified number of days per year was made available for free in order to build castles for governors, prisons for Africans, barracks for troops, and bungalows for colonial officials. A great deal of forced labor went into construction of roads, railways, and ports to provide infrastructure for private European capitalists. An international Forced Labor Convention was signed by all colonial powers in 1930 but again it was breached consistently in practice.

The causes of the Second World War were exacerbated by inter-colonial rivalries which struggled for territorial control. Germany and Italy sought colonial empires to conquer existing British and French colonies. And after the war, many colonial powers were significantly weakened, which did help Africans speed up the decolonization process. World War Two was the Wind of Change that blew down the Age of Empire: the European empires could no longer be maintained economically or militarily; morally and ideologically. In fact, Germany lost most of its colonial territory—notably, Tanzania and Namibia—to the British. As described in Marxism, by working within the global capitalist system, colonialism was closely associated with uneven development for Europe and Africa. It was an "instrument of wholesale destruction, dependency and systematic exploitation producing distorted economies, socio-psychological disorientation, massive poverty, and neocolonial dependency."[41] Yet, the historic irony also is not lost, considering the experiences of four Afro-Marxist states in recent history: Ethiopia, Mozambique, Angola, and Zimbabwe. The emphasis has been on consolidating the power and control of regimes rather than state, which also has led to failed economies and utter disregard for the agricultural economies in those states.

Africa's experience with colonialism has been nearly as dehumanizing as its experience with slavery. "Despite the success of his pacification, in spite of his appropriation, the colonist always remains a foreigner. It is not the factories, the estates or the bank account which primarily characterize the 'ruling' class. The ruling species is first and foremost the outsider from elsewhere, different from the indigenous population, the others."[42] Frantz describes how colonists dehumanized the colonized and they (the colonists) used zoological terms to describe them like slithery movements of the yellow race, the odors from the native quarters to the hordes, the stink, the swarming, the seething, and the gesticulations. The stark challenges of conscience are rendered more vivid by the simple and clear link between the ferocious exploitation of Africa and its peoples and the tremendous wealth of Europeans and the West.

Chapter 5: European Men who Reaped Wealth from African Colonies

"To tear treasure out of the bowels of the land was their desire, with no more moral purpose at the back of it than there is in burglars breaking into a safe." Joseph Conrad

King Leopold II of Belgium's (1835–1909) acquisition of the vast and mostly unexplored territory surrounding the Congo River was the most bizarre form of public-private partnership, a hyper-refinement of the colonial practices. As the royal CEO and sole shareholder of his corporation, he dictated the plunder and genocide of the lands known today as the Republic of the Congo. His legacy crippled the country in immeasurable ways that remain in effect today. Adam Hochschild, in the biography *King Leopold's Ghost*, has given a detailed account of how the European monarch, who was famously known for his "philanthropy" and was praised for investing his personal wealth in public works, looted the Congo of its rubber, enslaved its population, and turned the land into one of the world's major killing grounds. An estimated 10 million Congolese people were killed.

Congo exported its rubber, coal, iron, and gold—everything Africa was famous for—and King Leopold on its behalf only imported guns and ammunition.[43] The rubber boom was as much a curse to the Congolese people as it was a blessing to King Leopold with his privately owned Congo Free State[vii] as the world's main supplier of the material. The King did not flinch from dictating cruel measures to force the population into collecting rubber on his behalf, which then would be sold on the global market with no return or recourse to the benefit of the Congolese.

It is worth focusing our attention for a moment on the physical processes by which rubber—the emblematic resource of the Congo—was extracted and refined. A gatherer had to dry the syrup-like

---

vii   King Leopold referred to Congo as Congo Free State after assuring diplomats at the Berlin Conference that he was undertaking a philanthropic and humanitarian work.

rubber so that it would coagulate. Often the only way to do so was to spread the substance on his arms, thighs and chest—painful certainly for the first few times, especially if the man's torso was covered with hair. Unfortunately, the workers had no options for recourse because refusal led to horrific tactics of intimidation, as is recounted in *King Leopold's Ghost*:

> This officer's . . . method . . . was to arrive in canoes at a village, the inhabitants of which invariably bolted on their arrival, the soldiers were then landed, and commenced looting, taking all the chickens, grain, etc., out of the houses; after this they attacked the natives until able to seize their women; these women were kept as hostages until the chief of the district brought in the required number of kilograms of rubber. The rubber having been brought the women were sold back to their owners for a couple of goats apiece and so he continued from village to village until the requisite amount of rubber had been collected.[44]

Hochschild recounts these events in extensive detail. All along the rivers, columns of exhausted men, carrying baskets of lumpy gray rubber on their heads, sometimes walked twenty miles or more to assemble near the homes of European agents, who sat on their verandas and weighed the loads of rubber. When a village failed to supply the required volume, the king's *Force Publique* troops would raid the village and kill the men, and for each bullet the officer had to account for it by cutting off the hand of the dead man. They collected many hands in baskets. Some soldiers who lost track of their bullets would remove hands from survivors, so as to reconcile their accounting. When King Leopold fathered a son with his second wife Caroline, he was born with a deformed hand, and newspapers printed headlines such as *"Vengeance from the Most High."*

By the time King Leopold reluctantly succumbed to international pressure in relinquishing his private state and allowing it to be reconstituted as a Belgian colony, it was characterized by burned villages, starved hostages, and terrified refugees hiding in swamps, and the colonial process had reduced the country's 20 million population by half. Indeed the icon of the Congo Free State remains the severed hand. Scholars have estimated that King Leopold made 220 million francs in profits from the Congo—or, in present-day value, more than $1.1 billion. After his death, his two daughters tried to claim some of the booty but the Belgian government took it. Unfortunately, there was no lawyer to claim the money that should have been returned to Congo.[45]

Similar forced labor systems, especially those designed to extract rubber, existed in the French colonies of West and North Africas well as Germany's Cameroon and Portuguese-ruled Angola. Thousands of refugees who had fled North across the Congo River to escape Leopold's atrocities eventually returned, this time to escape from the French. Germany's Southwest Africa, now known as Namibia, was even worse and the atrocities had been classified as genocide as well. When Namibia's Herreros[viii] tried to rebel against German rule, Germany sent a heavily armed force with orders to kill every Herrero, whether found with a rifle or not, and no man was to be taken as a hostage.[46]

Despite this, Congo's case remains among the worst experienced in Africa and the country to this day still bleeds from the effects of global corporate greed. King Leopold's genocide only paved the path later, as automobiles began to be mass produced, to pillage Congo for rubber when the world needed tires. Belgians then initiated a war over control of Congo's copper to wire the world for electricity and communications. Recent conflicts in Congo arose because of the world's growing demand for tin to make conductors for electronic circuitry. Today the world needs cell phones, which makes the following relevant: Congo contains 60 percent of known reserves of an essential metal called tantalum and armed conflicts once again are common there.[47]

On the other side, British diamond prospector Cecil Rhodes, carved out a colony from blood and diamonds in South Africa, enforced de facto slave labor, where miners were locked up when not working to stop them from sneaking the company's gems out and

---

viii   The Herreros were originally an Ethnic group of people living in Central Eastern Region of Southern Africa or present-day Namibia.

monopolizing the precious metal and ore trade.[48] His power was entrusted with a royal charter akin to a legitimately operating government. Rhodes dispatched private armies to safeguard his corporate interests, similar to today's hired security companies to protect minefields for Western corporations.

The purpose of Colonialism was never to civilize. Europeans came to Africa to procure wealth and this remains the main reason for their continued dominance of African countries. They would never tell Africans how much they siphoned off, but it must be a figure bigger than what any calculator can handle. According to Fanon, Europe's existence is literally the creation of The Third World. The riches which are choking the First World are those plundered from the underdeveloped world. And as soon as European companies knew their governments planned to grant independence to the colonies they had founded, they hurried to withdraw their capital. Western bankers, who worried about any risk-taking in Africa, attempted to assure those who stayed after independence was granted that their first demands were for political stability and a peaceful social climate—an objective impossible to achieve, given the disaffected and abused masses. Paradoxically, newly independent governments which were unable to provide security, often asked that their former rulers keep a military presence—a situation bore that strange fruit in the form of complex economic and military trade-offs as private, foreign companies demanded that their interests be protected.[49] Independence turned out to be an illusion, and life was as bad or worse than it had been under colonial rule.

Chapter 6: Delusional Independence

"Nature has never read the declaration of independence. It continues to make us unequal." Will Durant

Independence to most African countries represented a colonist's fraud. The new African leaders had to reach an agreement with their outgoing colonial masters to keep the education system, economic models, culture, and even political infrastructure. The African leaders also were obligated to accept their young countries would pay large sums of money to the colonists as part of reparations for what they considered to have brought to the country as part of the colonization package.

A few leaders tried to resist these imperialist exploitative agreements with well-intentioned arguments reminding the citizenry how the colonists had exploited their countries' resources. They sought some form of reparations by taxing the infrastructure the colonists had built to carry out their enterprises. Nevertheless, these leaders almost always were immediately overthrown in military coups led by soldiers who had been trained by the colonists. Africa's long economic crisis strained the capacities and coping skills of political leaders. As a result, many countries experienced,

> Increased income inequality and [policies that] favored dramatic increases in luxury consumption among the nouveaux riches, the international businessmen and employees of international organizations and NGOs that have multiplied in numbers. This has intensified the sense of "relative deprivation." The dramatic increase in conspicuous consumption in the cities juxtaposed against deepening squalor has led to unravelling of the "social pacts"—be they populist, corporatist, or patron-clientelist—that until then provided a modicum of peace in the post-colonial era.[50]

Add in the mix the devaluation of a nation's currency, the suspension of agricultural subsidies, and dramatic increases in prices even for basic commodities and foodstuffs and the risks for riots and civil war erupted with quick fury. Liberia's example was among the worst, starting in 1979 after the rice riots. The soldiers would then "surrender" the country to colonialist corporations who resumed the activities of exploitation on a scale larger than ever. The amassed wealth for the privileged rose to the billions. And because this implied relationship guaranteed the rebels' long stay in power, they would send their children to colonial military academies such as The Royal Military Academy Sandhurst, as an assurance that even when they died their sons would continue to rule by the same expectations.

Puppet leaders (which are discussed in greater detail in the next chapter) did the West's bidding with metaphorical chains fastened on to their necks even if their public persona suggested uncompromising strength in order to instill fear among their country's citizens. Defense agreements guaranteed that the exiting colonial master would remain the main arms supplier and trainer of armed forces, as well as oblige independent colonies to ally with the colonizers in the event of any conflict or war, regardless of circumstances. The precedent was established decades earlier. In the Second World War, the military relationship between colonial master and servant went beyond the sale of equipment or the provision of training. Africans were expected to fight alongside their European overlords—and millions did—to defeat Nazism.

Meanwhile, African independence was to remain largely in symbols such as the national flag and anthem and passports but all critical matters of governance and policy-making required the advice and counsel of third-party groups representing old colonial interests. France established the CFA franc in the late 1940s, imposing the currency as legal tender in its African colonies. It is one of the most prominent signs of France's continued economic influence over its former African colonies. CFA, which is legal tender in 14 African countries, is pegged to the euro with the financial backing of the French treasury.

Bloomberg reported in 2014 that a hoard of cash from African French colonies using CFA sits in the Bank of France: $20 billion in African money held in trust by the French government and earning just 0.75 percent interest annually. This example of French economic exploitation of its African former colonies is one reason the French-speaking African countries are the least developed in Africa. And, it is why many African citizens aspire to escape their countries and go to France. Africans in these countries have staged several protests against the CFA and have demanded that the funds hoarded by France be returned and at a value calculated by the period dating back to the days when France's colonial empire ended.[51] Critics who espouse the anti-CFA movement, argue that in exchange for the guarantees provided by the French treasury, African countries have channeled more money to France than they have received in aid. They also argue that they have no say in deciding key monetary policies agreed to by European countries, which are members of the Eurozone.[52]

Other contracts signed prior to independence included those that guaranteed that companies and corporations from the colonial masters always would be given preference for public procurement and public bidding. Addressing a UK business forum in Kenya in April, 2018, Gregg Hands, the British state minister for international affairs, said that the UK was the largest foreign investor in Kenya and that one in 10 Kenyans work for a UK company.[53] Moreover, those British moguls were not only owners of businesses in Kenya alone but across all former British colonies. They are among the wealthiest owners in Uganda, for example. More than 100 British companies dominate Uganda's major economy sectors. For example, Tullow Oil and Shell dominate the energy sector, while Barclays and Standard Chartered dominate the banking sectors, and Unilever dominates the food and beverages sector.

In Francophone countries the streets are packed with mostly French-made cars, though one would hardly see such cars elsewhere. In fact, French car manufacturers were still in business thanks to the monopoly market their country secured in African colonies. It would be stunning news for an ordinary citizen in Togo or Gambia, for example, to learn that Toyota dominates the international automobile market. When it comes to the domestic African markets, colonial masters enjoy near-total economic freedom. And, it is their puppet government officials who ensure the exploitative relationship continues. The next chapter goes into further detail about the making of African puppet leaders.

Chapter 7: The Making of African Puppets

"Neither brutal assaults, nor cruel mistreatment, nor torture have ever led me to beg for mercy, for I prefer to die with my head held high." Patrice Lumumba

In the nascent period of Decolonization when Harold Macmillan's "wind of change" blew across the continent and the political consciousness of its peoples sharpened, Africans who aspired to leadership were faced with a number of challenges. Greatest among them was that of building nations that could survive without the colonial relationships on which they were founded.

As many anti-colonial African politicians rose to power, they immediately implemented policies to ensure Africa could thrive without the extensive involvement of European nations and the U.S. Unfortunately, most of those early populist leaders either were assassinated or overthrown by military officers who had been trained by their former colonial superiors.

Patrice Lumumba was one of the first populist leaders of that time, the first democratically elected prime minister of the Congo after the nation gained its independence on June 30, 1960. Lumumba's story and that of his country following his death can be seen as emblematic of the machinery that created the Puppet as a continental phenomenon and so deserves detailed attention here. One of the most impassioned proponents of pan-African solidarity, he believed that independence was not enough to free Africa from its colonial past without ending the continent's dependency on the West for the capacities of material prosperity. As mentioned previously, Europe and America had already established vast investments to siphon Congo's copper, cobalt, diamonds, gold, tin, manganese, and zinc. Many outside Africa looked on his speeches with alarm, fearing that Lumumba's clear, unconditional language was contagious enough to spread rapidly throughout the continent's independence movement.

Less than two months after being named the Congo's first democratically chosen prime minister, a U.S. National Security Council subcommittee on covert operations, which included the U.S. Central Intelligence Agency chief Allen Dulles, authorized Lumumba's assassination. After being arrested and beaten, the prime minister was shot to death in Elizabethville in January 1961. A CIA agent drove with Lumumba's body in his car, trying to find a place to dispose of it. Lumumba ended up like millions of Congolese before him—in an unmarked grave.

In 1975, an American investigation confirmed the CIA involvement in Lumumba's execution, which was carried out by a Katangan police unit with a Belgian officer supervising. In 2002, Belgium formally admitted its involvement, and in 2018, the Square du Bastion in Brussels, adjacent to the Matonge neighborhood, which is home to a large Congolese immigrant population, was renamed in Lumumba's memory.

Richard Bissell, CIA operations chief at the time, later said, "The president (Dwight D. Eisenhower) would have vastly preferred to have him taken care of some way other than by assassination, but he regarded Lumumba as I did and a lot of other people did: as a mad dog . . ."[54] The U.S. and Belgium spared no tactic in neutralizing Lumumba, even reaching out to the United Nations General Secretary (first, Dag Hammarskjöld and then Ralph Bunche) to help mediate buying the support of Lumumba's political rivals who would, in turn, work with the prime minister's killers. It should deeply disturb anyone concerned about the sanctity of any nation's right to independent rule how Western governments and multinational corporations believed it was their natural right to exploit African resources and markets or to take the most extreme measures to protect their interests when it came to political opposition.

The man who was chosen to *replace* Lumumba and the trajectory of his life and rule serve as exemplary of the African experience of post-colonial rule. Joseph-Désiré Mobutu (Mobutu SeseSeko), had also helped arrange Lumumba's murder. Western powers had spotted Mobutu as someone who would look out for their interests. He had received cash payments from a local CIA agent in Kinshasa (then Léopoldville) and Western military attaches while Lumumba's murder was planned. Wearing dark glasses and his general's uniform with gold braid and a sword, Mobutu later met President Kennedy at the White House in 1963. Kennedy gave him an airplane for his personal use and a U.S. Air Force crew to fly it for him. With American support in 1965, Mobutu staged a coup and he ruled the Congo for 32 years until the U.S. acted behind the scenes once again to replace him with Laurent-Désiré Kabila.[55] Kabila's rebel forces ousted Mobutu, who was suffering from advanced cancer. Mobutu fled to Morocco and died shortly after he went into exile.

Described by *Time* magazine in 2011 as the archetype of the African dictator, Mobutu, like many Western-controlled puppets, was desperate to portray himself to the masses as independent from his masters.[56] He changed the country's European chosen name of Congo to Zaire, banned Christian names including his own. He called himself Mobutu SeseSeko Kuku wazabanga. He banned European clothing styles, preferring instead his own design known as an *abacost*—a lightweight short-sleeved suit, often worn without a tie, which resembled the uniform worn by Chairman Mao.

A fate similar to that of the Congo befell Togo. In the early days of the independence movement. Sylvanus Olympio, like Lumumba, wanted to turn the future away from Togo's former colonial masters, the French, after attaining independence. He refused to sign the colonization continuation pact that then French president Charles de Gaulle proposed but he did agree to pay an annual debt to France for the so-called benefits Togo had received from French colonization. However, with the ball still in France's court, the French government levied high reparations to be paid back by the tiny country. Almost 40 percent of the country's budget was to be paid back to France annually in colonial debt resettlement. Olympio managed to mobilize Togolese citizens to pay off the French debt in two years and after it was paid, the revolutionary president demanded to move away from the CFA (francs) currency and institutionalize a new one for the young independent country. On January 13, 1963, only three days after printing Togo's new currency had begun, Olympio was assassinated in a military coup led by Etienne Gnassigbe, formerly a sergeant in the French Foreign Legion, who assumed the leadership and returned the country to France.

Most of the coups against post-independence African nationalist leaders occurred in former French colonies. In five decades, 67 coups were carried out in 26 countries in Africa, 16 of them from French-speaking countries in Africa. In many instances, ex-French Foreign Legionnaires carried out these coups against elected presidents. In every case after the coup, France would be the first country to recognize the coup leader as the respective nation's new leader. The following summarize a few examples.

Modibo Keïta, the first president of Mali, also decided to withdraw from the French colonial currency (CFA franc) claiming the colonization continuation pact with France burdened the country's efforts to strengthen its own economic independence program. He was deposed in 1968 after eight years by General Moussa Traoré, an ex-French Foreign Legionnaire officer, and sent to prison in the northern Malian town of Kida, where he died nine years later. Keïta's reputation was rehabilitated in 1992, shortly after Traoré was deposed in a coup, indicative of the ceaseless cycle of violent transitions of power that has plagued African politics for more than six decades.

David Dacko, the first president of the Central African Republic, was deposed on January 1, 1966, by Jean-Bédel Bokassa, again a former soldier in the French Foreign Legion. Dacko, however, had been one of the continent's most resilient politicians. In 1979, returning from France, he was able to regain power from Bokassa, ironically in a coup orchestrated with the help of French officials. Dacko's return to power, though, was short-lived, as he was unable to overcome criticism that his ties to France mattered more than his attention to the Gbaya, the Central African Republic's largest ethnic group. In 1981, he was overthrown in a bloodless coup by General André Kolingba, who subsequently enjoyed close relations with France. Many had believed, although it has never been confirmed, that Kolingba had gained the support of locally stationed French security personnel who had acted without orders from Parisian authorities. This occurred as France had elected its first socialist president, François Mitterrand. Dacko, meanwhile, became leader of the political opposition and remained active until his death in 2003 from natural causes.

In Benin (formerly Dahomey), Hubert Maga became the country's leader during the transition to independence. He survived numerous political crises, even when he was forced to resign or was deposed in a bloodless coup. In 1963, as the country's economy was in dire shape,

Christophe Soglo, the military chief of staff officer, took over, forcing Maga to resign. Maga went to Paris after being imprisoned briefly but returned in 1970 to serve on a three-member rotating presidential council. Two years later, Mathieu Kérékou, who identified as a Marxist-Leninist, deposed the council and imprisoned Maga along with the other presidential council members. Maga was released in 1981 and retired from public life permanently. He died in 2000.

Political stability in the newly independent African nations was well-nigh impossible to achieve so long was the shadow of the colonial past. The European countries did not just support coups against stubborn, unattached African presidents who endangered their corporate interests but also often engaged in rivalries with fellow European colonists for controlling the markets and business interests of African countries. These rivalries were not confined to the boardrooms or behind the scenes, as tremendous amounts of African blood were spilled. The Rwandan genocide, that has been portrayed widely as an intertribal conflict, was more accurately a war involving colonial rivals, with the British and America supporting Paul Kagame, president since 2000—through channels with Uganda's puppet dictator Yoweri Museveni, in power since 1986—to take over power from the French supported government of President Juvenal Habyarimana, who served in Rwanda from 1973 to his assassination in 1994. Kagame would enjoy the privilege of impunity even after the horrific scale of the Rwandan massacre, similar to that Museveni enjoyed after the Luwero war, which brought him to power.

British and American media reports consistently placed the blame of the killings on the defeated governments. The arc of the narrative is as infuriatingly predictable. In every war in Africa, the victor assumes the mantle of liberator in Western media while the defeated party assumes the mantle of the killer, genocide proponent, and terrorist. A 2000 International Press Institute report highlighted the problem, noting that many reporters likely hesitated to put their own lives at risk, trying to confirm details and facts of ethnic violence that were denied persistently by their perpetrators. As the "Kosovo Liberation Army wanted reporters to think that Yugoslav government violence prior to NATO's bombing was genocide or ethnic cleansing rather than counterinsurgency," similarly, "Rwanda's Hutu government wanted reporters to think that violence was civil war rather than genocide."[57] Alan Kuperman, an international scholar in security and politics, concluded that, "in both cases, Western reporters were fooled. They should take a lesson from this as they continue their vital task of informing Western policy makers and publics about violent conflicts around the world."[58]

Kagame's responsibility for the Rwandan genocide has been blurred to the point of obscurity. The world had to forget that Kagame opposed the deployment of United Nations peacekeepers one month into the hundred-day murder because he worried that the forces would interfere with his military campaign and prevent him from taking power. It was no surprise that after President Kagame's victory and ascension to power, Rwanda was admitted to the Commonwealth of Nations as its 54th member, even though the country historically had taken its place among French-speaking colonies. This act signifies that the particularly acrimonious relationship between France and Rwanda that has yet to be eased, even despite the 2017 meeting of Kagame with French President Emmanuel Macron. But France's hands cannot be seen as conclusively clean, either. Just days before this meeting, France's Constitutional Council had denied requests from human rights activists and scholars to open the archives from the genocide, which occurred during Mitterand's administration. This suggests just how difficult whatever grave sins have been committed, even new generations of leaders from the respective countries cannot resolve nor reconcile the differences to move forward.

In former British colonial states, just as in the Francophone countries, coups have been far too prevalent. In Uganda, my own country, General Idi Amin Dada, formerly a soldier in the British Colonial Army, toppled the socialist president Dr. Apollo Milton Obote in 1971. At the time, British Prime Minister Edward Heath told Obote, Julius Nyerere of Tanzania, and Kenneth Kaunda of Zambia during a Commonwealth conference in Singapore that one of them would not be returning to his country as president. Just a few hours elapsed before Amin had successfully deposed Obote.

Amin, despite having ousted a legitimately elected president in a military coup, had started out on a note that resonated well in Britain.

Publicly pro-Western, he facilitated Uganda's admission to the Commonwealth and was invited to an audience with Queen Elizabeth II. Less than four years later, he had turned completely against foreign investments in his country, expelling Asians and hijacking an Israeli plane, which ended in a dramatic rescue raid of the hostages carried out by the Israeli Defense Forces commando at the Entebbe airport in 1976.

His deepening madness, increasingly erratic behavior, and violent oppression of his own people became fresh headlines for the Western media. Once again, the West searched for a replacement leader and with the help of neighboring Tanzania, a bloody war was funded that toppled Amin in 1979. Nyerere, whose country was used as the base to attack and overthrow Amin, still wanted his friend Dr. Obote, who was among the Ugandan politicians behind the war, to lead Uganda again. Interim governments were formed but Obote, who enjoyed strong domestic influence, abstained from taking any transitional government post. Instead he contested again as presidential candidate in 1980 and won the elections. He resumed his prior socialist and nationalist post-independence agenda and Britain was disturbed anew by Obote's return. Yoweri Museveni, the rebel leader and now the longest serving president in Uganda's history, later would confess in his autobiography that he received "discreet" support from Britain to overthrow Obote in a bloody war again in 1986. I will discuss Museveni and the Western support that ushered him to power and has kept him there for many decades more in the next chapter.

The contemporary breed of African leaders who are supported by the West to stay beyond their legitimate terms in power, for the purposes of safeguarding external corporations' entrenched colonial interests, is equal to having chains fastened on the necks of Africans to restrain them from resisting neo-colonialism. The metal chains so familiar in the bygone colonial era have evolved into similar chains of leaders subjugating their citizens to accept the economic deprivation by handing over the continental resources and businesses to Western corporations with little consideration for the broader legitimate interests of citizen-stakeholders.

It is a perverse business arrangement in which these power-hungry leaders have submitted willingly to the Western governments and

their corporations to rule Africa, nearly as they had done in the colonial period. Those leaders protecting business interests have been
supported not only with weapons, intelligence, and funds to conquer
their respective country's leadership but also with the media's silence
against the atrocities they committed on their path to power. These
leaders are aware of the damage they are doing to their own people.
That is why they rely on large army battalions to protect them as
they move on streets. They understand the impact of depriving a
population of health care and education. When they require medical
treatment, they know well enough not to go to a hospital in their
country but to travel instead to the U.S. or Europe to be treated and
to send their children away to receive their education. Meanwhile,
the citizens of beleaguered African nations are compelled to migrate
to Europe to find jobs and cultivate the prospects for a decent life,
while their leaders travel free of conscience to Europe to cut exploitive deals selling their country's resources and businesses.

Chapter 8: The Endless Siphoning of African Wealth

"Every empire, however, tells itself and the world that it is unlike all other empires, that its mission is not to plunder and control but to educate and liberate." Edward W. Said

Africa is at once both the poorest and the richest of continents: on her soil many millions live in almost unimaginable squalor; but beneath her soil lie one-third of the planet's mineral deposits. The continent is a repository of 15 percent of the planet's crude oil reserves, 40 percent of its gold and 80 percent of its platinum. As we have already seen, for centuries that wealth has proven attractive to the Western nations of the old and new world and now in in the 21st century nation states situated all over the world are looking to join the U.S. and Europe in siphoning off Africa's wealth. Now there are African summits for the U.S., European Union, China, and even Israel.

However, these ostensibly economic summits have often proved useful to the agenda of putting military assets onto the Continent. In 2007, under the pretext of the undefined and unlimited War on Terror, the Bush Administration consolidated their various military operations in Africa to establish the United States Africa Command (AFRICOM). With a starting budget of half a billion dollars, AFRICOM was launched to engage with African countries in diplomacy and aid agreements. But, during the last 10 years, AFRICOM has been transformed into a central command for military incursions and interventions. U.S. troops conduct 3,500 military exercises and active combat operations throughout Africa annually. That translates to 10 events per day.

This remarkable rate of activity has gone relatively unnoticed. The American mainstream media rarely discusses continental political military presence thus giving the military ample space to destabilize any of the continent's 54 countries as it pleases.[59] The death of four U.S. Special Forces soldiers in Niger on October 4, 2017 generated a good deal of surprise among ordinary U.S. citizens because few knew that the U.S. Army was in Niger. At a White House press briefing two weeks after the incident, Chief of Staff John Kelly said the troops were in Niger to "teach them how to respect human rights." In the spring of 2018, a Pentagon report indicated that junior officers had mischaracterized the mission in question.[60] They said it was intended to be a meeting with tribal elders but it was actually a counterterrorism mission, which would have required senior officer approval and the assigning of more troops.

Currently, the U.S. has many military bases across the continent including Camp Lemonnier in Djibouti, an expeditionary base of roughly one square mile, which houses some 3,200 soldiers and civilians next to the international airport. In northern Cameroon at the Garoua airport an American drone base is used to target Boko Haram rebels in northeastern Nigeria. It houses unarmed Predator drones and some 300 soldiers. In Burkina Faso, a "cooperative security location" in Ouagadougou provides surveillance and intelligence over the Sahel. Likewise, Predator and Reaper drones are based in Chad's capital, Ndjamena. In Kenya, Camp Simba in Manda Bay is a base for American naval personnel and Green Berets. It also houses armed drones for operations in Somalia and Yemen. Another military base in Niger's Niamey handles large transport aircraft and armed Reaper drones. The base covers the Sahel and the Lake Chad Basin. In Somalia, U.S. commandos operate from compounds in Kismayo and Baledogle. Another drone operation base is in the East African nation on Seychelles on the island of Victoria while in Uganda PC-12 surveillance aircraft fly from the Entebbe airport as part of the U.S. Special Forces mission assisting the Ugandan army hunt for Joseph Kony and soldiers in the Lord's Resistance Army.[61]

The U.S. is far from alone in maintaining an extensive military presence on the continent. France also has a large military presence in Africa. This includes the anti-insurgent Operation Barkhane in Chad with 3,500 French troops that operate in Burkina Faso, Chad, Mali, Mauritania, and Niger. French military forces also are in Djibouti with 1,700 personnel while its other facilities at Port-Bouët, a suburb of Abidjan, in the Ivory Coast, has as many as 1,000 soldiers. Britain, which still trains troops of many African armies, has a permanent training support unit, based mainly in Nanyuki, 125 miles north of Nairobi in Kenya. Germany has an air transport base at the Niamey International Airport in Niger.[62]

China has established a military base at the port of Obock in Djibouti, across from Camp Lemonnier. Even the rich Gulf Arab countries have now joined the race on setting up military bases in Africa with Saudi Arabia putting roots in Djibouti and the UAE in Somalia and Eritrea. Russia although not physically *present* in the same sense is nevertheless the biggest arms exporter to Africa and, of course, African dictators have allocated more generous budgets for weapons than they have for food and medicines.

These military bases have several functions. They act primarily as forward operating platforms from which to protect their respective country's economic interests in Africa. They also have the secondary objective of assuring security for indigenous African people in the sense that they reassure the host dictator, who counts on his foreign allies to step in militarily should public disaffection turn to uncontrolled anger. But, the physical protection of African Dictatorship is in direct proportion to the loyalty any given dictator has to the agenda of the foreign power from whence that protection might come. Should a dictator try to pursue an unconventional path, the military bases will serve as a strong reminder that a recalcitrant leader can be replaced swiftly by a more willing puppet.

As a new player in African colonialism, China has aggravated the anxieties of Western governments and has brought a barrage of media coverage in Europe and America scrutinizing Chinese investments in the continent. The "no strings attached" development assistance protocol China has offered has drawn more African leaders to Beijing, thus opening up the continent's markets and encouraging new streams of exports of African natural resources. Despite the basic criticism of colonialism and economic dependency, Africa's relationship with China has engendered more benefits than what has been available with the Western benefactors. China's president Hu Jintao summarized the positives, saying China has built more than 100 schools, 30 hospitals, 30 anti-malaria centers, and 20 agricultural technology demonstration centers in Africa. It has met the pledge of providing $15 billion of lending of a preferential nature to Africa and China has trained close to 40,000 African personnel and provided more than 20,000 government scholarships.[63] Africa is reaping tangible economic benefits from China's presence but there is no doubt that China's interest in the continent goes beyond mere altruism. Economically, the private and public sectors in China are benefiting from this rapidly developing relationship. Chinese companies get new business investments, and the country as a whole gets steady access to much-needed natural resources.

There are clearly reasons to be concerned about China's heightened aggressiveness in Africa and its competition for procuring African resources. In 2011, delegates to the annual session of China's parliament debated a proposal to seek employment for as many as 100 million Chinese on African soil.[64] While it is past question that China's increasingly vigorous interest in the Continent will have diverse consequences for Africans, it seems unwise for them to look to the West for protection from or clarification of China's intentions. The European nations as well as the U.S. have offered ample proof over the centuries that their offers of assistance and security come at a high price.

In practice many Africans see the Chinese presence as a source of feasible solutions to some of the myriad problems that beset them and that Europe and the U.S. protest too much over China's *real intentions*. They would argue that the West could assist by discontinuing support for exploitative African dictators and that, in general, African leaders have behaved toward China according to type: accepting whatever they can in exchange for resources and access.

Expressions of shock and surprise from Europe regarding China's African adventures have often been hard for the average African to take. In January 2018, when the French daily newspaper *Le Monde* published a story claiming that technicians at the African Union's (AU) Chinese-built headquarters in the Ethiopian capital had discovered that China had been spying on them, Africans like myself were baffled. The report simply signified, once again, the possessive and protective nature of former imperialists to their colonies. The *Le Monde* report quoted anonymous AU sources, who indicated that data from computers in the Chinese-built building, at a construction cost of $200 million, had been transferred nightly to Chinese servers for five years. After the massive hack was discovered, the building's IT system including servers was overhauled. The report was dismissed by Moussa Faki Mahamat, AU commission chair, during a visit to Beijing. Mahamat said simply that some people "are jealous of China-Africa cooperation." And the pace of that co-operation shows no sign of slowing as China's investment in Africa deepens, as it regularly offers low-interest loans and gifts to individual nations. In 2016 alone China did $149.2 billion (120.3 billion euros) in trade.[65]

And what of the U.S.? President Trump also has acknowledged the potential of trading markets on the continent. "Africa has tremendous business potential, I have so many friends going to your countries trying to get rich. I congratulate you, they're spending a lot of money. It has tremendous business potential, representing huge amounts of different markets. . . . It's really become a place they have to go, that they want to go," the President said, while addressing a gathering of African leaders at the United Nations General Assembly in 2017.[66] The President's comments, even if given the benefit of the doubt as a message of congratulating Africans on their economic progress, nevertheless ring with the familiar condescending tone of the paternalistic language of colonial exploitation, which the continent has heard for centuries.

Johnnie Carson, U.S. Assistant Secretary of State for African Affairs from 2009 to 2012 under the Obama Administration, predicted that Trump's policy in Africa would be less interested in Africa than Obama's and despite his global network of hotel, golf, and tourism holdings, he appears to have placed no investments or business relationships in sub-Saharan Africa. "The one member of Trump's inner circle that may have an interest in Africa was the earlier Secretary of State Rex Tillerson," Carson said. "He has some experience in Africa because of his many years in the oil industry with ExxonMobil, most of whose successful dealings on the continent were with largely corrupt and authoritarian leaders."[67]

It is worth noting that the relationships between politicians in the developed world and those in Africa are corrupt in both directions, sometimes spectacularly so. One such came to light when former French President Nicolas Sarkozy was arrested in connection with allegations that he received millions of euros in illegal campaign financing from the regime of the late Libyan leader Moammar Gadhafi. Investigators examined claims that Gadhafi's regime secretly gave Sarkozy 50 million euros for his 2007 French presidential campaign. The sum would have been more than double the legal campaign funding limit at the time, which was 21 million euros. In addition, the alleged payments violated French rules against foreign financing and the protocol for declaring the source of campaign funds.[68]

Furthermore, the investigative journalism team at the Mediapart online journal published documents and an interview in which Ziad Takieddine, a French-Lebanese businessman, who said that in 2006–2007 he handed over three suitcases stuffed with 200 and 500 euro notes to Sarkozy and Claude Guéant, who was his Chief of Staff.[69] Sarkozy and Guéant—the latter a close ally of the former and once a minister—claimed that the documents that were obtained by Mediapart were false. A French court later declared that certain documents were authentic, allowing them to be used in the ongoing investigation.

The Sarkozy scandal is not the only case in which French politicians were reported as having accepted money from impoverished African countries for their career advancement. In an interview in *Le Monde*, French lawyer and political figure Robert Bourgi stated that he had collected cash valued at more than 20 million euros from various African dictators and delivered it to former President of France Jacques Chirac.[70] The 66-year-old lawyer said he delivered money concealed in suitcases or disguised as containers, ranging from African drums to advertising posters. The cash was donated, he said, by the leaders of Senegal, Burkina Faso, Ivory Coast, Congo, and Gabon. He named two leaders: Abdoulaye Wade of Senegal and Blaise Compaore of Burkina Faso and Chirac was arrested.

Soon after that arrest Chirac's friend the French billionaire Vincent Bolloré, Chairman of the Bolloré Investment Group, one of the most prominent businesses in Francophone Africa, was also detained and questioned by anti-corruption police. Investigators are looking into allegations that his Havas advertising agency provided discounted communications advice to Guinean President Alpha Condé and Togolese President Faure Gnassingbé at election time in return for the Bolloré Africa Logistics Company being given licenses to operate container ports in Conakry and Lomé. After the election in Guinea, Condé terminated the contract of Conakry port's existing operator and gave it to the Bolloré Group.[71]

On occasion the unhealthily close relationships between the African regimes and their erstwhile colonial overlords have been very far from covert: rather they have been blatant and bizarre; a source of embarrassment and shame to their citizens. Take for example the meeting of the Senegalese Cabinet that took place on October 18, 2017 in Paris, that was led by the French Prime Minister. After the meeting, the respective ministers of the two countries posed for photographs, as though proud of participating in such a disconcerting perversion of the norms of sovereign status.[72]

Shifting focus away from the client regime relationship, it seems that people, institutions, and states the world over see Africa and African potential in a depressingly cynical light. Africa seems to be viewed as a source of natural resources that come without the burden of sustainability, and cheap labor without the cost of socio-economic responsibility or health and safety legislation. Indeed, many nations treat Africa as a dumping ground both for actual rubbish and for cheaply made clothing, used electronics, or foodstuffs that were found to be surplus or that failed to capture Western markets—a sentiment strongly stated by Farida Bemba Nabourema, a Togo activist who has blogged frequently about Togo's dictator Faure Gnassigbe.[73]

Her concerns are not unfounded or exaggerated. Across Africa, second-hand merchandise from the U.S. and Europe constitutes the primary source of clothing. Likewise, Africa is the primary market for used cars, planes, hospital equipment, computers, and pharmaceuticals that have passed their expiration date. Even though used clothes can be appealing for their affordability many Africans hesitate to take them into their shops and homes. Few people are attracted by the prospect of wearing the discards of others, even if they are stuck in dire economic circumstances. That is why Africans have tagged such items the as "clothes of the dead" in Kenya or the "clothes of calamity" in Mozambique.

The phenomenon of the second-hand clothing trade is damaging not only to the dignity of citizens but also to industry; not only detrimental to the way Africans look and feel but to the possibility of their material prosperity. East African nations are striving to replicate economic success stories in Asia and the United States, where nascent industries of manufacturing and technology were initially incubated, protected, and nurtured before they were deemed capable and ready to compete on the global market. But importing vast quantities of used clothes and shoes—$151 million worth in 2015 alone, mostly from Europe and the U.S.—is clearly not the way to protect the textile industry. To that end East African countries such as Rwanda, Kenya, Uganda, Tanzania, South Sudan, and Burundi have teamed up to phase out imports of second-hand clothes and shoes by 2019.[74]

The U.S., which is the leading exporter of used clothes to these African countries, has already registered a hostile response to the proposed ban. It has threatened to reconsider the currently favorable trade terms that are part of the African Growth and Opportunity Act (AGOA) if any East African country proceeds with the ban. The response to such threats is contingent upon the nature of the relationship between the African country and the U.S., and the degree of dependency that exists in that relationship, and so varies considerably. Kenya was the first nation to backtrack and withdraw its support for the used-clothing ban. Uganda raised taxes for the import of used clothes, and it is difficult to discern Tanzania's position, as it has remained silent in the face of American bullying on the issue. Depressingly, the situation is further complicated by domestic politic troubles.

Rwanda's President Paul Kagame, however, has been firm and announced at a press conference that the ban would continue, despite American threats.[75] Kagame did not downplay the threat's seriousness but he said the ban would prevail even if it meant that Rwanda might have to sacrifice some potential for economic growth. It is painfully ironic that the U.S., with a president so intent on closing borders to immigrants, regardless of their legal status, would be so angered at African countries trying to close their markets to used clothes.

It seems that successive American administrations that have looked to retain the policy infrastructure that facilitates the used-clothing trade to markets in the developing world are far more important to protect their own industries than the rights of migrant human beings who seek to improve their economic lot while working hard for the benefit of the American economy. The American response reflects a desire to protect jobs and have open access to small but promising African markets simultaneously, but why then would it block African migrants from traveling abroad to fill some of the jobs that were created by the presence and demand of African markets. This episode has become one of a big brother bully who demands the unilateral exploitation of small African markets at the expense of its people with a moral setting in the same manner that King Joao III of Portugal in the 16th century had demanded the entitlement of African slaves for the benefit of Portuguese traders.

Behind the American response to the East African ban is a group of 40 used clothing exporters, known as the Secondary Materials and Recycled Textiles Association. It claims that 40,000 American jobs, primarily for sorting and packing clothes, are at risk. Clothing thrown away by Americans, the association says, will end up in U.S. landfills and cause further damage to the environment, if not sold abroad.[76]

Andrew Brooks, the author of *Clothing Poverty: The Hidden World of Fast Fashion and Second-hand Clothes,* noted how the current dispute over the trade deal has exposed the problems of globalization. Kenya, for example, had half a million workers in the garment industry a few decades ago. That number has shrunk to 20,000 today, and production is geared toward exporting clothes often too expensive for the local market. In Ghana, jobs in textiles plunged by 80 percent between 1975 and 2000. Many people in Zambia, which produced clothes locally 30 years ago, can now only afford to buy imported second-hand items.

As we close the historical chapter on colonialism and imperialism it is important to note here that Africans could have achieved a modicum of independence under the leadership of black presidents and prime ministers during the first wave of the independence movement. But, it became apparent quickly and often in brutal violent results, that the former colonial powers were not going to relinquish the fruits of economic activity to the newly independent countries with any speed or ease. This is what has continued to drive many Africans off the continent. Today when Africans try to complain about colonialism, they are always reminded that Black African people are now the leaders who control their own destinies, not white Europeans. And by doing so, media and scholars from those former colonial powers have publicized the aid they have given to Africans as exceptionally magnanimous acts of charity without mentioning that what they actually have taken from Africa always was much more than what they have given in return. African citizens also have accepted this fallacy without much rigorous analysis, looking at themselves as the wretched of the earth waiting for European aid instead of demanding that their wealth should not continue to be plundered by European corporations—now endorsed by a string of African corrupt presidents.

Streams of wealth still leave Africa at a rate that outpaces the inflows. African countries received $162 billion in 2015, mainly in loans, aid, and personal remittances. But in the same year, $203 billion was taken from the continent, according to an analysis by a coalition of UK and African equality and development campaigners.[77] The same report noted that African governments received $32 billion in loans in 2015, but paid more than half of that—$18 billion—in interest, with the level of debt rising rapidly and continuously. Another important source for the net wealth outflow is even more problematic. The U.S.-based Global Financial Integrity (GFI) and the Center for Applied Research at the Norwegian School of Economics released a study showing that since 1980 developing countries lost $16.3 trillion dollars through broad leakages in the balance of payments, incorrect trade invoicing and recorded financial transfers. The report notes that these resources represent immense social costs that have been borne by the citizens of developing countries around the globe.[78] "This report is the most comprehensive analysis of global financial flows impacting developing countries compiled to date," said GFI President Raymond Baker. However, the challenge remains how to translate the results of these reports into practical policy with real benefit for African citizens.

It is worth noting here that some commentators engage in false equivalence in order to dismiss the Continent's claim to unique suffering, arguing that Western exploitation through colonialism and neocolonialism occurred in Asia and the Americas as well as in Africa. The truth is that many countries in Asia and even the Middle

East have suffered to varying degrees under neocolonialism, with some enduring as much as have some African nations. The Middle East has stagnated politically and economically as ruthless dictators are most interested in doing oil deals with the west while suppressing all dissent at home. And while The Arab Spring succeeded in overthrowing a few aged despots and the revolutionary movement gathered momentum for a time, the West soon took over the reins and replaced the deposed dictators with still-more ruthless despots while simultaneously tightening the security details of their oil-rich Gulf allies who, though they had survived the Spring, can be numbered in the same class of those dictators who did not.

Africa's unique position in the league table of misfortune is secured by the duration and depth of her relationship with slavery and its descendant forms of exploitation. Certainly, countries such as Mexico, Guatemala, Jamaica, Haiti, and others in the Caribbean and Americas also endured their own involvement with slavery and still lag in economic measures and poverty persists because of the same exploitive policies. And many of the citizens of those countries like those of many African nations seek to migrate to the U.S. to find their own path of economic justice, and migration is the subject to which we turn our attention in the next chapter.

Chapter 9: European Migrations to Africa

"Europe has 'forgotten' that between 1840 and 1940 it exported 60 million migrants to Africa, Asia, and U.S., most of them illegally. Only 70 years ago, more than 5 million Europeans lived in Africa. They settled there without entry visas but with guns." Célestin Monga

Migration has been central to the narrative of every human civilization and that Europe in the age of exploration and empire is no exception. Europeans migrated to Africa in vast numbers but as Célestin Monga, the Chief Economist at African Development Bank, puts it: Europe has "forgotten" that between 1840 and 1940, it exported 60 million migrants to Africa, Asia, and U.S., most of them without the benefit of prior documentation. Indeed, just 70 years ago, more than five million Europeans lived in Africa, and they settled there without entry visas but rather with guns in hand to consolidate their legitimacy as migrants.[79]

Soon after decolonization, the polarity of that migration pattern was reversed, as Europeans returned to their respective homelands. The majority of European returnees were from French-controlled North Africa. After Algeria gained its independent in 1962, about 800,000 *Pieds-Noirs*—as they were known—of French nationality returned to France while about 200,000 chose to remain in Algeria. Of the latter, there were still about 100,000 in 1965 and about 50,000 more returned to France by the end of the 1960s.[80]

As soon as the Europeans left, the Arabs and Africans from the colonized states followed them, as the 1960s saw their independent states descend into war and chaos. Most Africans went to their nearest national colonial relative, with those from north and west Africa going to France and those from the eastern and southern regions of the continent heading to the UK.

Initially, European hosts were far from hostile to migrants in general and extended large migrant quotas to some former colonies in particular. The whole administrative climate differed radically from the conditions that prevail currently. Obtaining dual citizenship, for example, was then a relatively simple process that now can take more than ten years to complete. Such was the welcoming spirit that imperial countries formed organizations that fostered close political and economic ties with former colonies. The United Kingdom formed the Commonwealth of Nations; France, the Francophonie; The Netherlands, the Dutch Language Union and Portugal, Community of Portuguese Language Countries.

It was when the volume of migrant traffic ballooned going into the 1980s that changed the balance, as the ethnic profiles of European states grew more diverse. At first, France was the mostly affected with up to 25 percent of the population of Paris and 14 percent of the metropolitan region being Muslims from north Africa, mainly Algeria. Cultural and religious conflicts became more frequent.[81]

In response to growing popular discomfort with migrant numbers France and her continental partners looked to reduce net migration by imposing various restrictions but often simply narrowing the margins of validity in the conditions for applying for and obtaining a visa. 1985 proved seminal as ten European countries came together to sign the Schengen Treaty to ease border checks only for member countries.

The treaty disproportionately affected African migrants. A 2015 study examining a database of visa waiver policies for more than 150 countries, as compiled over a 40-year period ending in 2010, showed that citizens of the Organisation for Economic Co-operation and Development (OECD) countries and those with strong wealth economic indicators have gained substantially in their mobility rights, comparable rights have stagnated or diminished significantly in particular for citizens from African countries.[82]

The Trump Administration has provoked a furious reaction for irrationally stoking fears of migrants and immigration with his persistent calls to build a wall at the U.S.-Mexico border. But, African migrants have endured a *"Wall around The West"* far longer than the Trump Doctrine policies.[83] As we have already noted African migrants initially enjoyed easy visa requirements mainly because European officials saw it as a gesture of goodwill—a convenient substitute for other measures that might have involved significant investments in reparations and restorations in their former African colonies. What alarmed European officials was the robustness of the trend, as Africans gladly took the opportunity that was extended to them. It's worth closing this chapter and the section on a quote from the same 2015 study that illustrates the juxtaposed irony and hypocrisy of the situation:

> This, obviously, has changed, with the fear of irregular migration from Africa leading to an exclusion of Africans from enhanced forms of openness. Moreover, European countries harmonized their visa policies in 2001 and now have a common list of countries from which citizens have to apply for a visa before travelling to the EU. While strengthening the intra-EU process of policy making, this harmonization might have weakened relations between African countries and their former colonial powers in Europe.[84]

In the section we will see conscientious Africans fighting to bring democratic consciousness and institutions to their newly independent homelands, often alone and in the shadow of the knowledge that the organs of the state were already corrupted by wealth from the deep pockets of their former colonial masters.

SECTION III: A CONTINENT IN CHAINS

Chapter 10: Museveni's Ascent to Power on a Tide of Covert Western Influence

"The west won the world not by the superiority of its ideas or values or religion but rather by its superiority in applying organized violence. Westerners often forget this fact, non-westerners never do."
Samuel P. Huntington

In December 1980, in a scene he recounts in his autobiography *Sowing the Mustard Seed*,[85] Yoweri Kaguta Museveni, his wife and six-year-old son arrived at a military roadblock in Kireka, a suburb of Kampala. It was election time in the country, and he was one of the presidential candidates, although not one of the most popular. Two armed men in uniform ordered him out of his car and grabbed him and his family until other soldiers who recognized him intervened and demanded why he was being manhandled. Museveni recounted the scene in his book *Sowing the Mustard Seed*.[86] The men answered that they had orders from the Chairman of the Military Council to arrest and shoot Museveni because he was running a hate campaign in which he threatened to go to the bush and fight the government if the elections were rigged.

The event was a kind of epiphany for Museveni and left him deeply disturbed. For him it was at the very least symbolic of what was wrong with Uganda; perhaps even with Africa herself in the post-colonial era. Here was the Vice-Chairman of the Military Council—which effectively ruled the country—so the de facto Vice-President of Uganda(along with his family)—being harassed, apprehended, and threatened with abduction and murder on the streets of Kampala.

For our purposes the scene in Kireka is a tableau—an overture—that invites us into the story of Museveni as emblematic of the processes by which this generation of African leaders were formed: by experience, education, training, service, ideology, and conviction but also by a complex and dynamic relationship with the west.

Museveni was certainly right to be concerned about the elections. They proceeded as scheduled and Museveni contested under his new party known as the Uganda Patriotic Movement (UPM). But on December 11, 1980, Paul Muwanga, then President of Uganda, issued a decree pertaining to the election results that would have far-reaching consequences. It required electoral officers to submit their constituency results not to the electoral commission but instead to Muwanga, and barred the Electoral Commission from declaring any results until he had personally reviewed and approved them.

The numerical election results were unacceptable to Muwanga, who had backed Uganda's former president, Apollo Milton Obote. Despite their combined efforts to ensure that Obote, the flag bearer of the Uganda People's Congress (UPC) party, won the elections, the people of Uganda had decided otherwise: the Democratic Party headed by Paul Kawanga Semwogerere appeared to be victorious.

So Electoral officers were also required by the decree not to submit their constituency results to the electoral commission but instead to Muwanga. on December 12, Muwanga went on national radio, with the support of the army and police, to declare Obote the winner of the 1980 Ugandan elections. Muwanga assumed the post of vice-president and minister of defense. Museveni's UPM party won one out of 126 seats in parliament and he was ranked last of the four presidential candidates but so pained was he by what he called Obote's rigging of the elections that he declared war on the President he believed had stolen the crown.

Obote, whose prior administration has been defined by its communist ideology and trenchant criticism of Britain and its imperialist agenda, prepared to re-occupy these positions in the 1980s. However, Obote had failed or perhaps refused to accept the reality of the political situation on the continent: that while anti-imperial posturing was popular with the voters, it was not the material with which to lay the foundations of the future of a post-colonial state. Time and again African leaders had proven they were simply not strong enough to control their respective nation's political destiny without some kind of deal or understanding with the neo-colonialists or the erstwhile masters.

By contrast, Museveni's guerrilla war although clothed in the Marxist ideas and rhetoric that appealed to the average, was reliant on material support from the forces ranged in support of capitalism and the west. In his autobiography, Museveni recounts how important it was for him to establish contacts with British politicians such as Lord Carrington and Richard Luce, then Minister of State for Overseas Development in the Foreign and Commonwealth Office. Luce had reluctantly advised Museveni to accept the election results and to lead economic reform efforts, but Museveni insisted his strategy of challenging the results was worthwhile; Luce reversed his initial recommendation and a partnership of sorts was born.

The relationship was embarrassing and potentially destructive not only to Museveni but also to the British. Museveni recalls visits to London in which the British Government insisted that his presence in the country should remain discreet, concealing him in hotels away from public attention. But despite this reticence Museveni had won the undeclared support of the British government and soon he was in a position to speak to radio interviewers at the British Broadcasting Corporation (BBC), announcing that the U.S. as well as Britain would support his insurgent bush operation against Obote's Marxist-leaning regime. Indeed, Britain was among the first to allow Museveni's rebel group—the National Resistance Movement (NRM)—to establish an office of operations in their country. Soon after, the U.S. and Sweden also officially cut ties with Obote's government and allowed Museveni's rebel group to establish offices in their countries that later would become embassies for Uganda. Museveni's path to power though winding, was now clear.

Obote understood that Museveni's strength was generated by the massive support he received from foreign governments. Britain's patronage was as discreet as possible. This was, after all, interference in the internal politics of a sovereign nation that had only recently been her colony. And this in an era where the architecture of the post-world war order—based as it was on the principle of sovereignty—remained largely intact, at least in theory. Proxy wards were common, especially in Africa, but the plausible deniability remained de rigueur. African nations, by contrast observed no limits in professing their support for Museveni's rebel campaign, although the African leaders that supported Museveni were, of course, those with warm relationships with the UK: Kenya's Arap Moi, Libya's Moammar Gadhafi, and Tanzania's Mwalimu Julius Nyerere.

Obote was careful not to attack Britain openly but rather targeted his political rhetoric toward surrounding African governments, accusing them of advancing the West's imperialist agenda on the continent. Never diplomatic, Moi responded to the accusations during the 18th Kenyan National Day celebrations that he could if he chose topple Obote's teetering regime, in just minutes. In an even more personal provocation Moi addressed the absent Obote with advice that he should meet Museveni's rebels as they were only 10 miles from his Kampala residence.

Museveni was indeed busy as Moi and Obote jousted. He travelled to Libya via Nairobi after crossing Lake Victoria by boat and when in Tripoli he met Gadhafi, who was then still in good standing with the European powers. The two were once bitter rivals, as Gadhafi has been a principal supporter of Idi Amin, Uganda's notorious dictator whom Museveni had fought and helped to oust. Despite being divided by personal experience they were united not only in a political goal—the ousting of Obote—but in their roles as actual and aspirant client dictators. To cement this relationship Gadhafi assured the rebels that he would support them with money and weapons to oust the Obote government in Kampala. And he was true to his word giving them 800 rifles, 45 RPG launchers, 100 anti-tank landmines, as well as machine guns and mortars.[ix]

And so Nyerere of Tanzania had once been Obote's diehard supporter. In the 1970s when Obote and Museveni vied over who should take the leadership of the rebel groups to fight Amin, Nyerere sided with Obote, urging Museveni to work under him. And the Tanzanian army that had toppled Amin had stayed in Uganda to keep Obote's government firmly in control.

Nyerere was the last leader to abandon Obote but he recognized that times had changed. He was concerned about his own political survival and had no other option but to change course if he was to remain relevant in the continent's affairs. He embraced the new

---

ix   The consignment of weapons entered Uganda through Burundi.

dispensation of covert compromise with the West, and welcomed the new breed of Western puppet leaders here represented by Museveni. The West backed Museveni and Nyerere duly gave him 10,000 rifles and one million rounds of ammunition with which to attack his erstwhile ally.[87]

With his regime in its death throes Obote lashed out, seeking to avenge himself on Museveni's popular power base—generally speaking the people of Central Uganda. (Obote is from Northern Uganda) Paul Muwanga, Obote's Vice-President who was also from the country's central region, always would often remind audiences at government-sponsored rallies and functions that no matter how many people were killed, the grave can never be full but rather will always welcome fresh corpses—as blatant and graphic a threat as he could muster.

The violence wasn't limited to the provinces. Across Kampala there were roadblocks manned by Army personnel who had no respect for anyone's safety or personal welfare; who beat commuters, strip-searched women in a purported hunt for weapons, and demanded money, even from the children and the old. Obote's flailing was at times bizarre rather than gruesome. Before resigning the presidency and leaving the country, he set out to cast doubt on Museveni's citizenship, telling the BBC in a radio interview that Museveni was a Rwandan refugee.[88]

The outcome of such unchecked ruthlessness was never in doubt and Obote was finally ousted by General Tito Okello Lutwa, the Commander of the Army, who then held the presidential seat for a few months while moderating a national dialogue about Uganda's future, which was convened in Nairobi. Museveni was part of the dialogue but he did not pull back his guerilla adventure to grab power by force.

The cost of removing Obote had been high. The death toll for Museveni's bush war was estimated to be 300,000 by his Western funders and predictably enough the blame for those casualties was leveled exclusively at the defeated figure of Obote.[89] But power rarely pauses to mourn and Museveni was proclaimed not only the new leader of Uganda, but the representative of a new *type* of leader: someone the West could do business with; one of a new generation of Africa leaders to replace the "Big Men."[90]

Western patronage came with a certain amount of license. Museveni's alliance with the West during and after the war ensured he got away with war crimes, such as recruiting child soldiers and robbing banks to fund his guerilla war. Far from condemning him, the Western media blamed the carnage suffered during this violent transition of power in Uganda on Obote's earlier failure to compromise.

There was a widespread—probably genuine—failure in the West to see Uganda with a longitudinal perspective, one that is essential to understand how the perpetrators of one leader's dirty wars can find themselves transformed into the victims of another's. Colonialism had scarred the country with regional antipathy; wounds that did not heal with independence. On the contrary, ceaseless ethnic violence and the compulsion to settle scores perpetuated distrust, regardless of who occupied the presidency, and galvanized propaganda that turned abused civilians into convenient government targets.

Chapter 11: Europe's Man in Uganda

"Just because we have the best hammer does not mean that every problem is a nail." Barack Obama

On assuming power, Museveni's preeminent objective was to prove Uganda's reliability as a security partner to the West in East and Central Africa. As a consequence, the Ugandan President became directly involved in regional conflicts, acting as the political equivalent of a brokerage firm for rebels, insurgencies, and peace missions. Wherever there was a conflict in the region the West did not have to enter directly, Museveni was available to send in Uganda troops to support the side most amenable to Western interests, and acted as a principal negotiator on behalf of the U.S. or European nation involved. Under Museveni, Uganda had placed more troops abroad than any other country in the world barring the U.S.[91] And Ugandan troops were significant in determining the outcomes from conflicts in Somalia, South Sudan, Democratic Republic of Congo, Rwanda, Burundi, and even Kenya, after election-related violence erupted in 2007.

In 1991, after Somalia's dictator Mohammed Siad Barre was overthrown, the country went into a vicious civil war. The U.S. sent 100,000 troops to restore order in an operation they called "Operation Restore Hope," which began as an effort to underwrite the delivery of UN Aid by guaranteeing security in Mogadishu but ended as an unsuccessful manhunt targeting the Somali faction leader, General Mohammed Farah Aidid. On October 3, 1993, one of the bloodiest days of the conflicts and one immortalized in the annals of U.S. military legend, General Aidid's militia killed 18 Americans and wounded more than 70 others. More than 300 Somalis were killed. The battle proved to have been the bloody denoument of the American obsession with Aidid: the U.S. stopped pursuing him, unwilling to risk further casualties. The American troops pulled back into their encampments and compounds, dispatching few patrols until the politicians in Washington formally aborted the expedition.[92]

Thus bloodied the U.S. looked around and asked who in Africa was willing to take on the Somali war, and Museveni was the first to raise his hand. The Uganda People's Defense Forces (UPDF) provided about 6,000 troops leading the African Union Mission in Somalia (Amisom). Uganda's involvement drew the ire of the Somali Islamist militants "Al Shabab": in July 2010, a double suicide bombing in Kampala killed 76 people who were watching the World Cup soccer final on television.

As in Somalis so in South Sudan where Uganda acted as the intermediary of the American support to the Sudan People's Liberation Army (SPLA) in its war to separate South Sudan from North Sudan in the 1990s. Two years after South Sudan declared its independence, President Salva Kiir fired his vice-president, Riek Machar, and the political power contest snowballed into military clashes fought along the Dinka-Nuer ethnic lines representing Kiir and Machar, respectively. Museveni immediately deployed Ugandan troops, telling journalists the troops had been sent at the request of the South Sudan government, just in time to save Kiir from being toppled as the country's leader.[93]

Uganda was instrumental in regime changes involving its immediate neighbors. On his return from undergoing military training in the U.S., Paul Kagame—formerly a senior officer in the Ugandan Army—joined with other Rwandese exiled in Uganda, to form the Rwanda Patriotic Front (RPF). The RPF, supported by the Ugandan government, waged a war against the Rwandan government of President Habyarimana that would culminate in the Rwandan Genocide, which decimated the Tutsi population of the country. Kagame successfully overthrew Habyarimana's government, and has been the president of Rwanda since 2000.[94] Kagame had learned from Museveni's experience and immediately cast himself as the guarantor of the safety and indeed survival of the Tutsi minority, gesturing to the narrative of the genocide as his mandate, and transforming his country into a dictatorship. And Western backers have certainly indulged the exercise, continuing to fund Kagame's regime despite reports of widespread human rights abuses including the use of torture. Indeed the West has touted Rwanda as a success, an anomaly, almost a miracle, and this propaganda was unchallenged, becoming convenient proof that their aid was working for the good.

Whether this relationship will continue in such a mutually supportive vein is unclear. Until recently, the U.S. was Rwanda's largest bilateral aid donor, at $162 million, followed by the UK, which has provided $107 million. As David Himbara explains, "under the administrations of Bill Clinton, George Bush, and Barack Obama, the Rwandan dictator, Paul Kagame, became the American darling, receiving millions of dollars for both socioeconomic development and military aid."[95] But the Trump Administration has cooled to the idea of continuing aid to Rwanda at such robust levels, a decision based less on punishing the Rwandan government than it is for the president's penchant for reversing the policies his predecessors have endorsed. As Himbara notes, 70 percent of the aid Rwanda has received may disappear with the remaining portions being allocated for the purposes of treating AIDS/HIV and malaria. Himbara succinctly encapsulates the predicament, "Paul Kagame loves to boast that good aid is one that provides temporary support, as opposed to long-term aid that leads to dependency."[96]

Museveni and Kagame overstepped their role as clients and became kingmakers in their own right. But not all of their adventures have been welcomed by all sections of opinion in the West. One such is, their invasion of the Democratic Republic of Congo a resource-rich black hole into which the region was pulled for a decade. The conflict was triggered when the armies of Uganda and Rwanda, both key security allies for Western interests, turned against each other in the Congo. A 2001 United Nations report noted that Museveni and Kagame were "on the verge of becoming godfathers of the illegal exploitation of natural resources and the continuation of the conflict."[97] The report identified, as *The New York Times* article highlighted, "three dozen businesses, based in Belgium, Germany, Malaysia, Canada, Switzerland, the Netherlands, Britain, India, Pakistan, and Russia . . . as having imported minerals from Congo through Uganda and Rwanda."[98]

The allegations were substantiated. Following the war, the Government of the DRC Congo sued that of Uganda and Rwanda for plundering its resources and committing war atrocities. The International Court of Justice found Uganda guilty in December 2005, and the country was ordered to pay Congo $10 billion in damages.

Museveni's closest relatives, including his son Major Muhozi Kaineru-gaba and brother Lieutenant General Caleb Akandwanaho with the alias of Salim Saleh, were implicated in overseeing the plundering operations.

Unfortunately, this international lawsuit has not stopped the plundering of Congo's wealth by its regional global neighbors at the time of writing. Even now, Rwandan rebels in Congo, of which most of them are members of the Rwandan army, have served as the private army and resource extractors of diamonds, timber, gold, uranium, cassiterite, and coltan. They are not of course doing this for the benefit of the DRC or even for that of Rwandan but rather for leading global companies and the people and institutions they pay.

Rwanda is being used by Western nations as a proxy frontier for the pillage of Congolese resources and the laundering of the proceeds. Vast amounts of unaccounted-for resources are taken from the DRC and trafficked through Rwanda; a re-exportation process that comprises the bulk of Rwandan exports. For this service, Rwanda has been rewarded flattering public relations promoting the country as Africa's success story and its leader Paul Kagame as a pan-Africanist, who has brought capital inflows from foreign investors. Furthermore, corrupt politicians and militia also are investing their illicit spoils in real estate and facilitating government debt for public spending. Laundering of Congolese resources has brought about a real estate boom, along with the infrastructure development of Rwanda's capital Kigali, now being promoted as Africa's most beautiful city.

In Burundi, citizens attempted a coup in 2015 after their president Laurent Nkuruziza, Museveni's friend and another strong ally of the U.S., announced he was standing for a third term. Jubilant citizens thronged the streets after the coup announcement and news that the deposed president Nkurunziza fled the country, but that joy was soon darkened by the shadow of regional enforcer Museveni. Ugandan troops entered Burundi to overturn the coup and reinstate President Nkuruziza.

The ulterior rationale for the intervention is somewhat serpentine. Burundi, like Uganda, is a substantial recipient of U.S. military aid and many of its troops are fighting alongside Uganda in Somalia.

According to a section of the U.S. Foreign Assistance Act, if the people's coup in Burundi had succeeded, the U.S. would have been required by law to suspend its military assistance to the country,[99] This would have jeopardized Burundi's capacity and willingness to fight Al Shabab. Seen in this light, Museveni's reversal of the coup was little more than a favor to the U.S.

Museveni has been careful to keep his relationship with the U.S. secure. During the Invasion of Iraq in 2003, 20,000 Ugandans worked in American military bases.[100] And in 2018 he announced Uganda would send 8,000 troops into Yemen to fight on the U.S. side, led by Saudi Arabia and United Arab Emirates.

Somewhat counterintuitively, while it would be reasonable to surmise that when Uganda sent troops to neighboring countries and to the Middle East, the West was bankrolling the costs, the situation is not as simple as that. Certainly, the U.S. and some European countries contributed to the peace missions that were spear-headed by the Ugandan President, but much of the money for Uganda's adventures, comes from Uganda itself.

Indeed, soaring defense budgets and costs that dwarf government spending on health care and agriculture must be seen as a significant component of Museveni's legacy. With a population of approximately 42 million, Uganda often ranks at or near the top of the league table for defense spending among nations in East Africa. In 2011, it was first state in the region with an annual military expenditure that topped $642 million, more than $1 billion in the values current at the time of writing.

Unfortunately for the legacy of a substantial subsidy dedicated to military budgets, Museveni has not sought prior parliamentary approval and in the interim Western donors and their governments have remained silent.[101]

The recent unrest in Uganda erupted when pop star turned politician Bobi Wine was tortured by Museveni's personal security forces. Later he was welcomed in the U.S. for treatment where the embattled politician received enormous media attention and exposed Museveni's reliance on American military aid, a statement that likely will change the Ugandan political landscape.

The U.S., over the course of several administrations of different political complexion, has remained consistently both supportive and appreciative of Museveni. The U.S. has often looked away when questions about election fraud in Uganda have been raised and have accepted the Ugandan government's assurance that elections have been conducted freely and fairly.

Furthermore, the U.S. has done more than make supportive noises, demur when unsightly events take place, and send aid. In 2014, Barack Obama sent military aircraft and about 150 troops in cooperation with the Ugandan military establishment to track down the Ugandan warlord Joseph Kony, the most wanted suspect of the International Criminal Court at The Hague.

And the assistance though equally direct is sometimes somewhat more prosaic. Many troops in Uganda have been trained by the U.S. military, including in the use of sophisticated communications equipment, night-vision goggles and small surveillance drones—all of which are purchased from U.S. defense contractors. Ugandan troops deployed to Somalia travel in mine-resistant vehicles that once ferried American soldiers around Afghanistan. And Ugandan choppers engaged in operations against warlord Joseph Kony, powered by fuel paid for by the U.S., according to a 2016 article in the *Foreign Policy* journal.[102]

We close this chapter with another vignette: the hunt for Joseph Kony was led by the American-trained Ugandan Special Forces, which are commanded by Brigadier General Muhoozi Kainerugaba, Museveni's son, himself a graduate of Fort Leavenworth training.[103] The episode underscores Museveni's aspiration that, in a return to the feudal past at which he baulked as a younger man, he arrogantly believes that he eventually will be able to pass the mantle of power to his son, regardless of the opinion and of voting of Uganda's citizens.

Chapter 12: World Bank's Structural Adjustment Policies (SAPs)

"I love Trump because he tells Africans frankly that Africans need to solve their problems . . . America has got one of the best presidents ever." Yoweri Kaguta Museveni

Museveni has come to take for granted the support from the West that brought him to power and to a certain extent has kept him there. So much so that he has planned his succession—favoring either his son Muhoozi or wife Janet Kainerugaba—based on the assumption that the remarkably successful relationship between Uganda and the West will continue indefinitely.

The desperate, disillusioned, and exhausted population of Uganda certainly pose a threat to Museveni's dynastic plans and it is surely at least possible that population could attempt to wrest power without any reference or recourse to the West. But Museveni is probably right to think that the greatest threat to him is that the West will lose interest or faith in him and back someone else, however unlikely he may believe that to be.

That said, he has certainly had warning shots fired that should have shaken his cast-iron assumption of the permanence of his special relationship. In 2014, for example, when Museveni signed into law an anti-gay bill proposed by a parliamentary member of his National Resistance Movement party, the Obama Administration wasted no time in denouncing Uganda's government; a sentiment that was amplified by other Western powers. Western media reports followed suit, no longer referring to Museveni as the continent's new hope but instead being characterized as an aging dictator who had outlived his time in office. When Western rhetoric turned to genuine threats to shut off streams of aid, Museveni initially blustered, calling it blatant blackmail. But he soon realized his mistake and relocated his position, claiming that the bill had been rushed through the parliament without adequate research. However, in a parting salvo, he added, "Africans do not seek to impose their views on anybody. We do not want anybody to impose their views on us. This very debate was provoked by western groups who come to our schools and try to recruit children into homosexuality."[104]

So, Museveni has understood that he owes the West, especially the U.S., for his longevity as president despite the fact that Ugandans had tired of his leadership long ago. But, he also was aware that they could not mount any effective resistance to end his tenure without authorities catching wind of it. Regardless of the political provenance of the U.S. president, Museveni obliges his American benefactors with no protest, even when one (Donald Trump) flagrantly insults Africans. In January 2018 when President Trump had referred to African nations and Haiti as "shithole countries," some African leaders muttered mild disappointment. The governments of Botswana and Senegal summoned the respective U.S. ambassadors in their countries to explain the remarks. The African Union demanded an apology that never came but it was Museveni alone that welcomed the insults as "frank talk."

"I love Trump because he tells Africans frankly that Africans need to solve their problems. They need to be strong. In the world, you cannot survive if you are weak and it is the fault of Africans if they are weak," Museveni said while addressing members of the regional East African Legislative Assembly in the Ugandan capital of Kampala. "America has got one of the best presidents ever."[105] Unfortunately, Museveni's love for "frank talk" and vulgarity extends only as far his Western allies and not as far as Ugandan citizens. When Stella Nyanzi, a Ugandan academic and human rights activist called Museveni what can be transliterated to a "pair of buttocks," the president was really hurt and immediately ordered the activist arrested and charged.[106]

However, Western support for African dictators is clearly fickle and any such African who relies on it would surely have learned from the experience of others, most spectacularly Muammar Gadhafi who was deposed and then killed in humiliating circumstances. And there have certainly been rumblings. In April 2018, British MP Paul Williams asked the British government about taking advantage of an upcoming Commonwealth Heads of Government Meeting (CHoGM) to discuss how Museveni could be compelled to leave office. "Museveni has become a barrier to Uganda's development,"

Williams went as far to write in a Twitter post.[107] It seems at least possible that the British government has tired of Museveni, and downright likely that the British commercial world has: their corporations and parastatals were shuttering their doors in Uganda in frustration over the persistent incompetence of the regime. British Airways, for example, had taken over as the main air traffic provider at the Entebbe airport when Uganda Airlines was forced out of business by the World Bank's Structural Adjustment Policies (SAP). However, the British service provider later closed its own operations in Uganda, as it was no longer commercially viable. This is a significant indicator that the British government and businesses will no longer support Museveni's lifetime presidency bid if it is detrimental to their commercial interests.

It has not only been British corporations that have had to leave Uganda because of the worsening economic returns. UAE carrier Al Ittihad Airlines also halted its flights to Uganda and the America International Group (AIG) and other Western corporations have recently exited Uganda's failing economy. Their departure has had an effect on the government's income streams and to fill the gap the Museveni administration has had to rely heavily on taxing its citizens, something that they have shown some invention in doing. The government has previously introduced odd measures such as a social media tax in which citizens have to pay taxes for using Facebook, Twitter, or WhatsApp, something that would be laughed at in many other parts of the world.[x]

It is important to note in terms of domestic economic policy, there is little for the West to be disappointed about. Museveni still toes the Western line of liberalization, privatizing government parastatals, and embracing the World Bank and the International Monetary Fund's Structural Adjustment Programs (SAP), which his predecessors Obote and Amin had been reluctant to embrace. In Uganda, as in most of Africa, implementing the SAP in practice means handing over the whole country's economy to large Western corporations and a few of the President's cronies.

---

x   There also are the secondary effects of censorship to be realized by discouraging citizens to avoid using social media platforms, especially to criticize the government.

Progress on this agenda was steady. A few years into Museveni's presidency, as already noted, the country would lose Uganda airlines, local banks such as Uganda Commercial Banks would be privatized (or sold to foreign investors). Utility institutions such as Uganda Electricity Board would be dismantled and replaced with the foreign investors under the corporate name of Umeme. Today, the banking market is dominated by foreign banks and utilities in Uganda are owned by foreign corporations. Lint Marketing Board, Nyanza Textile Industries (Nytil), Uganda Grain Milling and Mulco Textiles that had employed thousands of Ugandans were all sold (and then mismanaged) by private buyers who were often foreigners or Museveni's family members and close friends.

Many critics of the SAP have wondered why the World Bank and IMF were so eager to force African governments to relinquish control over key economic institutions in their countries to the private sector. The policy only makes sense when seen as a continuation of the colonial project, then the logic is clear: the private sector has become the proxy for former colonially owned corporate enterprises.

Here is the essence of Neo-colonialism; perhaps a more pernicious form of exploitation than its progenitor Empire, in that it adds mendacity to violence and theft. Empire was what it claimed to be; neo-colonialism is not. African nations became nominally politically independent during the second half of the 20th century, but are yet to become so economically; and this is no accident. As political power devolved from the public institutions of Europe to those of Africa, Economic power moved from the public sector in Africa to the private sector in the West.

Some African leaders did indeed understand the logic of the machinery of neo-colonialism of course, and for that they were overthrown in bloody coups or assassinated. But, the majority embraced the new dispensation because they and their families were allowed to share in the neo-colonial spoils. Distinguishing between a complicit leader and a rebellious one is simple enough, have they ruled for decades while their citizens are starved of economic opportunities, or have they sincerely sought meaningful change and been overthrown, exiled, imprisoned, or killed?

There is no question that SAP policies have been bad for Africa. They have starved Africans of economic opportunities and forced them to leave their respective countries in large numbers. One reason African countries struggle with SAP policies is that SAP bring an unfavorable balance of trade. Take Nigeria for example. In the 1980s, Nigeria's demand for machinery and equipment accounted for nearly 40 percent of annual imports but when SAP measures were introduced the situation changed radically:[108]

> In 1990, $2,755 million (89.8 percent) of the $3,067 million of Nigeria's foreign exchange earnings was allocated to machinery, spare parts and raw materials. In 1991 this figure increased to $3,344 million (93.3 percent) of the $3,584.1 million total. This reveals that Nigeria is trying to achieve industrialization through a very slow approach—passive technology transfer. The mere erection of structures like roads and telecommunication networks, estates, banks, and industrial plants does not stimulate rapid technological development. The structures merely age and demand spare parts perpetually, decreasing in value over time.

In Uganda as in Nigeria, the effect of these policies is exacerbated by deeply embedded corruption on a vast scale, in the case of Uganda the center of that culture is the Museveni family.

Chapter 13: Corruption Runs in the President's Family

"We hang petty thieves and appoint great ones to public office." Aesop

Consider this scenario, the eldest son in the family goes to the wealthy neighbors to exchange his family's cow, a source of their livelihood, for a chicken. The neighbor, baffled by the offer, asks him if he is sure and the response is obviously yes: "if you give me that chicken it will be mine and the cow then belongs to all of us in the family." After sealing the deal, he again offers to keep the chicken as well with the neighbor and when the neighbor asks him about the eggs the chicken will lay, he says that he can eat the eggs and keep his chicken. And if the neighbor thinks this family will starve in their home and die then he is wrong. If they are to die of starvation they will die right at his doorstep, begging.

This is a parable of corruption that pervades Africa, with its politicians giving away all its wealth to foreign big corporations in exchange of shamelessly meager bribes. The western media has almost normalized African politicians as being inherently corrupt with little blame apportioned to the foreign corporations but genuinely all parties are guilty. By giving away this wealth the poor citizens are starved of economic opportunities and this desperation forces them to migrate.

Here is a true story, in November 2017, American media reported the arrest of two men in connection with plotting to bribe African delegates at the United Nations headquarters in New York City, during the tenure of Sam Kutesa, Uganda's Foreign Minister and brother-in-law of President Museveni, as President of the UN General Assembly.[xi]

Chi Ping Patrick Ho from Hong Kong and Cheikh Gadio from Senegal—both former Foreign Secretaries of their respective jurisdictions—conspired to bribe high-level African officials to secure business access for a Shanghai-based energy and financial conglomerate. According to a criminal complaint unsealed by U.S. prosecutors, Ho and Gadio engaged in a multi-year scheme to bribe Deby and Kutesa in exchange for business advantages for the energy company, a multibillion-dollar Chinese enterprise that operates in the oil-and-gas and financial sectors.

The two men were charged with bribery in violation of the Foreign Corrupt Practices Act (FCPA) and international money laundering. Ho is said to have paid a $500,000 bribe to Kutesa, the Ugandan Foreign Minister and Museveni's brother-in-law, in exchange for obtaining *business advantages* for the energy company, including the potential acquisition of a Ugandan bank.[109] At the time of writing, charges against Ho have been upheld while those levelled against Gadio were dropped in September 2018, no reason was given for this and the announcement seemed abrupt. It is believed that the charges were dropped in anticipation that the former Senegalese official would testify against Ho in his upcoming trial.[110]

Gadio's relationship with the U.S. Department of Justice will be of no slight concern to Kutesa not least because he has drawn this kind of attention before, having been at the center of corruption scandals in Uganda several times. Indeed, the International Consortium of Investigative Journalism (ICFJ) published a report in its Paradise Papers about Kutesa owning offshore companies created for the purpose of evading taxation, a report that featured Kutesa. He created the Obuyonza Discretionary Trust in the Seychelles in 2012, which held shares in the Seychelles company Katonga Investments Ltd. He also watched over its administration and was one of its beneficiaries. The money for Katonga was to come from Enhas Uganda Ltd., another Kutesa entity, Appleby's notes state. Kutesa has owned Enhas, a ground-handling service at Uganda's Entebbe Airport, since the 1990s. In 1998, a Ugandan parliamentary committee named Kutesa and another co-owner in a report criticizing the privatisation that helped create Enhas and led to its lucrative airport contract. The report concluded that the privatization efforts had been "manipulated and taken advantage of by a few politically powerful people who sacrifice the people's interests."[111]

The Kutesa bribery scandal is not unique to Uganda but across the African continent Western corporations also have been paying bribes to aides serving the presidents and kings in order to secure lucrative mining concessions or other contracts at less than market value. Investigators enforcing the U.S. Foreign Corrupt Practices Act have exposed several companies including Shell that paid a bribe of $2 million to Nigeria custom officials, a $5 million bribe paid by Kellogg, Brown & Root to build one of Nigeria's biggest oil facilities, the $6 billion liquefied natural gas plant at Bonny Island. That bribe was paid at a time when U.S. former Vice-President Dick Cheney was still the chief executive of Halliburton, an American engineering giant, of which KBR is a subsidiary.[112]

Kutesa epitomizes the corrupt politician, one of many who sold out Africa without a whiff of moral or social conscience. Their numbers might have been relatively small but the wealth and power they accumulated from these shady deals were way too disproportionate to consider that such deals had been handled above the table.

In the months following the 2016 elections, the Ugandan opposition would take on more heat as the country's prime minister, Amamma Mbabazi, had parted ways with Museveni and joined the opposition to oust his boss. Mbabazi was the "Mister Fix-It-All" character in Museveni's camp. He was one of his most trusted men from Museveni's days as a rebel as well as during his many years in office. He was the secretary general of Museveni's ruling party. Of course, the party's leader was the permanent president and political chair. In previous presidential elections the opposition had begrudged Mbabazi for being the man forging Museveni's victory. Now that he had separated from Museveni, the desperate masses easily were tempted to believe he was the man who knew how to forge election results and he would be the one to end effectively more than 30 years of Museveni's dictatorship.

But, Mbabazi had another battle to fight—seize the leadership of the opposition from Dr. Kizza Besigye, the Forum for Democratic Change (FDC)party leader who also had ended up several times as a runoff presidential candidate. Besigye, like Mbabazi, also once had been Museveni's close friend and personal physician. Ever since he parted ways with Museveni the masses had showered support over him, hoping that he could bring about change. However, he lost consistently to Museveni. The reason why many Ugandans hoped that the person capable of ousting Museveni was supposed to come from his own camp and tribe or among his close friends turning enemies is a baffling idea.

The battle for the opposition leadership between Besigye and Mbabazi was even tougher than that for the presidency. At a certain point the opposition leaders had to travel to the United Kingdom to have their former colonial masters mediate the question of which of them was qualified and capable of taking on Museveni. The UK meeting agreed on Mbabazi but when the duo returned to Uganda, Besigye insisted he was going to stand in the elections and disregarded the UK decision. It was political drama at its sharpest. Meanwhile, a less popular presidential candidate, Abedi Bwanika, indicated that the two rivaling opposition leaders had never left Museveni's camp or were just working for Museveni.

One could see this as a brilliant, even Machiavellian, strategy: Museveni trying to control the government and the opposition through his right-hand men. When he feared that Besigye lost his vigor for failing so many times, he decided to replace him with Mbabazi and thus he had managed to rule for so long, thanks to a fake opposition front.

These complex political machinations had rendered debate in any public forum pointless. Citizens were too exhausted from dealing with everyday problems to engage in political debate, particularly when living in the knowledge that their leaders and representatives had decided to use their precious resources for self-absorbed political drama rather than widespread economic improvement.

The political dramas essentially continued the same theater of public affairs that were so common in the colonial era. Meanwhile soul-crushing poverty remained a constant and Ugandans, tired of supporting losing political candidates and waiting for change that might never come, chose instead to emigrate to the very countries that are increasingly tired of them.

For a long time one tribe had dominated both the government and the opposition in Uganda but in 2017 that changed. For the first time opposition came from another tribe. The responses from Museveni as well as the opposition, as represented by his former personal doctor Dr. Kizza Besigye were as uncompromising as it was disturbing. Robert Kyagulanyi Ssentamu[xii], who goes by the stage name Bobi Wine, is arguably one of Uganda's best singers but decided to join politics as an opposition candidate. Although he had on several occasions supported Besigye, he was immediately rejected in the opposition circles largely because of being an outsider, not of the same tribe. He did not relent after being rejected, and he entered a by-election as an independent for member of parliament to represent Kyadondo East in central Uganda.

He beat candidates from the ruling National Resistance Movement (NRM) and the main opposition Forum for Democratic Change (FDC) of Dr. Besigye, scoring a landslide victory. After the victory, Bobi Wine doubled as a legislator and an activist, which frustrated numerous debates in the parliamentary chambers like the one seeking to uncap the maximum age limit that would allow Museveni to be president for life. Another contentious bill was the previously mentioned example of social media tax levies.

Bobi Wine's influence grew as he began supporting independent candidates (not from the ruling or dominant opposition party) in by-elections across the country and they all won. Bobi Wine beat candidates supporting Museveni and Besigye four times and both men's anxieties grew as they recognized that this man who was not from their tribe (Bayankole) started to accumulate political impact.

The tension surrounding the Wine phenomenon turned to violence when, during an election in Arua, supporters of Bobi Wine's candidate met with a motorcade carrying Museveni's entourage—a little ahead of the President himself—who were there in support of the President's selected candidate. As the motorcade passed through the crowd a stone was allegedly thrown at one of the cars in the motorcade, shattering its rear window. When the car in which Museveni was travelling arrived, eye witnesses say the president waved his driver through and was safely delivered to his waiting helicopter, but his security, smarting from embarrassment at the incident, returned later to inflict punishment, beating up supporters who had retreated to the hotel that was being used as a tactical headquarters for Bobi Wine's candidate.

xii   Bobi Wine is from Baganda tribe from central, which is the largest tribe in Uganda. Museveni, Besigye, Mbabazi are from Bayankole tribe of Western Uganda. Bayankole are currently the political dominat tribe in Uganda.

But this wasn't just some disgruntled hired thugs lashing. A soldier reportedly walked up to Kyagulanyi's pick-up truck and shot the MP's driver Yasin Kawuma, while other soldiers searched the hotel. Kyagulanyi was cornered, after being found hiding in a loft space. He was immediately beaten then whisked away to an army barracks where the abuse continued. His last action in the hotel was to tweet a photograph of a bloody body slumped in a car seat, with a message to the effect that police had shot and killed his driver in a case of mistaken identity. They were targeting him.

Three days later Wine was brought before a military court. He showed signs of physical torture and his lawyers said he was unable to walk, talk, or understand the charges read out to him. Social media was awash with videos detailing the torture he had endured.

According to his family, his face, torso, legs, and genitals were subjected to repeated heavy punches and kicks by Ugandan soldiers. He told his wife that he had been given so many injections that he lost count and consciousness, waking only when he was wheeled into his arraignment hearing—disoriented and unable to stand or speak. Even the military doctors are said to have told him that it is likely he had suffered significant kidney damage.

This was unprecedented: never before had treatment like this been meted out to an opposition MP. The judge at that hearing ordered that he be granted his constitutionally guaranteed right to medical care. But Wine was likely not to have been the worst instance of political violence that took place that day. Francis Zaake, the Mityana MP, was arrested on the same day. UPDF agents allegedly tied a rope around his neck and beat him unconscious since then he has been unable to leave his hospital bed because of dislocated discs in his back and a severely injured neck. In September of last year, the MP Betty Nambooze had her spine snapped in an attack by state agents—and that happened inside parliament. The stories go on and on.[113]

These incidents were clear indications that the Ugandan political climate was changing and any doubt as to that change was dispelled by Museveni himself. Addressing the members of parliament from his ruling party, Museveni threatened MPs that he could do away with the parliament, as Idi Amin had done.[xiii][xiv] Between 1971 and 1979, Uganda had no parliament. Museveni was quoted, "Don't think that you are in heaven . . . You should know where the power of that parliament comes from . . . in fact, I can do away with that parliament."[114]

Chapter 14: The Prospect of Eternal Rule in Uganda

"America cannot have an empire abroad and a republic at home."
Mark Twain

A year after he was sworn into office for his fifth term as Uganda's president, Museveni started a new campaign to amend the constitution to remove the provision for an age limit for serving presidents. It was an expression of intent to rule Uganda for life, and if his dynastic aspirations materialized and power were passed to his wife and son then in some senses, he would be ruling for longer even than that.

There is no material proof to support this claim regarding Museveni's intentions, but the circumstantial evidence is compelling. The age limit was not the first constitutional barrier that Museveni had lifted: he had already amended the constitution to reverse the two-term limit for presidential service. But, in his fifth term, he also realized the 1995 constitution had another limit to his rule—that is, no president could serve beyond the age of 75. Thus, at the time when his fifth term would expire, Museveni would be 77 and therefore ineligible to be reelected unless the constitution was amended.

Museveni's desire to change the democratic constitution so that it enshrines dictatorship is emblematic of the paradox of political life in Uganda. His efforts to do so are similarly pseudo-democratic. Ssemujju Ibrahim Nganda, the Ugandan MP for the Kira Municipality, estimated that Uganda spent 100 billion shillings (or roughly $26,139,500 in U.S. currency) on the campaign to discontinue the age limit and allow Museveni to seek reelection in 2021. "We are 451 MPs in parliament, which means at least 20 billion shillings was spent on them. The NRM (Museveni's party of the National Resistance Movement) MPs who sit on the legal and parliamentary affairs committee were each given 300 million shillings to sign the report on this bill. This amounts to 6 billion. In total, therefore, more than 40 billion shillings were spent on bribing MPs. Police and the military are on high alert nearly every day waiting to pounce on the protesting population. I think when you add all this, the total cost comes to over 100 billion shillings," Ssemujju wrote in his weekly column in the *Ugandan Observer*.[115]

Ssemujju also quoted his internal government cabinet sources that Museveni drove in at about nine am one day to chair a cabinet meeting called specifically to discuss the extension of the presidential term of office from five to seven years. Museveni told his cabinet that because the mandate that the population gave us was five years, extending the term of the current Parliament would bring a backlash. Ssemujju also cited General Moses Ali, the Deputy Prime Minister, himself a man of 84, as telling Museveni: "we are giving you something, let us also take something."

The blatant quid pro quo of the trade in the component checks and balances of democratic institutions for material gain is as bizarre as it is disheartening. When Museveni realized that unless they allowed MPs to extend their term by two years, they would sabotage his push for the removal of the presidential age limit. In Ssemujju's words: "If that is the case, a senior minister told me, Museveni said go ahead and give yourself two years."

The point here is that the entrenchment of dictatorship and its constant companions, cronyism, and corruption is a significant driver of migration. Some migrants are aspirant, some fugitive, but many are desperate in the most literal sense of the term: they are in despair. It is easy to blame migrants for abandoning their homeland instead of fighting to remove the likes of Museveni, but most of those who leave *have* tried—through political means at least—to make just that happen. But the odds are stacked. African leaders—supported by the West and protected by armies trained by the U.S. or the UK and armed with Russian weapons—rig elections, intimidate voters, arrest or bribe their opposition; even amend the constitution. After all that, they use wealth generated by natural resources to buy a clean image from western public relations firms, think tanks, and lobbyists. They are thus reinvented as *are so prohibitive for poor Africans to prosecute in protests. The dictators have rigged elections when the citizens tried to fire them at the ballot box. They have amended capriciously constitutions when the law was against their prolonged stay. They have dispersed demonstrations against their dictatorship with Russian-made tear gas and American-sourced live bullets. They have bribed leaders of the opposition and arrested political opponents. And, after committing so many atrocities in the name of fastening their grip on power they use the country's resources to pay western lobbyists, think tanks and media so that they have a good image in the world, as they take on the suspect labels of "reformers" and "philanthropists."*

This last point is far from idle conjecture. The U.S.-based Center for Public Integrity's review of records disclosed to the U.S. Justice Department in 2015 that the 50 countries with the worst human rights violation records have spent $168 million on American lobbyists and public relations specialists in a five-year period beginning in 2010.[116]

Western societies have long been concerned about the threat to Democracy posed by public relations firms and lobbyists, existing as they do in the shadows and corners of institutions and processes. But hitherto they have been accepted as an unsightly but permanent feature of the political landscape. The information revolution has changed all that as it has become increasingly clear that the potential for the manipulation and perversion of democracy by the invisible instruments of the internet, is almost infinite.

Elections are widely suspected of fraud and election monitors from the West always seem too eager to endorse the sham elections to keep their puppets in power. Kenya's 2017 presidential elections were among the most recent examples. Even worse, entities abroad played a chaotic role This phenomenon has been much scrutinized since the EU Referendum in the UK and the Presidential Election in the U.S. Less well-known is the involvement that Cambridge Analytica, the British UK data analysis firm that also has been implicated in swaying the outcomes of major balloting including the 2016 U.S. presidential election, had took on a surprising role in Uhuru Kenyatta's presidential campaign in Kenya. In 2018, the firm's managing director said, "We have rebranded the entire party twice, written their manifesto, done two rounds of 50,000 (participant) surveys," the firm's Managing Director in 2018 said in a statement that was covertly filmed by UK broadcaster Channel 4."[117]

Kenya had indeed proved to be fertile ground. The statement was covertly filmed by UK broadcaster Channel 4 in a report that aired in March 2018. Kenya's voters had adopted social media in an unprecedented level of activity and even the country's largest media outlet Safaricom said its most formidable journalistic challenge was neutralizing the waves of "fake news" that inundated the country's social media platforms. In light of the greatest exposure to smart phones and social media now available to more Africans than ever before, as long as African dictators know their citizens cannot vote them out of office or through protests or military means, these leaders will be confident and increasingly arrogant about their positions of power.

The stark truth is that dictators like Museveni, who have so blighted Africa and Africans, having the blessings of the west and remained there with it, will only leave when Washington decides that it's time for them to go. *Not so sure of this*

Not all the power resides in U.S.

Chapter 15: Political Assassinations and Torture

"Those who stand up for Justice will always be on the right side of history." Barack Obama

On a busy street in Kampala one evening in April 2012 at around nine o'clock after Muslims had completed their last prayers and were joining the commuter melee of cars and cyclists to go home, two men on a motorcycle, known as Boda Boda in local dialect, approached Sheikh Abdul Karim Sentamu, a renowned Muslim cleric and leader of the William Street mosque. The two men said the traditional Islamic greetings to the Sheikh before shooting him dead and then disappearing into the traffic.

It was a start of a series of political assassinations by men on motorcycles in Kampala. Sentamu, like most of the other victims, was a Muslim who had once been a member of a rebel group called Allied Democratic Forces (ADF), before receiving amnesty from Museveni.[xv]

Among these victims was Sheikh Mustafa Bahiga, shot five times at Bwebajja Mosque on Entebbe Road. Sheikh Ibrahim Hassan Kirya also was shot multiple times when he arrived at his home in Bweyogerere, Wakiso District. Sheikh Kirya had earlier informed police that he feared for his life after his colleagues were killed in related incidents by unknown assailants on motorcycles. Major Mohammed Kiggundu, one of the former commanders of the ADF rebel group who had joined the Ugandan Peoples Defense Forces (UPDF) after being pardoned, was also shot dead, along with his bodyguard Sergeant Steven Mukasa, one morning at Masanafu, a Kampala suburb. The two were driving to the city in a UPDF pickup truck. Kiggundu had turned into a strong advocate of the Museveni regime on radio stations after his amnesty and recruitment into the army. One

---

xv   ADF is a rebel group in Uganda whose commanders were mostly Muslims trying to overthrow the government of Yoweri Museveni. Most of these leaders abandoned the group in early 2000 and sought Amnesty from Museveni government.

time a caller during his radio talk show warned him in plain language that Museveni never forgives former rebels or anyone who has ever tried overthrowing his regime. Other Muslim clerics murdered by motorcycle assailants included Abdul Kadir Muwaya and Abubaker Kiwewa.

Most of the victims were those who had previously rebelled against the government of Museveni or were deemed politically inconvenient to the regime. Every time a politician was assassinated the police assembled a group of mostly Muslim men on television it had arrested as suspects. Most of those arrested were other Muslim[xvi] clerics of a rival faction. As they appeared on television some were limping with all the signs of torture. Most disturbing was that even after these arrests, the assassinations continued with other targets killed in a similar way that implied the real assassins were still at large. The police attempted to reassure the citizens and authorities reportedly conducted comprehensive investigations but not a single report was ever published.

There is no concrete evidence for the claim, but it seems at least reasonable to assume that the phenomenon of the assassination by motorcycle-borne gunmen was a weapon being used by the state. The collusion at all levels of official apparatus that was required for these crimes to be committed with total impunity makes it so.

Clearly the weapon was considered to be effective as its scope was broadened considerably to include high-profile political figures. Joan Kagezi, the Senior Principal State Attorney, was the first Non-Muslim target, shot dead in her car while shopping in Kiwatule, a Kampala suburb. Kagezi, who was a prosecutor in a July 2010 twin bombing trial, was shot twice at close range by the assailants while she was seated in her official car. She was known as an ethical independent prosecutor, more inclined not to take orders on what to investigate or ignore because of political sensitivities regarding the Museveni regime.

The peak of these political assassinations occurred when Andrew Felix Kaweesi, a police spokesperson, along with his driver and bodyguard were gunned down about 100 meters from Kaweesi's home in Kulambiro, Nakawa Division in Kampala. Then, Ibrahim Abiriga,

xvi   Uganda has about 12 percent of its citizens Muslims, according to the national census of 2002.

the Arua municipality member of parliament, and his bodyguard were shot dead, near the MP's home in Matugga, Wakiso District. An audio of an eyewitness account circulated on social media urged all Muslims in Matugga to flee the area to avoid being rounded up as purported suspects as far as they can after the shooting because the government likely would arrest any of them to parade on television. The audio reflected a general feeling among the population that the government was not interested in arresting the real killers but instead announced after every shooting the arrests of apparently innocent citizens on the streets, mostly Muslims as a coverup for the killers.

It seemed as if the motorcycle assassins could not and would not be stopped; and killings became more frequent. Muhammad Kirumira, an outspoken critic and a Ugandan police officer, was gunned down along with a female companion in the Kampala suburb of Bulenga. Kirumira, who was a key witness in a case against General Kale Kayihura, the sacked police boss,[xvii] had repeatedly told the media that he had become a target for assassination after having revealed that there were bandits of criminals in high posts of the Uganda police. "Expose the mafia to save the state. When you speak, you die. When you keep quiet, you die. Better speak and die when the message has reached the people," Kirumira said in a short video clip that went viral on social media after his assassination.

Kirumira's death had a profound effect on the people of Uganda as he had foretold his own death and even that was not enough to protect him. Clearly the assassins were working with no concern for conscience or law. Each killing would put gruesome pictures on social media and illicit a huge reaction from Ugandans.

Kirumira's assassination happened a few weeks after the army had shot and killed Kawuma, Bobi Wine's driver, and reports about the politician's torture had been circulated publicly. The international media focused intensely on the repressive nature of the Museveni regime for the first time. Museveni responded with acts of apparent concern: attending the scene where Kirumira had been gunned down and addressing parliament, blaming the assassination on elements in the police colluding with the criminals. Museveni also outlined new

xvii   Kale Kayihura is the former Inspector General of the Uganda Police Force, sacked after widespread outcry of increased insecurity with police cavorting with criminal gangs.

measures in his address to lawmakers that included setting up a modern forensic laboratory, installing CCTV cameras, shooting down unregistered drones, and banning hoodies.

It is true to say that in Uganda at least, the phenomenon of political assassinations carried out by gunmen on motorcycles was new, but only as a delivery system starting in 2012. Political assassination was familiar: politicians that had proved inconvenient to Museveni had been assassinated throughout the 1980s and 1990s. Gunmen would visit victims' homes and shoot them dead in sight of their family members. One of these victims was Dr. Lutakome Andrew Kayiira who had a rebel group also fighting Obote alongside Museveni's bush war. Museveni says in his book *The Mustard Seed* that during those times, his rebel group confiscated a consignment of guns that were supposed to go to Kayiira's rebel group. But Museveni and Kayiira had reconciled after Museveni came to power, and, in fact, Kayiira served as an energy minister in the Museveni government in the late 1980s, before his assassination.

Also, Major General James Kazini, former UPDF commander, challenged his government bosses. First, he was accused of disobeying the president, when he moved battalions of the Ugandan army under his command in West Nile without Museveni's approval. He then was accused of sending money to rebels of the Sudan People's Liberation Army (SPLA) in Southern Sudan and later Ugandans were told he had been beaten to death by his girlfriend in a brawl.[118]

Political assassinations in Uganda during the Museveni rule have not only occurred by putting a bullet in the victim's head. There have been an implausibly large number of unexplained deaths among the political classes and in some the suspected cause was poisoning. One such case is that of Brigadier Noble Mayombo, who was the Permanent Secretary for the Ministry of Defense and Chairman of the Board of Vision Group. In April 2007, Mayombo felt unwell and was admitted to Kololo hospital where he was diagnosed with acute pancreatitis. The next day, his condition having worsened, he was transferred to the intensive care unit at International Hospital in Kampala. His condition deteriorated further and on April 29, 2007, comatose, on life-support systems, he was flown to Agha Khan Hospital in Nairobi Kenya. He was airlifted to Nairobi in the Presidential

Gulfstream plane, on Museveni's orders, a courtesy because of what was supposed to be a relationship as mentor and trusted comrade. However, Mayombo died at the age of 42. Speculation that there might have been foul play prompted the government to launch an investigation. The team concluded its investigation and handed a report to Museveni in November 2007. As of today, the detailed findings of that probe have never been released to the public.[119]

Another suspected case of murder by poisoning was that of Cerina Nebanda, who at 24 was the youngest woman MP, serving in the Butaleja district. Nebanda criticized the president on his handling of corruption and unemployment. When she died of suspected poisoning, her parliamentary colleague Mohammed Nsereko was arrested for suggesting that the President was responsible for her death. Also, General Aronda Nyakairima, an MP who served as minister for internal affairs, died on a flight from South Korea while he was traveling through Dubai, a sudden death that followed the same investigative path as Nebanda's death.

The evidence that poisoning is being used by the regime as a political weapon is further strengthened by the fact that some politicians have survived having been poisoned. One such is Hussein Kyanjo, former MP for the Makindye East District. Kyanjo, one of the most eloquent legislators in Uganda, was instrumental in fighting government-proposed bills to make the government the sole land owner in Uganda. He called the proposal a land grab. But it was his investigations of suspected bribery in oil deals in 2011 as a chairman of a parliamentary committee that likely triggered the attempt to poison him, which he relayed to me personally. Kyanjo, who received treatment in Dubai and London, said he had been diagnosed with dystonia, a disorder that affects the control of body movements, but his doctors suspected he also had been poisoned. He has lost the eloquence that once moved crowds and has trouble speaking at all, but he is grateful to be alive.

The list of assassination victims in Uganda is as long as the years Museveni has ruled the country. Political assassinations are so common in dictatorships where dictators attempt to rule for eternity, but in Africa, Uganda during Museveni's tenure has experienced more political assassination than its neighbors. Every time someone was assassinated the Government promised to leave no stone unturned and to get to the bottom of the matter but each investigation eventually faded and what findings there were will never be made public, even when the victim was a public figure. This became the crucial yardstick for comparison, to distinguish assassinations carried out by dissidents and those likely perpetuated by the government.

Assassination became an understandably sensitive issue. People who demanded investigations or asked that results be made public soon became targets themselves. Ugandans understood that if the Government was not forthcoming with information about a given death then it was better to pretend that the victim had never lived. In some cases the President would give money to the families of the victims and showcase them as they publicly expressed their gratitude as when he gave 20 million shillings (U.S. $5,000) to the families of Yasin Kawuma and Muhammad Kirumira.

Neighboring countries have shared Uganda's troubles with political assassinations, and some have had their leaders who were killed when they departed from Uganda. One was Dr. John Garang of South Sudan who died in a plane crash, after attending peace talks in Uganda. Journalist Andrew Mwenda was arrested for suggesting the Ugandan government was behind Garang's death.

Political assassinations is not the Government's only tool of oppression. In September 2009, the Ugandan government sought to prevent King (Kabaka) Muwenda Mutebi, a cultural leader of the Buganda ethnic group from traveling to Kayunga, a town near Kampala where National Youth Day festivities were planned. His supporters took to the streets, and, in some instances, threw stones and set fires. The military and police beat demonstrators and quickly resorted to live ammunition, killing unarmed protesters and bystanders.[120]

The government maintained that 27 people lost their lives, largely as a result of security forces' stray bullets. Human Rights Watch (HRW) investigations of hospital records and local organizational accounts put the death toll at more than 40. Sources at Mulago hospital told HRW that they treated 88 victims, the vast majority of them for gunshot wounds. And more victims were taken to other hospitals. The government never investigated or charged any security force members for the deaths.[121]

In another violent incident, the Ugandan army and police raided the compound of the Rwenzururu King in the western town of Kasese. More than 100 people were killed, the bloodiest incident in the country for more than a decade. The king, Charles Wesley Mumbere, and nearly 200 people were arrested; they still await trial, on charges including murder, terrorism, and treason. The Bakonzo people, the main ethnic group in Kasese, straddle the borders between Uganda and the Democratic Republic of Congo, in the Rwenzori mountains. It is here, the Ugandan government alleges, that Bakonzo radicals want to carve out an independent kingdom. The King denies this, but people in these parts have long felt marginalized by the state. In Kasese there has been no investigation into the massacre. Peter Elwelu, the commander in charge that day, has been promoted. Maria Burnett, an HRW representative, said the killings illustrate the "entrenched impunity" of Museveni's regime.[122] That sense of impunity persistently degrades the quality of life for Ugandans and most people have decided to move to countries they think they would be safe.

Chapter 16: Deteriorating Lives among Citizens

"For some moments in life there are no words." David Seltzer

Ever since I shook hands with Al Hajji Ali Mawejje in a customary Islamic cultural practice and he agreed to give me his daughter in marriage, he has been a pillar of support in my family. He sat by my parents' respective deathbeds, unconditionally offering help and, when they finally succumbed, participated in their funeral ceremonies. Likewise, when he heard the news of my deportation from Dubai following the publication of my first book, he reached out to me immediately, consoling me with the thought that I could still make a handsome living and provide for my family in Uganda. He was supportive too when I ventured into agriculture, sending me a truck full of coffee husks to fertilize our pineapple crops. So, when my younger brother Wahab called to tell me that he had received unconfirmed reports of Al Hajji's death in an accident, I was devastated by grief.

A week after his burial, my wife sent me graphic video footage of the fatal accident. Two motorcycles, each with passengers, had collided on a tarmac road in the rain. Al Hajji had one passenger on his motorcycle as did the other rider. In the video all of their bodies are on the ground, some fatally injured and others fighting for their lives. A rescuer from a nearby village pulls Al Hajji by his arms to the side of the road where another body lies. That victim had died but one can clearly see my father-in-law shaking his head, indicating that he was fighting to stay alive.

My father-in-law's death is symbolic to me of what Uganda and other countries have lost or must do without; not only rights, and privileges but also the basic provision of health and safety that is the responsibility of any state. Al Hajji might well have survived if he had worn a helmet, but not wearing a helmet is notionally at least a minor traffic violation, but is not one that the police prosecute in practice. He might never have been in the accident if the traffic was organized and the roads maintained to a reasonable standard. But the government has never made road safety a priority. And after the accident—even with no helmet, poor roads, and chaotic traffic—he might have lived if there was medical help available. But there would not have been an ambulance near enough to help him or a system to get it there in time. Indeed, in the video the rescuers begged anyone who had a vehicle available to help carry the three survivors of the crash to the hospital.

I kept thinking as I watched the video footage again and again that if I was at the scene, I could have given CPR using the training I have undertaken in the U.S. for the work I do as a caregiver. Modern resuscitation techniques are a game-changer for emergency care and even individuals trained in CPR have been able to keep a critically injured person alive in the direst life-threatening circumstances. It is perhaps emblematic of the situation. I was watching his death from a world away wishing that—in the absence of the state—I had been there to save him.

A 2017 journal article in the *Journal of Injury and Violence Research* indicated that deaths in road accidents in Uganda occur at a rate of 28.9 per 100,000 population, the sixth highest in the world.[123] Indeed the British newspaper *The Independent* considers Uganda's Kampala Masaka road to be the world's most dangerous with more people dying on a single highway in Uganda than die on average each year on Bolivia's infamous "Death Road."[124]

Researchers pinpointed various reasons for these terrifying numbers. One focused on transportation conveniences because of their affordability and accessibility, the boda-bodas, in particular. The researchers characterized these motorbikes as a "silent killer." But, more importantly was the quick, close access to trauma care centers.[125] The researchers concluded that "it's irrefutable that timely pre-hospital care can reduce injury severity reducing the trend of [road] deaths by saving lives, treating injuries efficiently and effectively, preventing infections and injury-related diseases as well as preventing disabilities."[126]

For me as for many other Ugandans, this type of research only confirms what we have been saying for decades. After more than 30 years in power the government has not seen fit to build an effective system of emergency medical response. That, accident victims still had to be carried in rescuers' private vehicles to hospitals where they still could not have access to lifesaving measures would seem old.

Even if the victims of road traffic accidents make it to hospital then the care they receive will be patchy at best. Most hospitals in Uganda still don't have CT Scan technology to assess accurately the presence or extent of injuries The Kawolo hospital that is situated on one of the main highways linking Uganda to neighboring Kenya receives at least two Ugandan accident victims daily but there are no CT scans available to assess accurately the presence or extent of injuries.

One would expect that such widespread and profound concern about public safety and health would draw immediate attention and subsequent rectification from the Government. But there has been none. On the contrary, while these matters have been consistently ignored in the 30 years that Museveni has been in power, his enthusiasm for keeping the military well supplied has been unfailing. Bear in mind that Uganda's military is one of the largest and most capable in Africa, and as a sector of domestic spending bears no comparison being better funded than any other but contributing the least to the well-being of the nation as a whole.

This pattern of patronage and neglect only makes sense when seen through the prism of Museveni's rule. The military is an essential asset and therefore a legitimate destination for public money, healthcare is neither, because the government equates the regime and not the population with the Nation.

So public expectations have been systematically lowered to the point that public healthcare has come to be seen as something like charity. When popular Ugandan singer Mowzey Radio died in a private hospital, Museveni delivered the news of his death and added that he had personally contributed 30 million Ugandan Shillings (U.S. $8,000) to help pay for the singer's treatment.[127] In so doing he reminded Ugandans that their healthcare system had been relegated to a matter of personal donations for which they should be grateful. and he was being thanked all over the Ugandan media for using the Ugandans' $8,000 tax collections in the right circumstances.

Museveni made no mention, however, as to why he could not extend the same generosity to Ugandan referral hospitals—many of which lack drugs to prescribe—the institutions where millions of Ugandan citizens and taxpayers go to when seeking medical treatment. Even the Radio had had to be moved between various hospitals in the hopes of finding the correct treatment for the injuries he had sustained during a beating in a pub brawl. But, in each case there were no CT scanners available or other life-supporting equipment on hand. Eventually he was referred finally to an expensive, private hospital. Then, the president was quick to exploit the singer's popularity and cash in politically on his generosity.

Meanwhile, Ugandan drivers have become used to marking and dodging potholes rather than demanding that the Government fix the road or account for the billions of tax shillings that could have been spent on doing so. Instead they recoiled like desperate children, accepting without protest that they could not change anything, so their only option then was to leave the country.

Al Hajji wasn't the only person in our family to die during that period. Just three months earlier, two other close family members passed away: Musebeeyi, my maternal grandmother, who had pneumonia, and Uncle Badru Kikaawa, my mother's elder brother, who had gone to a Gombe hospital with malaria. And a month after Al Hajji's death my sister Aisha Nansukusa, the eldest daughter of my father, died of HIV/AIDS. As I announced their deaths in social media and it looked like everyone in my family was dying, it struck me that all these deaths could have been prevented if Uganda had a government that prioritized people's lives and health. Malaria, which already has been prevented if not eliminated in many countries, was still claiming people's lives in my country. Uganda receives some aid from the World Health Organization (WHO) program Global Alliance for Vaccines and Immunization (GAVI) to fight malaria but most of that is lost, due to corruption.

This dark period of bereavement was not the first time that thoughts concerning the relationship between good governance and preventable death had occurred to me. Neither were the losses of 2017 the only ones that had given me cause to think. My maternal grandfather Sheikh Hood Kabamba died in 1995, after being misdiagnosed; a mistake that remained uncorrected for two years at Gombe Hospital, one of the biggest centers in Uganda. When the doctors at the hospital failed to identify his illness he might—as many Ugandans do—have sought explanations in superstition. But the religious man he was, he always asked his family to return him home. When his health worsened Gombe hospital referred him to Mulago, the biggest referral hospital in Kampala. Here, doctors offered to do a spinal tap—a painful procedure with severe side effects—to establish the nature of the ailment: to no avail. After this he underwent a physical examination during which the doctors noticed a tumor at the back of his head large enough to be visible to the naked eye. No one, including family, had hitherto noticed the swelling. While the tumor was not cancerous, he needed surgery to remove it but his condition was discovered too late and Sheikh Hood died before receiving the surgery that perhaps could have saved his life.

The story of my Mother's cancer, which I told in my previous book *The Ambitious Struggle*, also involved an inaccurate diagnosis. Mulago physicians and their counterparts at Nsambya private hospital could not agree on her diagnosis, and the delay took away the window of opportunity to treat the disease effectively. She used to say, as we moved between the two hospitals, that "if the doctors cannot agree on the proper diagnosis then what is going to happen with the treatment." She turned down requests for a biopsy, just a few months before her death in 2012.

These deaths were preventable and they occurred because the health service as designed and maintained by the Government, failed to address these patients and their problems with a level of competence that would satisfy the most modest expectations. If you accept my experience as typical and then extrapolate it across the population of Uganda, then you can see the scale of the problem. Museveni's long rule has taken a toll of varying degree on virtually every family in Uganda. It is customary for families to maintain their own cemeteries in villages, and as I am looking at my mother's family cemetery, I realize that I knew nearly half of the people buried there, and I see the consequence of misrule; that the cost is many people's lives. Several people who are buried there died in the war that brought Museveni to power, while many more have died of diseases that could have been avoided with vaccinations or if treated in time.

It's hard to argue with anyone thinking that the most conclusive way of measuring an African president's legacy is by counting the dead at cemeteries. Perhaps, instead of naming themselves after major icons such as airports, hospitals, and stadiums, their names should be on their respective nation's cemeteries, for it is there where they made the most impact—negative as it is. Funny that even themselves the only institution they want to be part of is to be buried in our cemeteries. Meanwhile, they avoid our hospitals and seek treatments with their families in Europe or the U.S. They shun our universities and send their children to the Royal Military Academy at Sandhurst. Their fortunes accumulated from robbing our institutions are safely kept in European banks but when they die or any of their children die they hurry to bring the bodies into our soils.

Another big problem for Museveni's health sector has been—understandably enough—the morale of health care providers. Hospitals in Uganda lack skilled personnel and those there are demoralized, underpaid and undervalued. Strikes are common but whenever health care workers demand equitable pay the government responds with the laughable suggestion that it will import health workers from Cuba.

"Demoralized health workers" is a much more practical problem for patients than perhaps it sounds. It is they who are expected to close the gap between the expectations of the doctors and nurses and that which they receive from the government.

Again, my own experience as representing Ugandans in general, bears this out. My mother died in Mulago Hospital at around seven o'clock on an evening in July 2012, when the staff in the financial department had already left the premises. As a result, we could not pay and so get clearance to leave the hospital with my Mother's body. One of the duty doctors gave me the accountant's number and advised me that if I talked *favorably* with him he would come back to the hospital, take payment, and clear us to leave so that we could take the body that evening.

The accountant was rude on the phone, telling me plainly that the death of my mother was not special to him, indeed he had seen plenty of similar deaths, and that I should wait until the following day, which was Sunday. When I related this story to the doctor who had gave me the accountant's number, he blamed me for not talking *favorably* with him. It turned out that *favorably* meant offering the man a bribe. How that would have been possible over the phone mystified me. In the end the matter was resolved when a woman who had once been a colleague of mine when I was a journalist but was then working in PR at the hospital as called the accountant, who remained defiant initially but when she called someone at the top of the hospital's management team to call him, he turned up suddenly in a panic, offering condolences, before starting on our clearance paperwork and taking the necessary payment.

Chapter 17: Guns over Crops

"I'd like you to tell people in your place that the drink they are enjoying is now the cause of all our problems. We [grow] the crop with our sweat and sell it for nothing." Lawrence Segunya

I had always thought that I might try my hand at farming in Uganda. Agriculture is a huge sector and is at the center of our culture and consciousness. Uganda's agricultural potential is highly regarded among its African counterparts. Eighty percent of the country's land, according to the U.N. Food and Agriculture Organization, is suitable for agriculture but only 35 percent of the available land is being used for such purposes. More than seven of every 10 Ugandans work in agriculture.

Indeed, I had saved some money while working in the UAE and bought a parcel of land with the idea that one day I would develop the idea into a reality. So, when I was deported from Dubai for publishing articles that detailed the abuse of migrant workers, it seemed the right time to return home and try my hand as a farmer. I was to learn the hard way what the Museveni regime had done to Ugandan agriculture

I attended several investment workshops to get started. In the light of what I learned there I was attracted by the idea of growing passion fruit and pineapple. Domestic demand for fresh produce was on the rise and the course leaders at the workshop suggested that foreign interest would also be strong. While working in Dubai I had bought a five-acre parcel of land in Uganda for about $15,000, but there was a lot more investment needed to actually get the land working: an irrigation system, seedlings, fertilizers, pesticides, and labor.

At first glance the numbers looked promising. In theory an acre of passion fruit plants can yield up to 400 kilograms of produce weekly. Each 100-kilogram sack could bring 800,000 Ugandan shillings

($200). Actually, once I started harvesting, in practice these predictions were inaccurate. Harvesting was affected by the weather and market prices fluctuated in response. For example, it was difficult to harvest even just 100 kilograms in hot weather or when rain failed to materialize during the growing season. As in so many places, the weather in Uganda had become increasingly unpredictable, thanks to the steadily encroaching effects of climate change. And when the rains finally appeared, the yield was so large that prices could drop from $200 per bushel to $30. From my initial investment I made a return of less than $5,000.

So, I learned that while nature offers many challenges to the African farmer, in Uganda his principal enemy is the Government, which has no interest in making farming a viable or sustainable sector of the economy. And there is a great deal that could be done: investing agricultural infrastructure such as irrigation systems. These would benefit many rural villages with the crops which are dependent on the hitherto predictable but now capricious rainfall. In addition, storage facilities are few and far between, there aren't enough feeder roads in rural areas, and administration systems are heavily bureaucratized.

Furthermore, fertilizers and pesticides, which are essential inorganic elements in any high-yield agriculture, are very expensive in Uganda because they are imported from Europe and all the costs are passed on to the farmers. The consequences for farmers are predictable enough: increased financial risk and sometimes large losses. Compare this situation with that in some countries in the West like the USA where the cost of fertilizers and pesticides are subsidized even when they were being made within that same country.

The availability of machinery is also an issue. To take my experience as an example: I used to hire three or four people to plow my land with a hoe. They would do each acre in three days and five acres were done in almost two weeks; a small tractor could have done it in just a few hours. I tried to find a rental tractor but there were none in the nearby village. Eventually I found one in Kakiri, which is about 10 miles away, but the owner told me that it was booked for a full month and that he hated sending it to distant villages. Furthermore, he asked that I pay fuel charges in addition to the cost of the tractor. The demands were so excessive that I only rented the tractor once.

I found myself envisaging a government that would make rental tractors available in every district at a reasonable and regulated price. This would be especially important during the good, productive seasons during which there was a lot of rains and surplus crops. Similarly, the Government could help by finding foreign markets to sell off the surplus or at least provide suitable storage facilities where surplus crops could be preserved as a hedge against poor, dry growing seasons, measures that would off stabilize prices and prevent price crashes that are driven by a supply-flooded market.

The most damning evidence against the Government's agricultural policy can be found in the budget. In the 2015–2016 budget, the Museveni government allocated a paltry $165 million to agriculture, compared with the $533 million allocated to defense and security. Uganda is not at war. So why would buying weapons from Western corporations be prioritized over agriculture, which comprised the backbone of the country's economy? The question is of course rhetorical. As we have already seen the Museveni regime, like that of any dictator prefers the security of those in power with the benefit of the nation as a whole.

African farmers have long wished for a government that would prioritize crops over guns. Previous administrations—however brutal and corrupt—such as those of Dr. Apollo Milton Obote had put in place cooperative agricultural unions. Cooperatives were responsible for buying products such as coffee, and then processing and delivering the crop to the Coffee Marketing Board (CMB), which handled the international markets. The cooperatives bargained for better prices and ensured crop quality. When Museveni took over power and embraced the World Bank's Structural Adjustment Program, which I earlier equated to selling off the country's economy, he put farmers in direct contact with private buyers on an open market and stopped all government support to the cooperatives until they collapsed and vanished.[128]

* * *

"Mugged," a report compiled by Oxfam in 2002, gives us a window on another agricultural commodity: coffee; the world's second-most valued commodity after oil. But unlike oil producers, many coffee farmers see little or no profit, often a small fraction of coffee's prevailing retail price as a global average. Oxfam interviewed many players in the supply chain in Uganda to trace the rising price of coffee beans as they made their journey from the farmer's trees to the jars and bags sitting on supermarket shelves in the UK. They found that, in this case, the farmer received an average of just 2.5 percent of the retail price of the coffee. In the U.S. the figure would be 4.5 percent of the retail price. Today coffee farmers receive no more than one percent of the price of a cup of coffee sold in a coffee bar. They receive roughly six percent of the value of a pack of coffee sold in supermarkets and grocery stores.[129]

Lawrence Seguya, a coffee grower in Uganda, summed up the difficulty of growing the world's greatest cash crop in Uganda to Oxfam: "I'd like you to tell people in your place that the drink they are enjoying is now the cause of all our problems. We [grow] the crop with our sweat and sell it for nothing." Once Museveni allowed the cooperatives to die, the marketing of coffee was liberalized, which intensified competition among the private corporations who came to the country to buy the coffee beans.

There is no doubt that coffee is important to countries like Uganda. Coffee exports are Uganda's main source of foreign currency, accounting for about 80 percent of the country's total annual earnings. So, about a quarter of the country's population is dependent on the production of coffee in one way or the other. But the story of coffee—so highly prized in the West and so lucrative—is framed in desperation not only for many poor African countries like Ethiopia, Rwanda, Madagascar, and Burundi but also producing nations in Latin America such as Mexico, Brazil, and Panama.

Ethiopia's export revenue from coffee declined 42 percent, from $257 million to $149 million, in just one year. These were the 2002 figures from the Oxfam report, but the economic circumstances have been virtually unchanged. There is a double whammy here for producer countries: the price of their exports tends to decline over time, but the price of their imports, often manufactured goods, does not fall as fast, leading to a deterioration in their terms of trade.

On the positive side, however, several innovative Ugandans have tried to make a difference for coffee farmers. Shortly after the Oxfam report came out, Joseph Nkandu founded the NUCAFE (National Union of Coffee Agribusinesses and Farm Enterprises), which was a farmer-owned enterprise. On behalf of an estimated 800,000 individual farmers, Nkandu was able to fortify the network of local farmer associations and sought a partnership with Caffe River, and Italian coffee company. As Nkandu explained, "Instead, NUCAFE acts as a facilitator, providing farmers with the necessary services and facilities to successfully market their coffee, in exchange for a service fee that normally amounts to less than 1 percent of the value of the coffee processed and marketed. This has aligned the interests of both sides, as the organization strives to maximize returns to the farmers, and in the process grows its own income."[130] In the period 2013–2015, Uganda coffee farmers saw a 30 percent increase in their sale prices for graded green coffee beans. According to the Uganda Coffee Development Authority exports are growing: from only 3.2 million 60-kilogram bags of green coffee in 2016–2017 to 4.6 million bags the following year.

* * *

Coffee agriculture is benefiting from the independent efforts of entrepreneurs, but there is a shortage of such mentors in other key agricultural sectors. As a farmer starting out in my career I found this to my cost. Workshops and training are fine to give an idea of the landscape of the sector but every farmer needs the backing of well-intentioned domestic companies—with the commercial infrastructure they offer—as well as relationships with companies outside the country so that Ugandan farmers can have the confidence and belief that one day they will stand on their own feet and thrive.

To return to my own story—suffice to say that, frustrated with poor returns and keen to secure a steady income for my family—I looked for a job to provide for my family. I applied to be the Public

Relations Officer (PRO) for the Islamic University in Uganda. The then PRO, with whom I had attended high school and university, was leaving the country for a master's degree program in Pakistan. He encouraged me to apply and promised to put in a word for me. The job was in Mbale, where the main campus was located, so I had to commute and stay at campus during the week and return to my family in Kampala for the weekend. The monthly salary was $300 and the government took $100 of that in tax, leaving a take home of just $200 for the month. After two months at the job I realized what a dreadful mistake I had made in accepting the offer in the first place. I was stunned at how people in Uganda even in prominent positions, like that of a university spokesman, could earn so little. In the U.S., a comparable employee would be taking home between $4,000 and $5,000 a month. I resigned the PRO position and looked for opportunities outside Uganda. This chapter in my life was closing.

The country's poor performance in agriculture was not something that only people like me had noticed or were concerned about. Far from it. Even members of the political elite found it disturbing, but when they advised key decision makers in government accordingly, their advice was not taken seriously. As indicated earlier, Uganda's advantages in agriculture are real. And yet according to Professor Emmanuel Tumusiime-Mutebile, speaking at the CEO Summit Forum on October 30, 2012, agricultural productivity per worker in Uganda was at approximately $200 per year and among the lowest in the world.[131]

Furthermore, Mutebile warned that agriculture in Uganda risks being severely damaged when oil production comes online unless comprehensive measures are taken to modernize the sector, by raising productivity and promoting commercialization. While there are independent, individual actions being taken, Uganda is still without a nationwide government-led policy or program for agriculture. Mutebile also urged the government to allocate a much larger share of the budget both to agriculture and to investment in rural infrastructure. But this remains a remote possibility: Museveni's priorities remain as intractable as ever.

Chapter 18: Tribalism: An Effort to Reward a Few

"When two brothers are busy fighting, an evil man can easily attack and rob their poor mother. Mankind should always stay united, standing shoulder to shoulder so evil can never cheat and divide them." Suzy Kassem

Uganda's domestic problems are exacerbated by the dynamics of tribalism. Americans might be more familiar with this as racism. Insecure, ineffective, and incompetent presidents insist not only on cultivating a class system based on tribalism, but also on favoring their own tribe in distributing the country's wealth. Tribalism in Uganda, as in many other African nations, is treated as taboo, not all that different from the reticence to discuss HIV/AIDS, a problem where the discussion has improved only marginally since the 1990s. When a person dies of AIDS, everyone knows the cause, but no Ugandan says it out loud. Even eulogists are scrupulously discreet, explaining that the deceased had endured an occasional bout of high fever.

A similar dynamic applies to tribalism. In Uganda, the privileged tribe of the ruling Museveni dominates every key sector—a single tribe dominates both the government and oppositions. All key government institutions are staffed almost exclusively by a single tribe and so almost all the government-related higher education scholarships are awarded to members of a single tribe. It's almost as though there *is* only one tribe.

This is a sly political strategy because it is easier to secure more loyalty from one's own tribe in Africa than another because tribalism still rules in Africa. Once a single tribe has been elevated to form a kind of privileged class it becomes protective of the president; the source of the privilege. So, no one would suggest that he is overstaying his tenure or that he is taking the country on a wrong course by surrendering all the country's resources to foreign neo-colonialists. To do so would be to attack the vested interest of the entire tribe and by extension the tribe itself, the most powerful taboo in the culture.

The tribe protects itself even in matters of corruption. In the event of an investigation, any given person can count on tribesmen with superior rank in government to call it off. A tribe can act with total impunity in exchange for loyalty to the president.

This tribal perspective is, of course, fatally short-sighted. The president's tribesmen—even those benefiting from his excesses— are as expendable as anyone else and have sold themselves and their society so that the President stays in power and the country teeters. They are distracted with their meager rewards and fail to see that a nation is much larger than a single tribe and, once it sinks, everyone, regardless of tribal affiliation, will go down with it.

When the government fails a nation everyone's life is ruined and the few job openings or scholarships the dictator is willing to offer his tribes people will never be sufficient to save them from collapse or their children—their legacy. And that sacrifice has to be made now, for even the tribes of the rulers to join other masses into building a more just nation or their children as well as other children all will have to endure a more contentious, exploitive nation.

African leaders that relied on tribal loyalty did not hide it from their western enablers. In fact this system of hand picking a single tribe to dominate and rule over other tribes was initiated by largely the colonists as their divide and rule policy. In Uganda the British used the Baganda, the largest tribal group, to rule over other tribes. What has changed recently is that western powers today handpick mostly a minority tribe to dominate and rule the majority tribes. This is the case in both Uganda and its neighbors Rwanda.

For the two years I stayed in Uganda after I was deported from Dubai, I was so surprised that it had become normal for civil servants of all kinds—drawn from a privileged tribe—to ask for a bribe to perform tasks that they were actually employed to do— and doing so with a sense of entitlement and arrogance. It seemed to have become acceptable for officials paid to serve people to behave as though they were doing them a favor, and for desperate people of other tribes to react as though they were undeserving. The extent of nepotism in Uganda has reached the point where parents are afraid to retire before their children finish school because they will lose the leverage they have to place them in a job or in attractive training or an advanced educational program. It is just sad.

Latifa, my oldest daughter, was nine when she did something that taught me what justice really means. I was in my bedroom listening to my children playing outside, when one, my five-year-old niece Nakato whom we were taking care of, complained to Latifa that my three-year-old daughter Hadija, had run away with one of her toys. Latifa summoned Hadija and told her to return the toy to the owner and that if she ever wanted anything that is not hers that she had to ask the owner and not just grab it. Hadija returned the toy then Latifa told her to ask for it politely. If Nakato wanted to she could give it to her or if she didn't, Hadija then would understand that she could play with other toys. Luckily when Hadija asked Nakato this time, she gave it to her and the kids were happy again playing together.

Imagine if Latifa had taken the side of her sister against her complaining cousin who would therefore think Latifa unfair and avoid asking her for help should something similar happen again. At the same time her sister would be compelled to continue abusing her trust and misbehave with her young cousins. Justice is so plain in black and white that even young children can tell whether someone with power—be it a parent or a big sister—is being just or unjust. This is the same case with citizens of a country. It doesn't take highly educated people to know if they will get justice from their presidents or kings. It also is no secret that most Ugandans from the non-ruling tribes are the ones always leaving the country, risking foreign servitude in the hopes that their decision to migrate will improve their chances of at least finding a job to provide for their families back in Uganda. The disadvantaged tribes have found no other reasons to stay in their countries and apply for jobs when they are certain a few prevalent government jobs belong to only a certain tribe. So, they have always sought to go to foreign countries where the tags of their tribes will not affect their employment prospects.

It also is no secret that most Ugandans from the non-ruling tribes are the ones always leaving the country, risking foreign servitude in the hopes that their decision to migrate will improve their chances of at least finding a job to provide for their families back in Uganda. assume the role of the absent provider, as they remit their meager earnings so their children can go to school. One of my sons Ahmed who I left behind when I came to the U.S. was just a couple of months old when I moved. He thought that his Dad was actually a telephone or that dad was living inside it. Whenever he sees anyone speaking on the phone, he assumes the person on the receiving end of the call is his Dad. We pay a high price to achieve the most modest of economic stability, an expectation that our Government in Uganda has long forgotten because its priorities are centered around protecting only one person in the nation. It is an unfortunate story replicated in many variations around the African continent.

Chapter 19: Present-day Land-grabbing and Evictions in Africa

"Now, no matter what the mullah teaches, there is only one sin only one. And that is theft, every other sin is a variation of theft."
Khaled Hossein

In July 2015, a colleague from the Thomson Reuters Foundation contacted me by email as she wanted me to help translate and transcribe part of the interviews she had conducted in southern Uganda about the 14,000 villagers who were evicted from their land when the Ugandan government leased 8,000 hectares of land to a Norwegian timber company (Green Resources) in the forest area of Bukaleba. The villagers complained that they no longer had rights to the land on which they were born and have lived for many years.

There is no doubt that this was a flagrant case of land-grabbing but what struck me most about the conversation I translated,[132] was that it detailed the direct involvement of Museveni himself. It turns out that he had written a letter promising the village people 500 hectares elsewhere in exchange for theirs and their willingness to relocate. But the land was not demarcated and there was an endless debate about where exactly this land was located and who had a right to use it. The chairman of the Bukaleba village said the Norwegian company had lied and had planted trees on the land set aside for the evicted villagers. It all seemed endlessly confusing and the net result is that the people concerned have waited for years for the Ugandan government properly to allocate their 500 hectares as agreed.

The story of these villagers is symbolic of the position in which the disenfranchised African finds himself: between the rock of Corruption and he hard place of Nepotism. The fate of these thousands of people is to be rendered homeless and landless by a deal done above their heads and behind their backs between Ugandan and European elites, and then abandoned in a country where the monopoly on opportunity belongs to a single tribe.

Here then is another driver for migration and it is certain that some of the evictees or their children contemplated migrating to Europe, America, or the Middle East. But what success would they have? Little or none because the policy makers in these countries have insisted on blocking their entry. In another iteration of the paradoxical or cruelly ironic relationship between the continents: European corporations were evicting Africans from their land to pave the way for profitable agriculture projects while at the same time their governments were preventing them from migrating to their countries. It is the monolith of European vested interest: profit abroad and (perceived) security and stability at home that means Europeans both in the public and private spheres work relatively in sync.

Th case of Bukaleba's villagers is far from isolated. They are among millions facing an uncertain future across Africa where, according to a report by the U.S.-based Oakland Institute, an estimated 50 million hectares of land have been leased to foreign entities and 90 percent of rural land remains untitled.[133] The Norwegian company was among these foreign beneficiaries and has planted 41,000 hectares of forest in Uganda, Mozambique, and Tanzania and employs up to 2,500 workers.

Across Africa, dictators have rushed to introduce land reforms that take land away from their citizens in order to obtain quick cash from foreign investors. Bear in mind that land is both the only form of property and source of stable of income for most African families. Taking it means leaving people across the continent without either, and furthermore displacing them. Many will then try to migrate. In Ethiopia for example, thousands of people from the Anuak Gambella region fled the country as the government launched a program in which whole communities were forcibly resettled. They used threats, violence, and powers of arrest against those who resisted in order to give fertile land to foreign investors. Most of those relocated had limited access to food or farming, so much so that cases of starvation were reported.[134] According to the Oakland Institute, at least 3,619,509 hectares of land in Ethiopia have been transferred to investors, although the actual number may well be higher.

In another graphic example of this phenomenon, in 2008, South Korean conglomerate Daewoo announced it was leasing 1.3 million

hectares (3.2 million acres) of Madagascar for 99 years for about
$12 an acre—a small fraction of the cost of farmland in the Repub-
lic of South Korea (RSK)—in order to grow maize to be harvested
for ethanol-production in RSK.[xviii] To put it into perspective, that
amounts to one-half of Madagascar's arable land and is among the
largest land lease deals in post-colonial Africa. Bear in mind that
Madagascar is one of the poorest countries in the world where its
citizens frequently must rely on the World Food Program (WFP) to
save them from malnutrition and starvation.

It is only fair to mention that the land deal fueled popular anger
against Madagascar President Marc Ravalomanana that led to the
overthrow of his government in 2009. And his successor Andry Rajoelina cancelled the deal ahead of his inauguration. "In the constitution, it is stipulated that Madagascar's land is neither for sale nor for
rent, so the agreement with Daewoo is cancelled. We are not against
the idea of working with investors, but if we want to sell or rent out
land, we have to change the constitution; you have to consult the
people," Rajoelina told reporters.[135]

Meanwhile, many Western investors, including Wall Street bankers and wealthy individuals, have turned their attention to agricultural land acquisition in Africa. This shift places the food system in
Africa in the hands of a few Western corporations whose interests
are, first and foremost, economic gain, not feeding the millions of
the world's hungry. This again explains why the Western media is not
so keen at reporting these acquisitions.[136]

The American investor Philippe Heilberg signed a farmland deal
with Paulino Matip, a Sudanese warlord, to lease 400,000 hectares
of land (an area the size of Dubai) in South Sudan in July 2008 but
which was not reported until January 2009.[137] That same year Heilberg increased his acreage by 800,000 additional hectares. Heilberg
said, in his view, several African states were likely to break apart in
the coming years, and that the political and legal risks he took would
be amply rewarded. At the time, he explained that "if you bet right
on the shifting of sovereignty then you are on the ground floor . . .
I am constantly looking at the map and looking if there is any value."[138] Four years later, Heilberg, a self-described libertarian who is

also referred to as a "cowboy capitalist," had second thoughts about his gambit. As Vice media reported in a speech he gave to Duke University students, "There is no governance; it's a complete, utter disaster," he said to them of his dealings in South Sudan. "Until ministers found to be corrupt are hanged or severely punished, it won't be stopped."[139] Documenting the ongoing political crisis in South Sudan, journalists Robert Young Pelton and Tim Freccia concluded, "Who would have thought? Carpet bagging, double-dealing, back-stabbing, and blatant corruption in South Sudan? Africans outsmarted outsiders again and again, as Chevron, Rowland, Arakis, White Nile, Nile Trading and Development, and Jarch Capital all busted and then pushed away from the South Sudan high-stakes table."[140]

Western corporations were not the only players in a new race to acquire fertile African land and displace Africans. Asia and the Gulf Middle East were also aggressive in acquiring large chunks of African land to stabilize food supply in their countries and avert domestic social unrest and political instability. The only problem is that the political stability in their countries is being acquired at the expense of Africans whose corrupt governments do not prioritize domestic food supply or local production over foreign investment and production for export.

Qatar, with only one percent of its land suitable for farming, has purchased 40,000 hectares for $3.4 billion in Kenya to grow crops. Al Qudra, an Abu Dhabi-based investment company, also bought large tracts of farmland in Morocco and Algeria. No wonder that today the Gulf Middle East countries are among key destinations for African migrants robbed of their land and other possessions in Africa.

Even though it is important to invest in the African agricultural sector, the West's acquisition of continental land is a threat to African economies and livelihoods. Evidence shows that these land deals often lack transparency and are frequently mismanaged by governments. Smallholder farmers who are the majority in Africa are being displaced in the process. These farmers are starting to realize what the foreign investors are doing to their livelihoods, and with nothing much to do many are resorting to migration to these countries.

It is profoundly sad for the government or the president to be facilitating the ownership of land to be in the hands of European or

American foreigners as this is direct exploitation. If citizens do not even have ownership of land in their own country then what do they have? While several nations on the continent have tried to institute land administration reforms with varying degrees of success, several critical challenges remain. They can be summarized as:

The area formally recognized under statutory law is much less than the area to which Indigenous Peoples and local communities hold customary rights. Further action is needed to bridge that gap.

In many countries, laws may recognize community control but need to be strengthened to recognize more robust rights of ownership. Even where ownership is recognized, laws or regulations may limit certain uses of the land, particularly for commercial purposes. Incompatible laws governing other sectors such as extractive industries, agribusiness, and conservation can also adversely impact indigenous and community land rights.

Moreover, formal legal recognition of indigenous and community lands is not sufficient to guarantee tenure security. States and other actors must also respect, support, and enforce such legal protections.[141]

In Africa the European and American foreigners own the land, mines, banks, factories, fuel stations, airlines, and all the wealth coming from these sources are shipped or transferred to the West and what is left in Africa for Africans? What do the citizens of African countries have in their countries to keep them home not to emigrate—nothing or too little to sustain their families even on the most modest expectations. This is worsened by the fact that even prospective means like employment that would give them the opportunity to own their titles and deeds to land are nonexistent. At least they can see prospects of employment even in menial jobs in the West or in Middle East countries, much less than the potential to collaborate and start their own enterprises.

In 2017, the Ugandan government tabled a land bill amendment proposal on compulsory acquisition of land for public use, and that it may deposit in court a befitting sum for the land it wants to acquire from the owner. Museveni went on broadcast outlets to explain to the citizens that the amendments are framed for the country's better interests, and that the government taking over land from owners they deem not suitable for agriculture and giving it to investors ultimately will bring in more revenue to Uganda. Designating some parcels as public land has been the easiest way African leaders have facilitated the land grab in their countries and then they would hand over that land to foreign investors with not so much of a fair compensation to the previous African land owners.[142] More Africans stand to lose land that could be ascertained as being legitimately titled to them and without land and no employment they have no reason to stay at home.

The African leaders who are handing over fertile African land with easy access to water to Western corporations are doing the same thing that colonialists did in earlier times when they designated millions of acres as public land. In Kenya after the highlands were declared "crown land" the British colonialists handed over to Lord Delamere 100,000 acres at a cost of a penny per acre. Lord Francis Scott purchased 350,000 acres and the East African Syndicate Ltd. took 100,000 acres, all at give-away prices. In Liberia in 1926, the Firestone Rubber Company acquired a million acres of forest land at a cost of six cents per acre.[143] And in the Congo King Leopold II issued decrees that designated all free parcels as government land— in effect as his own property, sole proprietorship. He amassed all parcels that natives had not cultivated but instead set aside as hunting grounds or as a plentiful source of wood for building, or for mining iron ore to be used in tools and weapons. The 21st century has seen that practice continue, albeit in a different form.

As I close this chapter, I need to mention how this extensive exploitation exacerbated by long-ruling Western puppets like Museveni continues to affect negatively the future of the continent. African resources are fast becoming depleted and its population is growing at a faster corresponding pace. By 2050, it is predicted the population in most African countries will have doubled and the continent will have almost depleted all of its resources. The future is much darker than what even analysts have predicted and, for sure, more African migrants will continue trying to get to Europe or the U.S. where their resources have built stable economies. Europe and America are already definitely concerned about these demographics and more worried because even family planning strategies that have been promoted in the continent for a long time have not had any yields. Visa restrictions and border patrols are likely to be tightened but like I have always said, there are no restrictions that could ever be so rigorous to stop the wave of migrations that have determined our human history. Europe and the U.S. stand alone to address honestly the exploitation of Africa and demand from their corporations honest and decent trade practices with the continent.

SECTION IV: AFRICAN MIGRATIONS

Chapter 20: The Migration to the Middle East

"None of you [truly] believes until he loves for his brother that which he loves for himself." Prophet Mohammed

"In the spring of 2015, following my return to Uganda, a man contacted me to ask for help in repatriating the body of his daughter Faith Maryam Nandyose who had been working as a maid in Abu Dhabi when she died unexpectedly. The sinister circumstances of her untimely death beckon an invitation into the life of an African migrant working in the Gulf."

Pastor Moses Tebusweke told me that in the last communication Nandyose had with the family she told her brother that her employer's wife had suspected that her husband was attracted romantically to her. As revenge, the wife confiscated all of Nandyose's good clothes, ordering her to only dress in shapeless, nondescript attire. She also denied her food for two days, accusing her of instigating an affair with her husband in her home.

Nandyose's body arrived in Uganda with a death certificate issued by the Abu Dhabi Health Authority indicating that she had died of cardiac arrest, resulting from a fall from a high-rise building. But the conclusions of an autopsy commissioned by her family from the Mulago referral hospital were very different: her death had been caused by torture, including strangulation. Indeed, the body bore cuts that had been sutured signaling that the deceased was probably attacked with knives or similar tools.

"She used to work on the thirteenth floor and a body that falls from that floor would be completely smashed, which was not the case with my daughter's body," Tebusweke explained. "Also, there's no indication at all that her fall was reported in any newspaper, which like all other migrant suspicious deaths is a commonly covered item in the Emirate." He explained that the evidence confirmed his suspicions that she was tortured to death and that the cause of death indicated on the Abu Dhabi report as false. "I don't know how I can push for justice for my daughter," he said, adding that her tormentors and killers should be punished, "but I don't know how a poor man like myself can get that justice."

Her story is all too common. Similar incidents have been reported in the Ugandan media and others have simply never been covered. According to a report released in October 2017 by Uganda's parliamentary committee on labor and gender, about 50 Ugandans, of whom 32 were women, have died in the United Arab Emirates since January of that year. Thirty-five of these deaths were ruled suicides. Other causes of death include cardiac arrest, murder, drowning, meningitis, HIV-related complications, and liver failure.[144] Most of these people were young and healthy. If they weren't then they wouldn't have got the job and even if they did then they wouldn't be able to do it. So, the suicide rate is abnormally high.

Most Asian countries have already taken the drastic step of placing a moratorium on migration of domestic workers going to the Middle East because of the exploitation and abuses of workers in these places, so African countries have become the new recruitment ground. There they find no shortage of desperate people frustrated by moribund economies and long-term unemployment.

The relationship between African supply of and Arab demand for cheap migrant labor is more complex than it might seem. Migration is not only encouraged but also formally agreed by governments. Uganda for example signed an agreement with Saudi Arabia in 2015 for Saudi Arabia to send one million migrant domestic workers for wages as low as $200 per month. In addition, Uganda has little or no experience in managing labor migration outside the continent and has not put in place mechanisms for such migration to function safely. Without ethical recruitment practices and proper pre-departure orientation, citizens are vulnerable to exploitation like physical and sexual abuse, bonded labor, and human trafficking.

Furthermore, the policy prevalent in the Middle East known as *kafala*, which I covered extensively in my previous two books, requires migrants to secure a local sponsor to work or stay in many of these countries. This requirement gives employers enormous power over their employees who are unable to change jobs or leave without their consent. Under this system then, millions of workers have no means of escape and few rights of redress. They find themselves brutally exploited, their movements controlled, and their well-being disregarded. Reports of psychological, physical and sexual abuse, torture, and suicides are widespread. And there is often no way to escape without self-sacrifice.

I don't want to duplicate my work on *kafala* here, rather I want to draw attention to the ways in which African governments, like that of Uganda, have both abandoned their efforts to solve the problems of persistent unemployment and have behaved in the all too familiar pattern of Africa and earned a kickback commission for sending their most vulnerable citizens into servitude in the Gulf.

The only plausible motive for the kind of agreement mentioned above between Uganda and the Kingdom of Saudi Arabia would be the revenue generated by it for government elites. In Uganda at least, most recruitment agencies are linked to powerful men in the government. Middle East Consultants, for example, whose ownership is linked to Museveni's brother Salim Saleh. Even after being licensed, these agencies have continued to commit violations that equate to human trafficking, and these agencies are confident and arrogant enough to believe that they can do so with impunity. For example, making people pay for jobs abroad is illegal but has become standard practice. Agencies charge between $1,500 and $3,000 to get Ugandans to the Middle East. By the time a Ugandan migrant worker gets there they will have paid thousands of dollars in legal and illegal fees charged by these agencies, none of which is recoverable.

The five-year bilateral agreement Uganda signed with Saudi Arabia exemplifies the tenuous relationships that entrenched unemployment have forged. The agreement sets the minimum wage for Ugandan workers in Saudi Arabia at 700 riyals ($200) a month, lower than the minimum set for Filipino, Indian, and Bangladeshi domestic workers. This low wage creates an impossible economic chasm for workers to improve the conditions of their livelihood. The average annual salary in Riyadh, for example, is $84,000. A one-bedroom apartment ranges in rental costs from $700 to $1,500 per month. Even with private health insurance, a mandate for many ex-pats, the cost of a doctor's visit is generally between $30 and $60 per month. It is a mathematical impossibility that a

Ugandan worker in the Kingdom would have any discretionary income whatsoever.

The agreement was signed with little or no knowledge of or attention to the conditions in which migrants live and work in Saudi Arabia. As ever, the Ugandan Government was willing to ignore media reports of abuses as well as the fact that—at the time the agreement was signed—other countries had withdrawn their workers from Saudi Arabia, or forbidden them from migrating there. Museveni's government was too anxious to let domestic political tensions continue because of the country's poor economy. Just a few months after Ugandan workers started arriving in Saudi Arabia, voices of desperation surfaced with greater frequency in the media, and workers posted video and audio recordings of their plight in Saudi homes and prisons and homes and on social media.

The Ugandan government had few practicable ways in which to respond to this crisis. In January 2016, it announced a temporary ban on sending housemaids to Saudi Arabia after a barrage of complaints about workers being treated inhumanely. The country said the ban would remain until working conditions were "deemed fitting." The ban made the lives of those Ugandans actually working in the Kingdom more difficult rather than less. During my reporting on the agreement as well as the subsequent abuses and the ban, workers who stayed in Saudi Arabia told me they were being chastised by their employers for their country's women who were complaining and tarnishing the name of Saudi Arabia.

In practice the ban was untenable. Moses Binoga, coordinator of the Anti-Trafficking Task Force at the Ugandan Interior Ministry, told me the ban was doing more harm than good, as many traffickers went underground to take women to Saudi Arabia through neighboring countries such as Kenya. In fact, Kenya earlier had banned its citizens from going to work in Gulf Arab countries and their traffickers had been using Uganda as a transit point.

Furthermore, the relationships between African and Arab countries were not predicated solely on migrants but also several business deals. During the ban, Museveni went to Saudi Arabia for a two-day state visit and though the issue of Ugandan migrant workers was not on the publicly revealed agenda it was likely discussed. Museveni's visit was followed by two other visits of Uganda's Gender and

Labor Minister Janat Mukwaya and a few months later the ban on Ugandan domestic employees going to work in Saudi Arabia was lifted. Speaking to journalists at the time Mukwaya said increased supervision would lead to safer working conditions in the best interests of Ugandan migrants. "All domestic workers will be provided with a telephone SIM card on arrival by the government," Mukwaya said, adding the government would set up call centers and deploy Ugandan supervisors charged with the responsibility of monitoring the condition of Ugandans on duty abroad.

Meanwhile more videos of desperate Ugandans claiming to have been abused and trapped in Saudi Arabia continued to come out on social media. For example, in 2019 videos showed six Ugandan women living in accommodation owned by the recruitment company with which they were dealing, and they had asked for authorities in Uganda to intervene and facilitate their repatriation. "I have been deployed to work in seven different homes in the last six months I have stayed in Saudi Arabia. There has been no pay and when I demand to go back home, the recruitment company insists I should go to another family," said one of the women in the video. "Even here at the recruitment company we are being abused, the male workers are forcing themselves on us and we are being forced to drink water from the sinks."

Uganda is not a country with many high school—much less, college—graduates and many sectors still lack good qualified people. Governments that made a deal with Saudi Arabia to send a million of its trained people into Saudi Arabia servitude could not necessarily be equated to the African kings of the 15th century who sold their young, energetic people to European slave traders, but there's a looming similarity that appears on closer inspection. Today's African president is willing to preside over a state with no doctors, no nurses, no teachers, and no engineers because all of them have been sent to do menial jobs in Saudi Arabia. The sender pocketed a good commission—the same way the old kings were willing to live with large areas of uncultivated land because they exchanged their people as slaves for European factories making goods and guns on an unprecedented scale.

Chapter 21: South Africa and African Migrants

"If our goal is to slow migration, then the best way to do so is to work for a more equitable global system." Aviva Chomsky

In November 2016, in what proved to be a turning point in my life, I traveled to Cape Town for a training course in journalism relating to issues surrounding religion and LGBTQ communities. By this time I had come to realize—for the reasons we have seen in previous chapters—that I could not support my wife and four small children by living and working in Uganda and had started to consider relocating to South Africa to try to better our situation.

After the course, I moved to the home of my Ugandan host (let's call him Hussein for the purposes of the story). He was to brief me on the opportunities available to Ugandan migrants and show me the lie of the land in general. He bluntly told me that the best option was to be a *sangomas*, an African sacred healer, work that has attracted many Ugandans to South Africa. The phenomenon has built its own momentum: migrants often choose to do the same job as their compatriots, which for Ugandans was being sangomas. Put simply, most Ugandans were *sangomas* so all newcomers were likely to become *sangomas* as well.

We moved to the third floor of a multi-story building in the Bellville section of metropolitan Cape Town, where *sangomas* had rented two offices and converted them into a sacred healing shrine. I was shown both offices. The first appeared to be like any conventional office with a sofa for visitors and a table with a chair for the healer, similar to where an office manager might sit. A doorway connected both office spaces. The other office was divided by slats of soft plywood into one space for the shrine for ritualistic processional purposes and another where the supposed ancestral spirit would hide and wait until the *sangoma* called upon him to emerge. In the center of this plywood partition, a window hole had been cut which would be opened by the "spirit" when he enters the shrine.

At the start of the ritual, the *sangoma* would sit with the client and discuss a few details before inviting the ancestral spirits. The spirit emerges in complete darkness while the *sangoma* plays ankle bells held next to the client's ear. Although last this is a genuine tradition, it also serves to mask the sound of the "spirit" sneaking into the room. The "spirit" would then speak from a corner while playing ankle bells and then shift from corner to corner while changing voice tones and languages to create the impression there is more than one "spirit" in the shrine. The "spirit" might speak in English or the local Xhosa language.[xix] Indeed, it was essential for the person acting as the ancestral spirit to learn Xhosa.

After I had seen the shrine, we discussed the work in detail. Hussein suggested that I should listen closely because he was about to give me a comprehensive course in the work of sangomas in just one sitting. The way he spoke you could be forgiven for thinking that this was legitimate work that would require professional training at a university; that there might be a Bachelor of Science degree involved.

Hussein started by explaining that this business, like all others, is based on trust. The witch doctor work needs someone to build trust with his clients and once that trust is established then the client will believe everything the witch doctor said and would pay handsomely for their help. Trust, he explained, was built by being kind and by offering to solve the client's most pressing problems. Here I interrupted to ask how could I be sure that a woman who wants her husband back or a man who is looking for a job—common problems that a client might present to a *sangoma*—can be helped. Hussein answered with the confidence of an expert, adding that while one might not solve everything, one could always try, by studying the problem and attempting to find a solution. He said that one out of ten clients might have their problems fully resolved so the important thing is to keep the attention of the other nine by making promises and asking them to be patient, as they keep on paying. The person whose problems are solved becomes the example to all those waiting and sometimes that satisfied client is encouraged to offer a testimony to

---

xix   A Bantu tongue and of South Africa's official languages.

doubting clients. "The solutions we offer," Hussein explained, "are not spiritually granted but they are offered on a psychological point. You have to read through what people are thinking by interpreting their body language, using hypnosis and the power of suggestion. Whenever you get it right, they will believe you have supernatural abilities."

Returning to our ad hoc training, Hussein reminded me that men and women are treated differently. He said women were like gold because once a witch doctor mastered the skills of handling them, they would be the pipeline of prosperity for many other Ugandans who had decided to practice as *sangomas* in South Africa. Most witch doctors have used sex to build trust with their women clients. He said because their shrine was used by different clients, they would keep some condoms on hand so that those who used sex for building trust did not risk contracting HIV or other sexually transmitted diseases. He stressed that I should not be judgmental for fear of damaging the credibility of the practice. Hussein was honest, at least.

He said most women who visited the shrine were married or in a relationship that they wanted to cement or were searching for love. Other women visited because they thought they were being bewitched, or they wanted to find a job, or to help their children prosper, or to cure AIDS or other life-threatening illness. As Hussein spoke, I found it ironic that some clients—men and women—visited *sangomas* because of their desires to be rich although nearly every man who was a client came for the reason of finding great wealth.

Meanwhile, the women who visited the shrine to find love or re-kindle romantic feelings in their spouses comprised the easiest prey for witch doctors who used sex to build trust. The "spirit" would offer to improve their physical features of sexual attraction so men would find them irresistible and would provide a charm stick that women could use to lure men. Once a woman met a man to whom she was sexually attracted, all she would have to do is squeeze this small charm stick in her hands and invoke the name of her sexual attraction. As for the physical aspects of the body, that required services to be conducted at the shrine.

Hussein said that sex was used not only to build trust but also blackmail some women. He said that most women who visited the shrines with financial problems were first lured into sex and then blackmailêd to continue bringing money to the witch doctor to keep their sexual activities at the shrine a secret. Married women would even be advised to seek divorce and have a share of their husbands' wealth brought to the witch doctor. The whole thing was a scam.

For men the trick was always to convince them that "spirits" could make them richer and resolve all their financial problems. Hussein picked up a briefcase from the shrine room and opened it on the floor to demonstrate the trick. What did I see? I replied, "newspapers." There were pages from as many as 100 copies of newspapers stuffed into that briefcase. Hussein explained that they would put a few currency notes on top and they would show the briefcase to their client, explaining that it was all his money that the ancestors were helping him to reclaim. Then, they would instruct him to sell something that would act as a cover should authorities query him about how he obtained his new wealth from ancestors. After selling a house or a car, the client was instructed to bring the proceeds of the sale to the witch doctors who would then mix it in with the handful of currency notes in the briefcase. The witch doctor told the client that he would take the briefcase to the seashore so that its contents would be blessed by ancestral spirits and a week later, it would be given to the client. Anyone who asked the client how he obtained such riches could safely answer that he had sold his car or house and invested it well. The client would then become useful in providing testimony of success, adding to the stories of countless other men who had followed a similar path. Some clients were financially comfortable but were just greedy. This, too, demonstrated how all of this was an outright scam.

Unsurprisingly the natural prey of a witch doctor—the poor and desperate migrant who had left their homeland in search of productive employment elsewhere also unwittingly led them to scams that set them back even further. Meanwhile, these so-called *sangomas* operated with arrogant confidence, knowing that only a few public officials genuinely cared about protecting the most economically vulnerable people.

After our discussion, we went to a nightclub for the evening and left after midnight. On our way back home, Hussein drove around the poor neighborhoods of Khayelesha, Phiphi, and Delft to show me the city's nightlife. We found a young woman in her early twenties walking on the streets, who was crying and had evidently been attacked because of blood and bruises on her face. Hussein stopped the car and asked her why she was crying. They exchanged a few words that I could not hear but the woman joined us in the car.

I learned that she was a South African from a Xhosa tribe, and she had fought with her Zimbabwean boyfriend and she was going to the police to report him when we found her. Hussein offered to take her to the police station but as he drove, he also tried to convince her to go to a nearby hospital, instead of the police. I stayed in the car while Hussein helped her to the hospital's emergency department. I noticed there were several other women coming to the hospital that night and most of them appeared to be domestic violence victims. When the two returned, Hussein told me the woman was going to stay with us for the night because her husband likely would beat her up if she returned home. As he drove to his home in the Belhar area he told me about the incident in Luganda when this woman discovered that her Zimbabwean boyfriend was cheating with her sister and that is how the fight had started. He told me he was expecting the woman to be his client and they had agreed on the arrangement at the hospital. He would bring her to the shrine in the morning to consult with the "ancestors" on how she could bring her husband back and kick her sister out of their home. Unfortunately, this was a common occurrence, as I had discovered how willing so many people had become to escape such dire circumstances because they knew that few authorities would bother to help them out in the best way possible. Vulnerable victims became even more vulnerable.

After that night, I knew there was no way I could live and work in South Africa under these moral and physical conditions. I returned to Uganda before my travel visa had expired. The probability of my staying on the continent had diminished significantly.

Chapter 22: Anger Directed at the Wrong People

"Never, never and never again shall this beautiful land experience the oppression of one by another." Nelson Mandela

South Africa is among the most favored destinations in Africa for economic migrants and political refugees who are fleeing war and poverty. As one of Africa's economic powerhouses, the country has been in receipt of migrants from its less fortunate African neighbors since the times of apartheid; many of them coming to work in the mining industry. Since Apartheid ended political upheaval and military conflict have only increased the number of Africans going to work in South Africa. Indeed, the fall of Apartheid has, for reasons that will be obvious, made South Africa still more attractive to the African migrant.

Africans come to South Africa from a range of countries to do a variety of work, but for similar reasons. About three million Zimbabweans, mostly professionals, have fled to South Africa from their country, despairing of their leadership, and sickened by corruption and hyperinflation. These college-educated professionals have been working as housekeepers and menial laborers in South Africa. Ethiopians and Somalis work mostly as shopkeepers, and Ugandans as witchdoctors. The country also has seen a significant number of other nationalities and ethnicities including Chinese, Bangladeshi, Indians, Middle Easterners, and Europeans who live and work there.

It is hard to tell with any degree of certainty how many Africans migrate, or attempt to migrate to South Africa although there can be no doubt that the number is high. The very statistics are a political minefield. Africa Check, an independent research group, reported in 2018 that there were 381,754 applications in South Africa for asylum according to its review of the backlog volume, which makes the country second in such cases, only exceeded by Germany.[145] One of the officials quoted in the report said the large number of open asylum applications in South Africa is a result of "slow and ineffective asylum processing which keeps people in asylum limbo for many years; instead of processing them so that applicants are either granted or refused asylum."[146]

The numbers are important, according to Africa Check, which publishes regular reports and factsheets relating to migration in southern Africa. The group contends that both governments and nongovernmental organizations have a vested interest in exaggerating immigrant numbers, either to justify stricter immigration controls or secure increased donor funding. Africa Check, for example, has disputed claims that more than 1.5 million Zimbabweans live in South Africa, or that almost one-third of Malawi's population live and work in the country. The factual discrepancies fuel anecdotal rhetoric that may amplify negative stereotypes about foreign-born migrants in South Africa and heighten fears that, for example, migrants are "stealing" South African jobs.

There can be no doubt that migration is a source of social and political turmoil in the country. In 2017, the Southern African Migration Programme published a case study focusing on the double impact crisis caused by the mass exodus of citizens from Zimbabwe, many of whom head for South Africa, and xenophobic violence in the country.[147] To put the report in context: xenophobia has become common in South Africa, with local citizens going on the rampage, killing foreigners and burning their homes and businesses, and demanding that migrants leave the country. The first outbreaks of this kind of violence took place in 1994 and 1995 shortly after the country had gained independence and another major wave of broke in 2008, when tens of thousands of migrants were displaced, their businesses, homes and properties looted, and 56 people were killed.

These violent convulsions were not simply a spontaneous expression of anger. In 2015, Zulu King Goodwill Zwelithini was reported to have made comments that foreigners should go back to their home countries, sparking yet another wave of xenophobic attacks. The Zulu king blamed foreigners for changing the nature of South African society and enjoying wealth that should have been reserved for local people.

The 2017 report, which the European Union funded, was commissioned by the International Centre for Migration Policy Development, which is based in Vienna. The report indicated that as many as three out of every 10 migrants from Zimbabwe make their livelihood in the informal local economy, with many of them predominantly males under the age of 35. Most of the current migrant entrepreneurs came to South Africa in the first decade of the new millennium. Most of the migrants rely on their personal savings to start their businesses and many previously had worked in the formal economy. The report indicated that "business expansion has occurred despite the prime obligation of the entrepreneurs to support family still in Zimbabwe. Instead of reinvesting all of the business profits into further expansion, a portion is therefore diverted into remittance channels. Over one-third remit funds at least once per month and only 12 percent never send remittances."[148] Yet, many of these entrepreneurs have become victims of violence and crime, including looting, robbery, abuse, and police misconduct.

The 2017 report also examined the South African government's response to the migrant crisis and concerns about xenophobic violence. Former President Jacob Zuma's son has spoken publicly against immigrants and would support mass expulsion, indicating that foreigners in South African represent a time bomb in the country. The South African government launched Operation Fiela (which translates as *sweep clean*) that led to mass arrests and deportation of immigrants. The operation was denounced by human rights activists as institutional xenophobia.

Indeed, the 2017 report added the disturbing context to these statements. The report summarized:

> There is a strong official line that these attacks are not motivated by xenophobia and indeed, that xenophobia does not even exist. This is clearly contradicted by the migrants who view the attacks as motivated by xenophobia. A second element of the official response is that the migrants are partially to blame for what happens to them as their business success builds resentment amongst South Africans. Government has yet to acknowledge that migrant-owned informal enterprises make a valuable contribution to

the economy of the country, including through job creation for South Africans.[149]

The point here is that ordinary black South Africans direct their anger towards African immigrants in error, not only because the latter do not threaten their livelihoods or culture but also, and far more importantly, because indigenous political elites are their real enemy and one on which their ire would be focused more productively.

Africans mostly run small shops, vending, and service industries, which do not siphon off significant revenue potential elsewhere in the South African economy. Whites in South Africa make up about 8.7 percent of the population but control more than 85 percent of the country's wealth. African immigrants don't own land or hold secured titles to property, don't run companies, don't own mining companies, don't operate trophy hunting companies, or do not ship out capital to European banks. Indeed, the anger of Black South Africans turning to African immigrants is completely misplaced. if all Black Africans who are not native to South Africa were deported right now, then there would be little change for the ordinary native South African.

African migrants are not the source of the problem. The gap in wealth and income that once was a signature evil of the apartheid regime has widened in the post-apartheid era. What has changed is that there is now a small group of black native elites who benefit from an established system and have joined their wealthy white peers. These elites are the ones refocusing the black political energy that fought and won against Apartheid and transforming it into hatred against other black people who are considered foreigners.

The 2017 report zeroed in on the importance of the South African Human Rights Commission (SAHRC), which has played a major role in the past in holding government to account and articulating extensive recommendations for remedial action, "most of which have not been taken up and many of which are still highly relevant." The report concluded:

> International organizations have tended to target integration and education programming at the community

level but there has only been one systematic evaluation (of the UNHCR's response) which was highly critical of the organization. These organizations and other governments are considerably hamstrung by xenophobia denialism at the highest level because it means that government will avoid the kinds of partnership that are urgently needed to address this endemic crisis.[150]

The more South Africans accept this destructive myth the longer the elite will continue to exploit the economy and the suffering will continue as poverty in wealth, health, education, and expectation will deepen further. The sooner South Africans see this situation with clarity and demand justice with the same vigor they used to end apartheid, the better and sooner their deliverance.

Chapter 23: Israel and the Deportation of Eritreans to Uganda

"The stranger who resides with you shall be to you as one of your citizens; you shall love them as yourself, for you were strangers in the land of Egypt." (Leviticus 19:34)

In 2016, I was in Uganda and still struggling to resettle at home after my Middle East career had ended in disaster and deportation. During this period news broke that, under the terms of a secret agreement, Israel had deported several Eritreans to Uganda. One of my old school friends, Sharif Migadde, a lawyer trained in the United Kingdom, had a number of Eritrean clients who had been recently deported from Israel to Uganda, who were in need of legal advice on a range of issues regarding their resettlement including how to go about setting up small businesses. On many occasions I accompanied Sharif as he met these new clients at the airport and then escorted them to his office or their temporary homes.

Many of them settled in the center of Kampala in areas including Old Kampala, Najjanakumbi, Nsambya, and Namasuba. I took the opportunity of talking to them about how and why they were forced to leave Israel. One of them told me how he and his compatriots had paid smugglers between three and five thousand USD—a considerable sum for an Eritrean migrant—to get to Israel so as to escape the civil war in Eritrea. The Israeli government offered him an option of taking $3,500 to leave Israel and be resettled in Uganda or be held in an immigration detention camp for the remainder of his life, a place where he already had been staying for three years since he entered Israel. They had no option of ever going out to mingle with other people and make out a living on Tel Aviv streets because in Israel, the official position was that they were infiltrators, not refugees seeking asylum.

There had already been speculation in the media regarding secret, high-level deals between Israel and both Uganda and Rwanda in which the African states would accept refugees in return for arms, military training, and other aid. Though Israel readily admitted the arrangement, Uganda was at first hesitant to do so seemingly doubting that there was any benefit in so doing. Ofwono Opondo, a spokesperson for the Ugandan Government, frequently appeared in the media to deny that they made the deal or the Eritreans in question existed. As I had met and talked to them, I knew this to be untrue and was once again flabbergasted at the shamelessness of the Museveni regime in the face of such potential benefits.

It is certainly true that Museveni had been praised for accepting refugees at a time when the richer countries were refusing them—at first the U.S. and the European nations and now South Africa and Israel. Indeed, it appeared that the richer the country was, the tighter it closed its doors to newcomers and the only countries that could open their doors to other people were poor, struggling nations such as Uganda, who did so out of self-interest and not altruism.

In public Museveni has been keen to personalize his relationship with the migrant issue, telling the press his own story of having been a refugee in Tanzania and Malawi during his long struggle to become Uganda's president. He plays the role of the humanitarian accepting any number of refugees into his country, but fails to mention the arms deals he has brokered with Israel in exchange for taking on its unwanted asylum seekers, or indeed the fact that the refugees have been cared for by aid donated by international NGOs rather than by the Ugandan authorities who would have left them to survive on their own. Museveni has made hosting unwanted refugees his core national policy, earning the political capital from Europeans and American politicians that helps him to retain power.

During the previous presidential elections in 2016, the Ugandan opposition also complained that Museveni's government was registering refugees to vote. Candidate Kizza Besigye warned refugees against voting in the country's elections almost in every region he visited that hosted them.[xx]

Political clout is not the only benefit that Museveni's refugee-hosting policy brings the regime. The aforementioned aid generated by the policy is wholly unaccountable and therefore vulnerable to the predations of an endemically corrupt political class: Museveni's

xx   See https://ugandaradionetwork.com/story/sudanese-refugees-warned-against-voting-in-this-months-elections.

government received $200 million in humanitarian aid in 2018 and there is no way of telling how much of that ever reached the refugees for whom it was intended. At the time of writing, Uganda plays host to 1.4 million refugees and is considered by the United Nations as one of the most welcoming countries in a world where the richer countries in the West as well as those of Africa and the Middle East—including Israel are pulling up the drawbridge. This narrative has been simplified to the advantage of the ruling elite and to the disadvantage of the refugees who are being offloaded onto another African country that is unfamiliar to them in all but standard of living and quality of life and left to start from scratch; a country from which its own citizens are leaving in large numbers.

Chapter 24: Africans going to Europe

"We do not support planned search and rescue operations in the Mediterranean." Baroness Joyce Anelay

I have only ever been to Europe while en route to another destination; in air transit. In 2006 when I traveled to Canada to cover the international AIDS Conference, I passed through Birmingham, England, where we stayed in transit for four hours. I thought I would have been granted a visa to stay overnight without much trouble, not least because the migrant crisis and the anxiety it generated were yet to sweep Europe.

In 2014 when the European migrant crisis was raging, I had another chance to travel to Europe. The Thomson Reuters Foundation selected me to attend its anti-slavery reporting workshop in London. I was working in Qatar at the time as an online editor for a local daily called *Peninsula* and writing my second book *Slave States*. My application for a British visa had to go through the visa processing office in neighboring Abu Dhabi (UAE) because there was only a courier center in Qatar from which visa applications were posted. A decision would be forthcoming in a month. My visa was denied because the visa officer was not convinced that I was financially stable enough to want to return to Qatar after my training in London, and so to them I represented a threat.

The rejection frustrated and surprised me. I told the conference organizers that the embassy turned me down simply because I was not rich enough to attend. They encouraged me to try another application, this time giving me a detailed letter explaining that they would take responsibility for my financial obligations in London as well as assuring authorities that I would return to Qatar afterward, where—after all—I had a steady job. The organizer also promised to call the Abu Dhabi embassy on my behalf once my second application was submitted. Despite all that, the second application was rejected on the same grounds. They added that while they understood that the Foundation was paying all the expenses incurred on the trip, the new visa requirements stipulated that all applicants must prove that they are financially stable in their own right. At this time, I had not even thought of trying to stay in Europe apart from the training time, as I was still working on a book project I loved and my editorial job in Qatar was better than the factory and caregiving work that would have awaited me in London.

The reality was that a system trying to block migrants coming into Europe had unfairly victimized me. When I discussed the incident about the rejection online with some Ugandan friends who live in London, they all put the blame on me. One of them told me that they could have helped with the documents if only I had let them know because the only way a person could travel to Europe, even for a visit, was to prove that their bank accounts held funds sufficient to reassure the authorities that they were financially independent.

This was a time when European politicians believed that the number of people—migrants as well as refuges—trying to settle on the Continent illegally had become unacceptable. In Britain and across Europe, governments were not only tightening visa restrictions but also closing their borders. Across the Continent there was a shift in consciousness towards nationalism, which values national identity over humanity. Politicians were besieged by it and found it to be politically advantageous to dehumanize people by refusing them sanctuary, even though they are in desperate need of shelter and protection. Of course, sealing European borders did not deter the migrants. Instead the cost in all sense of the term simply shot up and refugees and migrants fleeing violence and poverty tried more dangerous routes and more unscrupulous smugglers.

The European Migrant Crisis has been in the news for several years and analysts have proposed solutions such as creating safe routes for the migrants, spending millions of dollars to rescue and shelter them, breaking the networks of the smugglers or giving these people legal refugee status. None of these solutions will put an end to the human exodus of our generation. The real solution lies with those powerful and stable countries to which people look to escape the corruption, poverty, war, and despair that I have tried to detail here. If those countries changed the politics of plunder and proxy that have so undermined development in general, then potential migrants would find what they're looking for—what everyone looks for—in their homeland.

Nowhere has the sting of European rejection been felt more keenly than in the Mediterranean where authorities look the other way as hundreds of thousands of refugees, including women and children, take overcrowded boats with faulty engines only to drown. Baroness Joyce Anelay, an erstwhile UK Foreign Office Minister, clearly stated her nation's position: "We do not support planned search and rescue operations in the Mediterranean," she said, citing "an unintended *pull factor,* encouraging more migrants to attempt the dangerous sea crossing and thereby leading to more tragic and unnecessary deaths."

Public opinion polls across Europe have shown how migration, especially that coming from Africa and the Middle East, has become an overriding concern to ordinary people; ordinary people who vote. Politicians running on anti-migrant rhetoric started winning elections, from Italy to Britain, Hungary and Austria. The question of migration has dominated European Union debates and politicians have sought to articulate a continental policy in which refugees and migrants should be considered to be the responsibility of other continents, not that of Europe.

European countries have launched media campaigns including ads in foreign countries to discourage more refugees from seeking asylum. Among these include Spain's campaigns in 2007, targeting refugees from Africa and warning against the dangerous travel across the seas. Likewise, Germany and Austria have posted advertisements in newspapers in Kosovo, explaining that human traffickers are lying about grounds for asylum in Austria. Germany published a similar message in the Albanian papers: "NO economic asylum in Germany." Denmark has a campaign aimed at Syrian Muslims fleeing the civil war, with messages posted in Turkish and probably major Arab media, to deter asylum seekers from coming to Denmark.

European politicians have discussed African migration in terms that would suit an impending hurricane. And watching the news or reading the newspapers one might think that the entire population of Africa was waiting for boats to migrate to Europe. This public discourse blows the situation out of all proportion, but more importantly fails to acknowledge that many African refugees move to other

Africa countries and not to Europe. Indeed, according to the UN, more than 80 percent of African migration today occurs within Africa itself, either intra-regionally (particularly within the West, East, and Southern African regions) or inter-regionally (from West Africa to Southern Africa, from East/Horn of Africa to Southern Africa and from Central Africa to Southern Africa and West Africa). Africa also hosts more than a quarter of the world's refugees. African countries that are in the top 10 refugee-hosting countries in the world (including the Democratic Republic of the Congo, Chad, Ethiopia, Kenya, and Uganda) accounted for 21 percent of the world's refugees in 2016.[151]

Of course, not all Europeans are hostile to refugees and migrants. In fact, despite the populist anti-migration propaganda, the attitudes of Europeans to newcomers are complex and open to influence, as was clear from the reaction to the drowning of the Syrian child Alan Kurdi, the image of which was shared around the world. Similar images of a child who drowned along with her father while trying to swim their way into USA also elicited sympathies even from anti-immigration politicians. The voices of the populists have drowned out the more rational voices in Europe, but they are certainly there. Today nearly all of the people that have had to flee their own countries to escape wars that European countries are involved in are being sheltered in poor countries. It is only common sense that if everyone else is sheltering refugees, then Europe should also do its bit. It would be something that European voters could feel proud of, and not cynical about, if it is explained to them properly. Likewise, those dynamics can be replicated in the U.S., despite the current administration's nativist rhetoric.

SECTION V: U.S. MIGRATION

Chapter 25: The Rise of Anti-immigrant Nationalism

"Remember, remember always, that all of us, and you and I especially, are descended from immigrants and revolutionists."
Franklin D. Roosevelt

The destination of choice for most African migrants is the USA. Indeed, that dream never dims even for those who have already made it to the Middle East or Europe. A recent survey (2018) by the Pew Research Center[xxi] adds statistical weight to this generalization, concluding that most Africans planning to migrate cited the U.S., as opposed to Europe, as their preferred target. For example, among the 42 percent of Ghanaians who said they plan to migrate abroad in the next five years, four out of ten (41 percent) identified the U.S. as their intended goal, while three out of ten (30 percent) name a country in the European, usually Norway or Switzerland. Similarly, shares of potential migrants in South Africa (39 percent vs. 22 percent) and Kenya (39 percent vs. 12 percent) say they intend to migrate to the U.S. rather than Europe.[152]

It is not only African migrants who feel this way. These sentiments are shared by citizens of the troubled Middle East where neocolonial wars have displaced hundreds of thousands of people and also by citizens of countries that are regional neighbors of the U.S., many of which, like their African counterparts, experienced the negative and durable impact of colonialism and the Slave Trade. Despite lack of healthcare, massive social disparity, a flawed justice system, trigger-happy police, gun crime in general, the U.S. remains the world's favorite destination for migration.

The upsurge in migrants has unsettled at least some in the U.S. and Europe as there is in both a strident and extremely vocal minority, who have become uneasy about the issue of migration and

---

are routinely holding aggressive protests and even resorting to violence. This mood has proven to be fertile ground to politicians on the make as they compete for the crown of being the toughest on immigration; the most willing to impose travel restrictions, and the most enthusiastic about boondoggle projects such as building walls.

President Donald Trump has led the field in this race to the bottom offering, in jingoistic rhetoric, measures that have virtually no basis in fact or constitutional law. In late 2018, he ordered thousands of troops to the U.S.-Mexico border to protect against entry of a caravan of migrants from Central America, even as their numbers progressively diminished and they remained 1,000 miles from the border. Just a week before the midterm Congressional elections, he suggested in a television interview that he would sign an executive order revoking the claim to birthright citizenship. Neither he nor the U.S. Congress has the constitutional authority to act upon that suggestion, as that right was articulated in the Fourteenth Amendment to the U.S. Constitution and has been upheld essentially as irrevocable by the U.S. Supreme Court since the 1890s. As Dara Lind an immigration reporter for Vox explained:

> The existence of a large, settled unauthorized immigrant population in the U.S. has distorted the center of gravity in the immigration debate. Restrictionists who simply want less immigration, and people who worry about demographic change, often claim they simply want less unauthorized immigration—that they're motivated by a neutral concern for the rule of law. (Some restrictionists really do want this.) But rhetorically, the concerns about birthright citizenship often recycle longstanding racist tropes.[153]

President Trump's sentiments have been echoed by other nationalist leaders in the world, including Viktor Orbán, prime minister of Hungary and Brazil's recently elected president, Jair Bolsonaro. Trump, whose wife is an immigrant and whose Grandfather was too, has repeatedly threatened to shut down the American Government if Congress does not pass legislation calling for more restrictions on immigration. In one message posted on Twitter that exemplifies his public stance, the President wrote, "CHAIN MIGRATION must end now! Some people come in, and they bring their whole family with them, who can be truly evil. NOT ACCEPTABLE!"

He has resorted to pejorative terms such as chain migration to replace family reunions of immigrants. But it was his description of Haiti as well as countries in Africa as "shithole countries" that have ignited the most volatile opposition. As leaked by White House insiders, Trump allegedly demanded to know in a meeting why he should accept immigrants from the afore-mentioned "shithole countries" rather than from places like Norway. Trump had made similar statements before, in which he complained about admitting Haitians to the country, saying that they all carried AIDS, and for the Nigerians, he said they would never go back to their "huts" in Africa.[154] In comments about the aforementioned caravan moving through Central America in late 2018, he said erroneously they were carrying diseases such as leprosy, which is unlikely and is easily treatable by inexpensive antibiotics, and smallpox, a disease that has been eradicated across the world. It has astounded many Americans and others abroad about how the designated leader of the Free World would be so willing to level such preposterous and easily refuted accusations.

As has become customary, there was condemnation from world leaders about President Trump's statements. "The African Union Mission wishes to express its infuriation, disappointment and outrage over the unfortunate comment made by Mr. Donald Trump, President of the United States of America, whose remarks dishonor the celebrated American creed and respect for diversity and human dignity."[155] But, there was one president from Africa who differed with the African Union and instead praised President Trump for being frank and sincere: Museveni.

I am an immigrant from Uganda, numbered among the shithole countries, and I would prefer not to see my fellow citizens endure what I and others have experienced in navigating the asylum process in the West even though the vocabulary used to describe my country is sufficiently respectful. However, I would like to see a fair share of this blame going not only to Africans fleeing their countries but also to the European countries and America for their contributions of making Africa a less livable continent by holding it financially hostage, by enslaving our grandfathers and cheating the continent's labor for many generations, by plundering their natural resources and by supporting African dictators such as Museveni who facilitate further exploitation and suppression of the masses.

The widespread condemnation of President Trump's inelegant choice of words did not alter his anti-immigration stance. On the contrary, the Trump administration has continued to pursue a travel ban that is based on blatant discrimination and stands in disregard for the tenets of the U.S. Constitution. In June 2018 the U.S. Attorney-General Jeff Sessions signaled that victims of domestic abuse and gang violence generally could not qualify for asylum under federal law. This decision was an affront to tens of thousands of foreign nationals—most of whom were women—who were seeking safety in the U.S. To give a personal experience as an example: at the time of announcing this decision, a Ugandan woman who worked with me at a rehabilitation home of intellectually challenged children and who had applied for asylum on the grounds that her husband was abusing her, asked me for some advice. I told her to keep her fingers crossed in prayer, in the hopes of waiting for women activists to jump on the case and help to reverse the decision. She responded that "women activists rarely stand up for migrant women, especially when the new oppressor is a powerful government like the USA." Sadly, she was right. They ignored it.

Similar to that systematic exclusion of women asylum seekers, was President Trump's "zero-tolerance" policy, that separated immigrant children from their undocumented migrant parents. The policy meant that any adult who crossed the border illegally would face criminal prosecution, which meant that parents were taken to federal jails while their children were sent to shelters. During six weeks in April and May of 2018 about 2,000 immigrant children were separated from their parents, and even after they were deported some of those parents were unable to recover their children.[156] Taking children away from their families is a heartless policy that does permanent damage to the children.

It was some consolation that American politicians and activists this time stood up against this inhumane policy, which was eventually reversed. However, many children have yet to be accounted for and many cases remain in limbo.

The news has negatively affected the opinions of Hispanics in the U.S. There are 59 million who identify as Hispanic living in the U.S., and they represent the nation's youngest and fastest-growing group. Overall, about one in three Hispanics were born outside of the U.S. In an October 2018 survey by Pew Research, 50 percent said their situation has worsened since Trump's election in 2016 and 55 percent worry about a family member or close friend being deported. The key finding was that, "two-thirds (67 percent) say the administration's policies have been harmful to Hispanics—a much higher share than during the administration of either Democrat Barack Obama (15 percent in 2010) or Republican George W. Bush (41 percent in 2007)."[157] However, it should be noted that similar opinions are being found in polls conducted with immigrants from other regions of the world, most notably, Asians and Pacific Rim countries.

Immigration phobias have intensified after President Trump assumed office and have led the U.S. Citizenship and Immigration Services (USCIS), a division of the U.S. Department of Homeland Security, to rewrite its mission statement, eliminating language characterizing the agency's purpose as securing "America's promise as a nation of immigrants." The federal agency that grants visas and U.S. citizenship now refers to itself as an organization that "administers the nation's lawful immigration system." The new mission statement also eliminates the word "customers" to refer to visa applicants.[158]

It is not only Trump and those who voted for him who are hostile to migrants. Take for example, statements by Catherine Woollard, secretary general of the European Council on Refugees and Exiles, an alliance of nearly 100 refugee rights groups, who explained that while still moderate in tone, some leaders are pursuing policies that are Trumpian in spirit. "There's a denial among many European leaders that they're anything like Trump—while they promote measures that will have the same impact," as Mr. Trump's restrictions, she said.[159]

One such leader is Orban of Hungary, who criticized non-Christian migrants and then built a wall to stop migrants from entering Hungary. Organizations such as the European Union that were founded on values of economic integration are now disintegrating

142

because some members states don't want immigrants to possess the right of free entry into their countries. Across Europe anti-immigrant politicians have swayed support. Immigration was one of the main issues that led to the UK voting to leave the EU. In Denmark the Danish People's Party (DPP) was founded with the near exclusive purpose of limiting immigration. Politicians across the Continent are competing to claim they are the toughest on immigration and so the legitimate voice of populism and nationalism. They want free markets for goods where they are sold in Africa but do not espouse free labor markets where African migrants can work in the U.S. or Europe.

It is interesting to note that nativist rhetoric and politics in Europe it is at odds with the statistical realities of both actual immigration and concern regarding it among Europeans. European immigration has slowed to levels last seen before 2015, when the infamous surge began and a recent survey conducted by the European Union's Eurobarometer shows that immigration as an issue of the highest concerns has fallen from a median of nearly one-half in late 2015 to a median of just 23 percent in 2018.[160] Despite all that nationalist politics continue to shape attitudes across the continent: Laura Silver a senior researcher focusing on global research at Pew Research Center said;

> "But while anxieties have decreased dramatically across the EU as immigration flows have slowed, immigration still remains a top concern for many Western Europeans. For example, in both Denmark and Germany, more people name the issue as a problem facing their country than any other (34 percent and 38 percent, respectively). And while only a minority of people are concerned in most countries, they do tend to be vocal. Immigration issues, often raised by far-right parties, have rocked coalitions in Germany, and been front and center in recent elections in Italy and Sweden."[161]

These findings also suggest that Western Europeans are comfortable with the presence of immigrants if they are committed to integrating culturally with their new home. But what is most concerning are attitudes about immigrants and matters of the economy and security, which seem to divide along demographic lines that include education and income, among other factors. Most noteworthy is the following: "Concerns about the economic effects of immigration are somewhat related to people's financial circumstances. In most countries surveyed, those with lower incomes are more likely than those with higher incomes to feel that immigrants burden their economies. But, in most countries, even those with lower incomes feel that immigrants strengthen the economy more than they burden it."[162]

Indeed, this is an enlightening point relative to the dangerously sweeping generalizations articulated by nationalist politicians who seek to whip up the fervor of their constituencies, despite their own policy failures to lead responsibly on the issue. Immigration remains a multi-faceted complex issue that does point to a more positive consensus than what politicians would be likely to admit.

Chapter 26: Beating the American Immigration Restrictions

"There are no restrictions that could ever be so rigorous to stop the wave of migration that has determined our human history."
Yasin Kakande

In June 2015, at an old house opposite the Buganda government offices in Mengo, located in the middle of Kampala, I met Nsubuga, a local man helping Ugandans to obtain visas for the U.S. and Canada. One of my relatives was planning to pay him and wanted me around because I knew enough to know if he was being cheated. Nsubuga arrived fresh from teaching a class of about fifteen how to conduct themselves during the interview for a visa at the American Embassy in Kampala. I interrogated him, firing numerous pointed questions to find out if he knew anything that would genuinely help these people—and my cousin. I approached this process hesitantly wanting to ascertain if he was authentic knowing that I would soon be looking to get a U.S. visa. I felt that if I gathered enough information from him, then I could navigate the visa process without his assistance. I quickly gathered that he was training prospective immigrants to be confident: to look directly into the visa officer's eyes, and lie to them that they were rich enough in Uganda and their trip to America was just for business; and, most importantly, that they will return home after it was completed. *Confidence* was the magic bullet in the hunt for an American visa, he said, and, clearly, he emphasized this point every day of the entire month of training.

He demanded nine million Ugandan shillings ($2,700) from my cousin and wanted three million more ($1,000) to start the process with the balance to be paid on the successful completion of the process. Among the services he offered was that of securing a letter of invitation from America. He accomplished this by applying to an international conference or workshops. He would then create supporting documents in Uganda that would be relevant to this U.S.-based conference, including the employment authorization letter for the client's travel. I asked him what would happen if any of this were to be discovered to be fake. He told me that that was unlikely because the visa officials never have enough time to verify all the papers that came in front of them. He said that success depended upon the applicant's ability to present the documents with confidence. He said the ability to exude confidence is not easy, which brought us to the last point. He explained that learning to transmit confidence was the core skill and the one for which his clients paid. He said each student was expected to attend three weeks of classes of preparations and only then could he complete the student's visa interview application; safe in the knowledge that he was confident enough to pass the test. He claimed to have trained students who had never gone to a university or college to pass themselves off as physicians and surgeons. Furthermore, he contended students of his method managed to secure visas while bona fide surgeons (who hadn't attended his classes) are refused for lacking the necessary confidence.

Confidence was required even after receiving the visa it seemed. Nsubuga impressed upon his students the need to put his lessons into practice at every stage of the physical process of migration: as they travel, and while they navigate airports. At this time, scrutiny airport immigration checkpoints had become more rigorous, due in part to respective governments' more strident anti-immigration policies. Appearing nervous in the face of authority asking basic questions before stamping one's passport would be an expensive mistake; a point Nsubuga stressed repeatedly. His students were reminded to keep the details of their accommodation and the conference to which they were travelling at their mental and physical fingertips. Furthermore, they should make it clear that their stay in the U.S. would be brief, only long enough for the duration of the putative conference that they planned to attend.

He also advised them to carry the bare minimum of luggage and to use JFK airport in New York City, as it had more traffic and so less scrutiny. So even a student going to a *conference* in California or Orlando would enter the U.S. at JFK. Once the student made it to New York, they could abandon their plans to go to Orlando or California and take a bus to Boston, Massachusetts or any other city or state that took their fancy. It seemed that Nsubuga had the game figured out completely.

Chapter 27: The Last Conversation with My Father

"Everybody becomes better writers after their parent dies."
Lisa Harris

The day before he died, my father learned that I had a master's degree. I had visited him at home the day after he had suffered a life-threatening incident triggered by his hypertension. He had summoned his children so he could have what he called a "last word" with each of us.

I arrived a few minutes after my elder half-sister Sauya had left the home. He was lying in his sitting room on a small mattress with a bed sheet covering his lower half. After exchanging the usual Islamic greetings, he asked me to loosen two buttons on his white shirt because he felt hot. The room was packed with 50-kilogram bags of rice, destined for the neighborhood mosque at the end of Ramadan.[xxii]

Our conversation that day was difficult. He was in great pain, which had been made worse by the application of a catheter by an inexperienced physician. I told him I understood both the severity of his pain and the fact that he needed to be in a hospital, but I could no longer afford to pay for the treatment he needed alone. I mobilized my siblings and Sauya told me that she would have enough money the following day for us to get him into hospital. My Father told me repeatedly that he did not want to be a burden on his children and that his time was up; that he was dying and that no amount of money could stop the inevitable. I urged him to stay strong, reminding him that he had survived several bad attacks in the past, but I knew he was right: I too had accepted his fate.

He changed the subject and we discussed my own struggles, in particular my shaky finances. He reiterated a familiar complaint that I had brought my financial problems on myself when I published my first book *The Ambitious Struggle*, a move that got me deported

---

xxii   My father had been treasurer at the mosque for many years and his home occasionally served as a store for mosque-related materials.

from Dubai. He had already asked what I was doing to find a job in Uganda, if my farm of passion fruits was bringing any income, how I was coping with my children's school fees and upkeep, and so on. I knew that none of the answers represented good news, and that that wouldn't help his situation, and I tried several times to change the subject, but he wouldn't let me. On the contrary, he continued to interrogate me with evermore incisive questions.

My Father had solutions of his own, such as going back to school to do a master's degree. I told him that I had been working on it even as I worked as a journalist in Dubai. He was both happy and disturbed, as he extended his fragile, weak hand in a gesture of congratulation. He said that his experience was that anyone with a master's degree would be guaranteed success and happiness, as they would be employed in well-paid management positions. Though, he was worried about Uganda's future which might make those even with a Ph.D. unemployed and mired in debt. He said that he had come around to the opinion that the only option was for everyone who could to migrate to other countries where they could find work and build lives. He said: "having a passport to flee Uganda is more important than having a university certificate." He was only half joking and his words have stayed with me.

Continuing in this vein, he asked me if I would consider trying to Europe or the U.S. My half-brother Wahab was in the U.S., would I consider joining him? I told my father that I would indeed follow up on his suggestion. Speaking even more faintly, he returned to his earlier point, warning me not to write another book, especially if I made it to America. He said I was going into battle with only my pen and that forces arrayed against me would crush me. He said—rightly—that politicians as a class were willing to neutralize their critics by any means at their disposal; and if they killed me it would be bad news for my children. He said we had to accept that we were poor people and in his experience the poor cannot change anything. He implored me not to risk my job for the sake of publishing a book or a critical news story that by the time I got to the U.S. he would be long-dead. He knew that in his absence nothing and no one would be there to caution or restrain me, save his advice.

I did not know my father well when I was a child. My mother had separated from him and she raised our family as a single parent. I stayed with him and my stepmother for a few school holidays and knew him primarily as a tough disciplinarian who enforced the rules with military discipline and swift retribution. I and my thirteen siblings knew that stupidity or mischief in his presence would have consequences usually involving a stick he kept in his bedroom. But as we grew into young adults, my father became a caring, loving, and polite parent. He wanted to hear both of our progress and our setbacks, and always offered advice. He offered advice not only on my career, but also on investments and on women who did not match up as marriage material. I often disagreed with him, but I fear that it was mostly to prove a point that I was grown and independent.

He was a man who wanted me to see the world through his eyes and while I was always willing to the hear suggestions, options, and alternatives he offered, we would sometimes descend into argument. Eventually, one of us would resign, not out of a conviction but simply to avoid escalation. During one such conversation that was rapidly turning sour he blurted out that my Mother thought I was the smartest guy around, that whatever I said was brilliant, and what I chose to do was for the best. He added that while there might be some truth in that, I was nevertheless a young man who needed a lot of guidance. I would do better, he said, if I could do more listening than talking. I certainly listened that day to his advice regarding how I should conduct myself should I make it to America. These were the words of a man who knew his life was ending and was trying to advise me on preserving my own and being there for my children; it was not worth falling out over it.

He asked me if I could still read the Quran with a good voice. Whenever I visited, he always let me lead him in prayers, but this was the first time he complimented me on my Quran recitals. He asked me to read for him some parts of the Quran and I read him the whole of Chapter 17 (*Surat Al-Isra*). It was a relevant scripture to recite, as it talks about the legacy of Muhammad's prophecies and how they would sustain all children even to the farthest points or mosques in the land. I helped to feed and reposition him and after I'd spent about three hours with him, I said goodbye promising to return the next day with Sauya and take him to hospital.

Our appointment to take him to hospital was at two o'clock but Sauya called at around ten in a panic. Our father was having another attack and he had asked for me but a few minutes later my half-brother Ibrahim, the youngest of my siblings, called and said, *Innah Lillah Wa Innah Illaikhi Rajiuna* (From God we came to Him, We all Return), the Islamic statement announcing a death. When I arrived home, mourners had already gathered, and a small tent was being erected. I rushed inside where I saw that my father's body had been moved from the place I had left him yesterday. He was still lying on the small mattress but the bedsheets that had covered him halfway now enshrouded his entire form. The two buttons that I had loosened on the day before were just as they were. He appeared to be sleeping; but my father Edirisa Kalule, aged 70, was dead.

The first time I laid a dead person in the ground was years earlier with my Father's assistance. I was a freshman at university and my Father insisted I join him in washing the body, wrapping it and lowering it into the grave. In so doing he taught me how Muslims bury their dead and told me that I should do the same for him when he died. That time had come, and I was standing in the four-foot grave with my brothers Musa and Ibrahim preparing to lower his body in the ground. I was concentrating on remembering the protocols of carrying the dead and trying to handle him the same way I had seen him handling others, but more than that I recalled our last conversation. I grieved not only for him but for that fact that I wasn't there in time to take him to hospital, for the knowledge that I had paid a high price for raising my voice in defense of migrants in the Middle East.

While I had no intention of obeying my Father's injunction against writing books or articles that held truth to power, I knew he was right about leaving Uganda; it was time to go. Soon after his funeral I began preparations to get a U.S. visa and to emigrate once again. Only when you lose a parent do you feel the gravity of being an adult in a difficult and complicated world.

Chapter 28: The Thorny Road to Asylum

"Give me your tired, your poor, Your huddled masses yearning to breathe free, The wretched refuse of your teeming shore. Send these, the homeless, tempest-tossed, to me: I lift my lamp beside the golden door." Emma Lazarus

The easiest ways for migrants to gain legal entry to and then citizenship of the USA are through a spouse or relative, but after those the most logical and popular route is to claim asylum. Both the definition of a refugee and the number of them that would be accepted by the country has varied in line with American foreign policy at any given time. Prior to 1980, the United States defined a refugee as a person fleeing a communist country, a communist-dominated area, or the Middle East. The Refugee Act of 1980 re-defined the term meaning a person who resides outside his country of nationality and is unwilling and unable to return due to a "well-founded fear of persecution on account of race, religion, nationality, membership in a particular social group or political opinion."[163]

One should be prepared to tell Asylum officers a most compelling account for being persecuted in a home country to gain asylum. Poverty and unemployment—albeit the most common reasons for why many immigrants leave their country—do not count among the *acceptable reasons* for gaining asylum. That is why most migrants who are indeed motivated by just those reasons must invent or adapt a story that includes some form of politically affiliated persecution to form a part of their application for asylum.

In many countries the process has become an industry: various communities employ specialists to advise and coach potential refugees on how to tell their story in order to persuade the relevant officials to advance or process their applications in a timely manner. In the case of Ugandans, U.S. immigration officials usually believe the story of the purported homosexual fleeing community reprisals, because the international media extensively covered the failed anti-gay bill that eventually was tabled in Uganda's Parliament. One such story might go something like this: "My community learned that I am homosexual. They killed my partner and I narrowly made it out of the country; if I go there, they will definitely lynch me." Or, for a woman applicant: "My male neighbors suspected I was sleeping with a girl. So, when they saw my girlfriend entering my apartment, they all crowded the door demanding I open the door and tell them what we were both doing. They broke down the door and took turns raping me and my girlfriend: there were about ten men; I almost died. The police saved us and as we were being hauled into a police van to go to the station the men continued making threats that they will rape us again and again until we learn that a woman sleeps with a man, not a woman. At the station, the police also raped us, and they charged us. I only just managed to get out of that country."

These examples should be understood to emphasize that the official does not have to believe the person genuinely is gay or lesbian. If it was just a story that will secure asylum, then one would tell without asking further questions. But Immigration officials require all sorts of evidence. Still the experts in the community would advise the individual on how to fabricate realistically looking evidence documents. These consultants will advise an individual to join some LGBTI groups in America and obtain a letter explaining their predicament to immigration officials. Some people fear that by joining such groups they may fail to portray themselves genuinely as gay or lesbian. Sometimes they hesitate out of fear, maybe that a possible suitor is a spy.

The best bet for Ugandans seeking asylum is to focus on political persecution. The strongest stories are related to the Lord's Resistance Army of Joseph Kony's such as that the rebels had killed their family members. Another strong suit would be that the person in question had been a member of one of the opposition parties to which the Museveni Government had turned hostile.

Some stories submitted for asylum have of course bordered on the absurd. One Ugandan who could not read told me how the *story-makers* had written a laughable story for his asylum application; so much so that he was afraid to go to the interview. The story was that a neighbor's cat had run into his house and climbed on top of a chair and that he had beaten it to death in the process of evicting it. The neighbor wanted revenge and threatened to kill him, so he would need to flee to the US to save his life. The ghostwriter told him before posting the application to officials that the Americans love cats so much that his story would endear him to them immediately. After he posted the application, other people told him that people do not get asylum in America for killing a cat. In fact, they face criminal charges for it and they told him that he risked such a fate if he went ahead for the interview.

Arranged marriages are an easier path to American citizenship than applying for asylum. Many African immigrants would rather pay to get married than go through the hassle of finding documents as evidence for the asylum process and then waiting years for it to be completed. Still, even these marriages had their challenges. The putative spouses demanded large sums, and documentation indicating shared accommodation and utility bills proving that the two were cohabiting as a married couple were sometimes difficult to compile because immigration officials could easily verify their authenticity or lack thereof—a discovery that would lead to serious consequences.

There was also the performance required at the relevant meetings. The couple had to turn up holding hands, looking in one another's eyes and willing to display the appropriate gestures of affection. In a shared house I stayed in when I arrived in America, there was a woman in her fifties, renting one of the rooms in the house because she was having trouble with her arranged spouse, an African-American citizen. She had paid in installments to a sum of $10,000 to this man for the fake marriage and after completing the payments the man demanded sexual intercourse from her. Frequently, they would meet in the living room of the boarding house before going to the immigration meetings and the rest of us could hear them arguing. The man told the woman that it was the last time he was going to the meetings and having to put on a show of fake smiles and kisses if she didn't let him into her bed. And, the woman would retort, in a pleading tone, reminding him she had paid all the money he asked for and sex was not part of the package. She had a son almost his age, and she told him that she could not agree to his request.

In many other countries—such as those in Europe—migrants are enrolled in social welfare on arrival, but in the U.S., most end up on their own almost from the time that they are admitted. Most migrants arriving in the U.S. quickly find work or already have a job so they can support the families they have left behind. This independent arrangement did not seem to concern officials. The main challenge was to start working but the employment authorization for many migrants was only issued five months after an immigrant filed for asylum. It was easier for immigrants who arrived with lottery green cards or those with spouse-arranged visas/green cards. For those who sought asylum and had to wait for five months to obtain employment authorization there was still a way out to work while they waited. This often involved using someone else's documents like the work permit and Social Security number. One had to adopt the details of the generous person offering the work documents from names, date of birth, and the last 4 digits of a legitimate Social Security number.

At first it is intimidating, if not downright scary, to take someone's documents, including their photo ID and pass them off as one's own despite the fact that your friends and co-workers tell you that white people think all black people look the same, and so they don't often spot a difference. Sometimes the employers don't even look at the photo on the ID and if they do, they don't look at the applicant. Few bothered to look at both and ensure that the comparison matches. Memorizing the date of birth was the key challenge that most immigrants noted most often because this the employer would ask without warning. Understandable the person's first instinct was to state their actual date of birth, not the one listed on the card. Most people who shared their documents with newcomers demanded a certain percentage of their paycheck every week. Others were eager simply that the newcomer generated more taxes for them, because in the U.S. taxes are collected on every paycheck and at the end of the year the rightful owner can claim a tax rebate. Using other people's documents to secure employment was common among several migrant communities. In December 2018, a couple of undocumented workers came forward to claim they had worked at President Trump's golf club despite his strident anti-immigration rhetoric. For example, Victorina Morales told *The New York Times* that she had made Trump's bed, cleaned his toilets and dusted his crystal golf trophies and she had been awarded a certificate from the White House Communications Agency for her outstanding work.

Chapter 29: The Immigrants Workplace

"The land flourished because it was fed from so many sources—because it was nourished by so many cultures and traditions and peoples."
Lyndon B. Johnson

One of the many good things about America is that the sign *we're hiring* is almost everywhere. It is not hard to find work if your (or someone else's) papers are in order. Also, an immigrant has to contend with the fact that regardless of their academic or professional achievements, the jobs they will do will be classified with one of the 3 D's: "Dirty, Demanding or Dangerous," the kind of jobs most U.S. citizens will refuse to do. For the sake of completing this initial picture: most jobs for immigrants are paid hourly and at the minimum wage of $10 to $12 per hour, depending on the state.

The ubiquitous demand for labor coupled with the endless supply of migrants looking for work has shaped both America's economy and society. A 2017 Pew Research study, relying on U.S. Census Bureau data collected in 2014, shows that immigrants make up roughly 17 percent of the U.S. workforce and that many are employed primarily in specific jobs, including sewing machine operators, plasterers, stucco masons, and manicurists.[164] The industries with the biggest shares of immigrant workers include private households, with 45 percent of the nearly 950,000 domestic workers coming from migrants, and textile, apparel and leather manufacturers with 36 percent of the total workers. In agriculture, nearly one-third of the 2 million people who work in this sector are born outside of the U.S. Another Pew Research study indicated that without working-age immigrants at current levels, the levels of the total working-age population in the U.S. would decline by 2035.[165]

In hospitals, immigrants work as cleaners and nursing assistants. Direct caregivers for the elderly and disabled represent the most common employer for African migrants. These jobs readily are obtained in nursing homes, rehabilitation centers, and group homes, as well as in the private residences of elderly patients and disabled individuals.

These jobs are relatively easy to come by. There are several direct care agent offices across the state of Massachusetts that recruit daily on a part- or full-time basis. Direct caregivers are classified under the Fair Labor Standards Act (FLSA) as hourly workers entitled to minimum wage and overtime. The largest group among the direct caregivers are Home Healthcare Aides (HHA), who carry the burdens in many private homes. With an increased number of aging and disabled individuals choosing to stay at home, many will have to hire a HHA at some point or else it becomes a family member's responsibility. While it's true that Certified Nursing Assistants (CNAs) also provide direct care, that's mostly in nursing homes. HHAs are required to take just a one-day training in accomplishing simple tasks such as changing a client's dressing and assisting in routine activities. The training in Massachusetts costs $100 and this simple procedure is the reason why many new migrants have found HHA as an easy entry into the U.S. job market. To qualify as a CNA one has to do a 3–4 week course that costs about $1,000 and then pass state exams. CNAs generally earn $14 to $15 per hour, slightly ahead of HHAs who earn $12 to $13 per hour in homes. Many migrants who started as HHA eventually upgrade to CNA after earning enough money to complete their training and others will even continue to upgrade to senior positions such as Licensed Practical Nurse (LPN) or Registered Nurse (RN).

Despite the relative ease of availability, these jobs carry a good deal of responsibility. Direct caregivers are responsible for high-risk elderly people such as those suffering from Dementia, Cancer, Parkinson's Disease, and other chronic and progressive illnesses. A caregiver's tasks often involve tending those physical needs known in industry parlance as the Activities of Daily Living (ADLs). These include transferring patients safely from bed to wheelchair, toilet access, showers, feeding, and sometimes being able to spot and care for wounds.

There is an increasing number of elderly people who need care, especially as the first wave of Baby Boomers (the pop-demographic term for the post-war generation) will mark their 80th birthdays in the 2020s. Despite this increase in demand, it seems likely that the supply of willing and able labor—from immigrants at least—will shrink exponentially as restrictions on migration increase. So, in this sense those restrictions seem to make little economic sense. In 2017, Betty Yee, California state controller, said "undocumented immigrants" labor is worth more than $180 billion a year to California's economy—about equal to the 2015 gross domestic product for the entire state of Oklahoma. Labor from undocumented immigrants is fundamental not just to agriculture, but to childcare, restaurants, hotels, and construction."

However, economic reasoning has been overwhelmed by rancorous nativist political rhetoric that comes from some unlikely corners of the political landscape, rather than just the usual suspects. Trade unions historically ensured that people work only 40 hours in a week and if one had to work extra that time should be paid in higher hourly rates such as 1.5 times the regular hourly pay. The problem has been these rules helped neither the immigrant nor the ordinary working citizens. Cash-rich employers who paid workers the minimum wage of $12 an hour could afford an extra $6 per hour for overtime pay. In fact, immigrant workers, many of whom juggle paying the bills in the U.S. and sending remittances to their relatives back home, are often eager to do overtime but sometimes trade union rules about seniority and work performance, disadvantaged them. And, then in cases where companies hesitated or sometimes even refused to pay overtime, many immigrant workers and native-born lower-income workers would take on additional employment and end up working far more hours—80 to 100 hours per week to earn the same amount of money.

The shift-cycle of work dominates the daily routine of many migrant workers. There are some who do not think twice about working two shifts a day, seven days a week. In fact, this practice of a long day toiling at two or maybe even three jobs, is one that has united immigrants with their American-born peers. The 21st century workers in America are toiling longer hours than even their slave ancestors of the 18th century or the white peasants of the 14th century.

For immigrants, the long day is not just about paying bills for living in America. In addition to the remittances they send to their family, immigrants will receive an emergency call or additional request from a relative or friend back home, who asks meekly and politely for money. The immigrant feels the pressure of the social obligation and often picks up more hours at work to fulfill these requests. One might suggest the person should refuse any requests but there also are cultural and social expectations that might not be apparent to many Americans. Immigrants feel obligated because the separation from home was an economic necessity. And no one makes a call and expects the person in the States to refuse or make the excuse that money is tight. To everyone back home, America remains a country of wealth, even as it is more than apparent that economic equality has become even harder to achieve here in the States. The connecting thread becomes money.

As a consequence, social dynamics change for the worse. Once the immigrant arrives in the U.S., relatives and friends back home lose interest in making small talk or sharing stories or gossip. When the immigrant answers a call from home, they know it will not have been made for social reasons call to lighten one's spirits, or to remind one of the absence of connection. The main—often only—topic is money. And if the immigrant refuses the request from a relative or friend, it is almost certain that they will never speak again. In order to sustain the friendship, money is an essential and non-negotiable requirement.

Chapter 30: Immigrant Direct Caregivers

"From caring comes courage." Lao Tzu

Approximately one million immigrants work in direct care, according to PHI, a New York City-based organization widely considered to be the nation's most authoritative source about the direct care workforce.[166] The current global debate on migration has heightened the need for informed discourse about migration, especially regarding the rapidly growing long-term care industry. Policies that limit immigration could worsen existing shortages of direct care workers across long-term-care settings. One such policy was framed in the Reforming American Immigration for Strong Employment (RAISE) Act, which was proposed by Republicans in the 115th U.S. Congress in 2017. RAISE was designed to reduce legal immigration from one million people per annum to around 500,000.[167] [xxiii]

The precise effects of these policies on the supply of direct care workers is unknown, but it is reasonable to assume that immigrants working in the direct care industry are likely to be distressed when they are threatened with deportation, or when they see friends and family similarly removed or prevented from pursuing legal immigrant status. The demand for more caregivers does not just call for policy makers to relax their harsh attitude towards migrants but also to look into the circumstances of employee welfare and pay for migrant caregivers. This workforce lives in poverty and relies on public benefits like state health insurance and food stamps. And that's true not only of the migrants working in the sector but also of the natives. Across the country, American families struggle to support their families when working as direct care workers and often leave

---

xxiii   Despite the legislation receiving President Trump's endorsement, no other Congressional members signed on as co-sponsors for a revised version proposed later that year. The proposal died when the current U.S. Congress adjourned in late 2018 and it is highly unlikely that a similar proposal would pass, as the Democrats took control of the U.S. House of Representatives with the 116th U.S. Congress.

the industry as a result. In turn long-term care providers can't find enough workers, and the existing workers can't make ends meet.

So, what is the pay in real terms? U.S. home care workers earn a median hourly wage of $10.49 and—because of inconsistent work hours—typically earn $13,800 annually. Nursing assistants working in nursing homes earn moderately higher hourly wages ($12.34 median wage) and annual incomes ($20,000 median annual income) than home care workers, but wages for both occupations have stagnated or barely kept up with inflation over the last 10 years.[168]

As someone who has worked as a direct caregiver in the homes of elderly Americans, I have witnessed another dimension of numerous vulnerabilities that I had never imagined. In many cases, an elderly individual did not have a single living family member available, either afar or nearby. Understandably, the patient comes to consider the immigrant working in his or her home as family. Some elderly people who still had family struggled with their (geographically) distant relatives to get doctors to increase their morphine intake or to urge physicians not to resuscitate them when their lives were on the line. About 10,000 Americans will turn 65 every day until 2030; the overwhelming majority of them likely will take the option of remaining in their homes with the help of direct care aides, many of whom likely will be migrant workers.[169]

I once worked in the home of a 90-year-old man in Needham, Massachusetts. The man was still quite aware of his surroundings and was conscious, but his nieces, the apparent heirs to his property, asked doctors several times not to resuscitate him. They even tried to kick him out of his home and place him in a long-term nursing care facility. He told his story to every worker who came to his house. His wife and a single daughter died previously, and his only surviving relatives were his brother's two daughters. As he talked about them, I could see the frustration in his face. He asked me if I had a car and a valid driver's license because he wanted me to take him to Springfield about 80 miles to see his childhood home where he was raised. I explained that traveling such a distance was not permissible, but then he requested to be taken to his lawyer's office so he could change his will. I told him it was Saturday so no lawyers would be present. His last plea was to drive him around just to see the neighborhood. He mostly wanted to see the school where his deceased daughter was a student. But I could not do that without permission from those supervising his care. So, I called the office of the agent who had recruited me, and the request was refused and our communication for the rest of the weekend was strained, at best.

The following week, the agent asked me to come and work again and I told her how the patient had demanded to leave his home, even if it was just for a brief drive around the neighborhood. The agent checked with his nieces, who agreed. They made it clear that I was never to take him to his lawyer or to his childhood home in Springfield, Massachusetts, explaining that it was a personal family matter. When I helped him into my car and started the engine, he immediately fell asleep. Even when I stopped at key neighborhood landmarks such as the church and the school where his daughter attended and asked him if he remembered them, he briefly woke for a brief moment, grasped awkwardly for a few words that I couldn't understand, and then went back to sleep. After about an hour of driving around we went back to the house, but he was so happy he had been able to leave his home.

One of the first jobs I had in Boston was as a caregiver for a poor elderly white couple who were living on government social welfare. The wife, 68, had been completely paralyzed since her birth and she lay in bed most of the time unless she needed to be lifted and put into her wheelchair. She weighed 90 pounds and many caregivers had not been able to lift her out of bed. Her husband, 70, was frail after having suffered five strokes and required a walker. He had converted to Islam under the influence of the people who were involved in the Boston Marathon bombing several years before. They had worked in the couple's home prior to their suicidal mission. The wife was shocked to learn I was Muslim, as she had been upset with the bombers and when they left she never wanted other Muslims in her home. But with me being the only caregiver who could lift her into her wheelchair and said I did not look like someone who would use obscenities, she hired me as their personal care assistant (PCA). The job required one to have at least a certified nursing assistant (CNA) certificate but I did not have one at the time. I had only managed to prepare for myself an online home health aide certificate (HHA) after attending a few hours of internet training. CNA certification required one to attend traditional classes for one month and complete written and practical exams that are administered at the state level. Most African immigrants and their cousins from Haiti have a CNA certificate, as it is among the easiest ways to kickstart a career in caregiving in America.

After getting the PCA job without a CNA certificate I became reluctant to sacrifice a month going to class to obtain the certificate. I was always trying to convince myself that I was doing the job only temporarily for a few months, as I continued to search for a stable, long-term assignment as a journalist—that objective having become increasingly more difficult to achieve.

My PCA job was more like what a housemaid or house boy position would be considered elsewhere in the world. I would do all the house chores for the couple. This included vacuuming the carpets, preparing meals, washing dishes, cleaning bathrooms, helping male patients with showers and bathing, changing adult diapers, and giving sponge baths for the woman. I would carry her to the wheelchair, escort her to doctor's appointments as well as other outings, including social dinners and church services.

Despite her physical limitations, her mind was clear and vigorous and she considered herself the supervisor of her own workers. She instructed me to take 30 minutes for a lunch break and she would always start timing it on her Alexa device at 2 pm, as soon as I finished her afternoon diaper change. While I took my lunch break, she took a quick nap and would be refreshed after the break to issue orders to me. If she was awake during my lunch break, she would send her husband during my lunch break to remind me that I had just 15 minutes, then 10 minutes and, finally, five minutes left for my lunch break. Her husband sat in his bedroom with his metallic walker nearby so I could hear the banging noises as soon as he set foot to come out to the living room and remind me how much time I had left on my break.

My employer was so uncomfortable spending anytime without her worker. She was eager to see every minute the government paid for her care had been well earned and used. No moment of idleness was allowed in her home and this is why many workers never return after a single day's work. Whenever there was nothing to be done in the kitchen or living room, I would sit with them to watch television, discuss politics, and share in her gossip about her family, friends and neighbors. Her conversations were mainly about her daughter and her black husband, a marriage for which the couple apparently did not approve. In the evenings, we would listen to audiobooks together and when there was no audio format available, I would read a chapter or two for them from their books before they went to sleep for the night.

The repetition of chores was the thing that bored me most. She demanded her diapers be changed every two hours even when they were still clean. Her therapy would be done several times in a day whenever she wanted and when she thought there was no more work for the aide she would ask to wipe her nose every five minutes. One day, I counted wiping her nose 60 times from 9 am to 11 pm She did not have a runny nose but it simply was intended to ensure I was busy every moment and not risk being idle in her house. When we went out to doctor's appointments, she would introduce me to everyone as "my Ugandan worker," in a boastful manner as if to remind others that she should not be demeaned and that she takes pride in "owning" a worker.

Worse still, I struggled to refuse her consistent pleas to take photos while feeding her so that she could share them on Facebook: I didn't want to advertise the low, migrant life I had assumed in America. I was in their house for three, consecutive days every week, for the other four days of the week, I worked at other jobs. The practice of staying overnight during such work was always called "live in" and was very much sought after simply because one had the chance to work more hours. During my time in their home, I had marked a birthday and the wife bought me the book *Uncle Tom's Cabin* by Harriet Beecher Stowe, the famous novel on the life of slaves in America, as a gift. I have never had birthday gifts before. It was not so common at home to celebrate birthdays. I was grateful to receive the gift, but it also reminded me that life in their home was not anyway comparable to that of the slaves Stowe described.

Another senior client I attended to was on home-based hospice care. She had a medical emergency and I immediately called her nurse. As I was leaving the room after the nurse arrived, the patient was struggling to say something. But the nurse could not make out her words. I told the nurse she's saying that I should not leave the room. She thought that if I leave her alone or with a stranger, she will die. The nurse noticed her smiling as I spoke these words. She said, "Oh, she's smiling, so she understands fully what we are talking about." She died a few minutes later, while I held her now-cold hand, reassuring her that she should stay calm and that she will be fine. After she had died at home, her surviving family were notified along with the local police and fire authorities. When they arrived, they initially ignored me (like most people do to caregivers) but the nurse kept redirecting their questions toward me.

Her children did not invite me to the funeral, but they kept calling me to gather details about her last moments, as they prepared her eulogy. I was struck by how they treasured even the smallest detail. I could not help but imagine how hard the final moments of life must be to some Japanese—a country that has blocked migrants like me and where there have been many reports of Japan's elderly dying alone. Their bodies are sometimes discovered several weeks after they have passed.

The most challenging case I worked on as a direct caregiver was that of a quadriplegic man in Waban, Massachusetts, who weighed 260 pounds. It was a live-in job for four days starting on Monday morning and ending on Friday morning. The agency that handled the assignment was owned by a Russian man and the agency supervisor was also Russian. The supervisor received me at the client's door to help with orientation. He emphasized how the client was so special to the agency and that he himself had chosen me because he knew I would give 100-percent effort in the role. The wife and supervisor explained to me how to transfer manually the man from his bed to his wheelchair without using a Hoyer lift, which was in a corner of their bedroom. They referred to this kind of move as a "pivotal transfer," claiming it would minimize the lifting weight pressure on my back and that my spinal cord was not in any danger of injury if I did it right. They told me he didn't want to use a Hoyer lift so that is why they wanted to hire a male aide who could handle the weight requirements to move the patient. They asked me to put him in the wheelchair in their presence to see that I understood their instructions. I lifted the bed with a remote control until he was in a sitting position. Then I turned him around by grabbing his pants at the waist so that he faced the bed edge and had his legs on the floor. Once his feet were on the floor, I placed a transfer belt around his waist. Then I had to face him and use my knees to push his knees as a leverage to lift him and to stand up, using the belt wrapped around his waist. When I did this, my left knee which always has caused me to walk with a slight limp did not push his knee with the right effect and fearing that I might injure my knee more, I found myself putting more effort in lifting him using my back and the energy from elsewhere than my knee. Then I turned him around to have his back on the left where the wheelchair was and I placed him into it. In the first attempt, he placed his buttocks in the middle of the wheelchair and I had to half-lift him again, pushing him to the end of the wheelchair. After sitting him properly the wife and my supervisor all clapped their hands, congratulating me that I had done it so quickly and so smoothly.

Then it was time to demonstrate the lessons for transferring him back to the bed and once that was done, they asked me to return him to the wheelchair for the rest of the day. Even though I was congratulated for doing the maneuvers so well, I felt my back aching and I thought it was not right for me.

I didn't want to complain in front of the client's family, so I attracted the attention of my Russian supervisor in private before he left. I told him the job was not right for me and my back was aching. He told me in a mocking tone that he thought I was a real African man and that he had never seen an African complain about lifting anyone. He also reminded me that the PCA aide who worked on the weekend was an African and he never complained about anything. He then offered to replace me as soon as they found another man for the job, but that he wanted me to stay and do the job that day and that he would be in touch the following morning with news of a replacement.

I was supposed to lift him three times in a day—in the morning from the bed to the wheelchair, in the mid-day before his lunch to change his diapers on the bed and then put him back into the wheelchair, and at night around 9:30 back to his bed for sleep. Besides the lifting I was supposed to give a sponge shower every morning, clean his dentures, change his diapers during the day and at night he did not put on diapers because they caused him skin sores, so if he had a bowel movement it was supposed to be cleaned from the disposable linens spread on his bed. The first night (a Monday) was the most challenging because he had severe diarrhea and I had to clean his bedding twice during the night. I realized how even turning him in the bed to clean him after a bowel movement was a heavy, exhausting task, because of his size.

In the middle of the night I wrote a group email to the agency explaining what I had discussed with the supervisor during the day that the job was not right for me and I needed to be replaced immediately. On Tuesday, the Russian supervisor visited me at the home, and he told the client's family he was doing a routine check on me to see that all was good. He found the client in the wheelchair and asked him how the transfer went, and he told him, "very well, good work." I had not indicated anything to the client or his family that I was having any troubles with transfers and the whole family liked me a lot for putting their father in the wheelchair and they could see him wheeling around the house.

After talking to the family, the supervisor asked to speak to me privately outside where he chastised me for betraying his trust in African men. His insistence that all African men were strong was fascinating and disturbing, as it was a racist comment. He told me if I wanted to be replaced, they would just fire me and never consider me for any future openings.

On Tuesday night I wrote another group email to the group and said I accepted the supervisor's decision to fire me but I still wanted to be relieved from the job I was not comfortable doing. I wanted them to do it the following day (Wednesday) or else I would take actions in my own hands. This time it was the agency owner who replied with a text on my phone, saying he had received my email but if I ever leave the client's home without them finding a replacement for me he was going to file a complaint in court, accusing me of abandoning a quadriplegic patient. I understood from the text we had started exchanging threats to each other but even though I had

written a message just to put pressure on them to replace me I realized they had perceived my taking actions in my own hands to have
met running away from their client's home.

I spent a lot of time thinking about the agency owner's text and
realized how I was powerless in this escalation. Such employers
know so well the best way to exploit their immigrant workers. They
just mention "court," as they know no immigrant wants to be placed
close to either a cop or judge. I thought that it was far-fetched for
the owner to file a court complaint based on my protest to do work
I could not do but I still feared that if such a case ever went to
court—a black migrant facing a white man—the odds were not in
my hands, as the fate of many cases of black people in American
courts has demonstrated.

For all I had read about the Black Lives Matter movement in
America, I understood clearly why it always was better for a black
person to avoid meeting a judge or a police officer under any circumstances. The judge's perceptions of black people were not much different from that of the cops who impulsively shot and killed young
black people on the streets. And if justice could be so difficult for
American blacks to obtain, the probabilities were even worse for
black African migrants in America. There were no forums whatsoever to even put out their voices with the expectations their concerns
would be addressed satisfactorily.

In the light of this understanding I remained prudent. Waiting
for my asylum application to be processed, I knew that any case
filed against me could be detrimental to my status. So, I relented and
stopped asking to be relieved and reassigned. On Wednesday, while
still at the couple's home, the supervisor again came, this time telling
the clients that I had complained about the workload and that I was
threatening to discontinue the assignment. From the room in which
I stayed I could hear the wife explaining to the supervisor that they
did not believe they had requested tasks excessively. She said the job
was principally the transfer of the husband between wheelchair and
bed at various times during the day. After the supervisor left, the
family's attitude toward me changed completely and this complicated
my work even more, at a time when I had no further options. The
client spent most of the time on his computer and when I was on

my own in my room I simply stared. I could not read the book I carried nor could I continue on my manuscript. I just stared. At night I could not even sleep; I only stared and counted the time I had remaining in that house and even this seemed to move at a snail's pace.

I soon learned about my wider situation. On Thursday, as I had abandoned the idea of leaving the house, the supervisor didn't come, so I chatted with the client's son who was in his mid-twenties. He told me that his father was annoyed because they were paying the company $35 per hour for my service and I was complaining. The son also mentioned they were paying $20 per hour for their personal care assistant and he never complained about anything. I resisted the urge to tell him that out of the $35 per hour they paid the agency, I was only paid $12 per hour to do the work, far less than their PCA. But that would have sounded like I was protesting the poor pay and not being able to do the heavy lifting. Friday finally came and I was scheduled to leave the client's house, and I happened to meet the African man who was the PCA on my way out. He appeared to be in his mid- to late-twenties and have a frame that was bulkier and more muscular than mine, sort of like a weightlifter.

It is perhaps easy to forget or ignore that working as a home health aide or CNA incurs risks of injury similar to working in a factory. The vast number of injuries occur because of lifting clients. The Bureau of Labor Statistics (BLS) reports that health care aides suffer injuries at nearly twice the rate of all private industries combined. An analysis in Washington state found that home health workers were injured 50 percent more frequently than workers in all industries. In the National Nursing Assistant Survey (NNAS) 56 percent of CNAs reported they had been injured at work.[170]

Injury is not the only downside. I also worked for several recruiting agencies in Massachusetts that place workers for elderly care. In addition, I worked at an elderly care facility. Jobs for elderly care taken up by African migrants are associated with changing adult diapers. In fact, in Africa, some communities look at returning migrants as "buttock washers." One elderly patient I worked with would take stool softeners when I was at work because she said I was the only worker who did not make faces and squinch his nose while changing her diapers. Therefore, she planned on having her bowel movements only when I was on duty. Some patients needed to change their diapers up to eight times a day, because of diarrhea or incontinence. Diaper changes could not be delayed because a soiled garment could trigger infections or severe skin rashes, which would be noticed by examining physicians or nurses looking for bed sores. Honestly, the act of changing diapers was the most overwhelming task I endured as a caregiver even though I always struggled to stay as civil as I could while doing it. I heard stories from other migrant caregivers about the challenges of coping with the uncomfortable nature of changing diapers. Working in an elderly care facility meant that an aide might be changing the diapers multiple times each day for five or ten patients. Many workers complained how the odor stayed with them even when they were having their meals or when they left work.

Taking care of an ailing individual encompasses challenges that many families know well. And, the caretaker aide often absorbs many of those challenges. The roles include being a house cleaner and family members act like a nanny supervisor, ensuring the stranger in their home acts with the utmost dignity and respect in carrying out difficult tasks—such as changing a diaper, one that many family members would never do on their own. Communication is especially difficult when an elderly patient struggles to make a request clear and plain as possible so the aide is left to second guess and delay trying to make out what the patient is trying to say or the request being made. Second-guessing the person or making a mistake only agitates the uncomfortable patient and creates stress for both the patient and the aide. Hopefully, the aide can guess correctly and avoid the risks of a stress-inducing ordeal for both of them.

I should emphasize that not all caregiving aides deserve such consideration or defense. Every human being has their shortcomings and such difficult situations where the comfort of health care is paramount should be made easier for both aide and patient. In Massachusetts, there are scores of stories about aides hired to care for the elderly, chronically ill and disabled people at home who have faced allegations that they took advantage of their clients, including swindling them out of their life's savings, stealing their medications, neglecting their care, and inflicting physical abuse.

A *Boston Globe* investigative reporter who visited more than three dozen courthouses across the state of Massachusetts found up to

47 recent alleged abuse cases against home care workers. Of those, 45 allegedly robbed their clients of money, valuables, and/or drugs in schemes that were sometimes as brazen as they were heartless.[171] Most scholars and activists have concentrated on the shortcomings of caregivers but a clear look at the figures presented above as compared to the number of caregivers in the state reveals how infrequently these cases truly occur. In fact, though it is not possible to achieve 100 percent zero violations on the side of caregivers but with better regulations in place and training that emphasizes work ethics and respect, the few reported cases of abuses can be greatly reduced. Migrant caregivers understand the severe risks of their fate should a single case of abuse or neglect be filed against them and most avoid as much as possible being accused of violations of which they might be aware. Consequences such as "a ban not to work again in human service" that stains their work record or not being able to work anywhere or deportations and prison terms become so common and remorseful that any clear-thinking migrant will avoid even the slightest appearances of doing anything wrong.

One of the main challenges is reshaping the negative community and policy maker attitudes that consider caregivers as life failures, limited in intellectual capacities or as people unsustainable to learn anything meaningful. How can the most developed nation in the world treat its senior citizens and the people who care for them in this way. It is because of these attitudes that they have not even bothered to put in place options for better training and compensation for these important workers. For the time I have worked as a caregiver, I realize how disrespectful the community, policy makers, and health care practitioners are. Paul Osterman, arguing a point regarding the widespread disrespect of caregivers in the U.S., noted in his book *Who Will Care for Us*, that health care practitioners do not consider caregivers as part of the medical team even though they spend the most time with patients. In one case he noted how the rules that forbade caregivers from doing anything proactive regarding the health of the patient had one aide place eyedrops in the patient's hand and put their hand over the patient's eye to guide the drops towards their intended target, but they were not permitted to administer them directly.

To conclude, caregivers—unvalued, mistreated, marginalized, and working in dreadful conditions for low pay—have to fight to stay in the U.S. As a category, *caregivers* are not among those professions or skills that are eligible for employment-related Green Cards. Such visas go mostly to researchers, professors, engineers, or multinational managers, but not to caregivers. And this, despite the fact that there are more job openings for caregivers than there are for professors and researchers. As a result of this structural iniquity, many caregivers remain on employment authorization permits for several years without ever getting permanent residency and are unable to travel home because doing so without Permanent Residency or a Green Card would mean that they would not be allowed to return and would have to build the whole project from scratch. So, these immigration restrictions harm not only migrants but also senior citizens and people with disabilities. The situation seems to be about to get worse as the Trump Administration looks to cut the flow of migrants further still.

Chapter 31: Facilities for Patients with Mental Health Disorders

"There are wounds that never show on the body that are deeper and more hurtful than anything that bleeds." Laurell K. Hamilton

Private group homes across America have today replaced the institutions similar to prisons where people with mental illnesses were kept previously. The facilities, most of which are part of developmental disabilities rehabilitation centers, are recognizable in the sense that they are used by the state as a dumping ground for categories of people in which they are not interested. There is little funding for these facilities; they survive mostly because of their (cheap) immigrant workforce, which always is understaffed. There is no political will to invest in the institutions or the people who work in them but rather politicians simply want governments to spend only the minimum to keep this workforce alive and working. There is little understanding among the political classes about the conditions for patients and workers alike; who neither will or can vote.

Like other immigrants, I have worked in one of these group homes or schools for people with mental health disorders or those who are developmentally disabled. Immigrants work in many roles: as residential counselors, teaching assistants or supervisors, which means taking care of patients round the clock and doing almost exactly the same tasks as when working as a home care aide. Employers routinely mention a minimum requirement for a high school diploma but then fail to ask the applicant for documents or proof of educational attainment. They offer 1–2 week courses in the relevant disciplines—the proper use of restraints in emergencies, medical management, First Aid, and so on.

Most Ugandans, including me, prefer to work night shifts, a preference that appeals to many employers. I took a position at a group home for children from 14–22 where the shift started at 11 pm and ended at nine the following morning.

While in most group homes the staff slept on sofas or chairs, especially those with adult clients, sleeping was completely forbidden in homes with children or teenaged patients. Surveillance cameras were evident, but they were rarely checked unless an incident occurred. Most staff worked multiple shifts and more than 15 hours a day at these *No Sleep* homes, so they had to devise a means of catching an occasional power nap. They would avoid being detected by studying the surveillance camera angles. This allowed them to put a blanket or cape over their heads while in chairs with their backs facing the camera. Some bolder staff would catch a quick nap on sofas. Actually, they never checked the cameras regularly, only when there was a fight and staff needed to restrain a patient who had become too violent or aggressive. So, if a staff member slept at night, that person also likely prayed that no young person misbehaved to warrant a restraint and a subsequent review of video footage.

Most of the nights I would stay awake, writing this manuscript on my laptop. I was working both day and night to get more hours and pay. The most challenging task for the night shift was waking up young people, preparing and driving them to school in the morning rush hours. After staying awake for the full night, one understandably would not be comfortable driving in the morning traffic.

If you were caught sleeping, the punishment was immediate and severe. A female colleague who had been with the facility for more than five years was abruptly terminated because she was found asleep. A newly hired overnight female staffer found her sleeping in her chair at around two am. The newcomer didn't know that most staffers always found ways to nap in their chair, so she decided to report the incident. She came initially to me so I could be her witness. I replied that it was the role of surveillance cameras to watch over staff members, and mine was to oversee the young patients.

A few minutes after the incident had been reported, the night supervisor—a young Ugandan man—called me asking to wake the sleeping staff member. He wanted to avoid having to make a report that could lead to her dismissal. I told him I couldn't do it because the new staffer was watching everyone. When he arrived, the sleeping staffer was woken by the doorbell and so it seemed as though it would be ok. But the supervisor relayed bad news: the CEO had called and asked him to relieve the sleeping staffer of her duties. According to protocol the staffer had to leave the house immediately and the supervisor was supposed to take her seat for the night.

I was struck at how easy it was to fire an immigrant worker in the U.S. without a hearing or indeed any opportunity to consider the circumstances. The fired staffer, after learning her fate, said she was praying that they don't describe her sleeping on her profile as "neglect," because that was considered an abuse of children's rights. Thus, in any attempt to find new employment, she would fail background checks and might not be able to land a job even in a retail or grocery store.

Another female colleague quickly found trouble in an interaction with one of the young people, a 17-year-old male. He stood in front of her as if he wanted to ask for something but instead, he spat in her face. She responded with the natural and unconsidered reaction of slapping; she burst into tears as soon as she realized what she had done. The whole thing lasted less than a minute but the damage to her employment status already was irreversible. She was terminated and banned from working in any human services setting anywhere in the U.S.

The most challenging moments came when dealing with violent, young patients. Unlike adults, the younger patients had volatile mood changes. One moment they may be playful and the next violent and dangerously impulsive. In the case of a display of violent behavior, staff were required to restrain the patient on the floor and allowing the mood to pass and the episode finish. In the home where I worked, one patient, who was about 20 years old, frequently acted violently towards fellow patients and the staff. If the incident involved another patient, staff were instructed to separate them and to restrain the one who instigated it. An incident report would be followed up by an investigation. It was not always easy to chronicle the events in the reports, because they happened so quickly and they often involved retaliation between the patients, and so were quite complex interactions. Before a staff member jumped in to separate them, one could see the marks on both individuals.

Investigations often would conclude that the staff did not act quickly enough nor in a sufficiently compassionate manner against the patient who started the scuffle. In most cases, it was easier to fire and replace a staff member rather than complete an investigation that accurately captured and documented everything that had occurred in the incident.

So, when a patient who had previously been involved in a violent incident approached another patient in a situation that could escalate quickly, the on-duty staff member's anxiety level skyrocketed. Likewise, scuffles between patients and staff members were even worse and truthfully some staff members acted unprofessionally. In such instances, staff members would be fired and then either prosecuted or deported, depending on whether they had violated the conditions of their immigrant status. Even if a staff member avoided being deported the incident would go on his/her record, indicating that they had abused a child with special needs. Thus, the migrant would find it extremely difficult if not impossible to land employment wherever criminal background checks were conducted prior to hiring.

Staff members bore the burden of ensuring that the number of violent incidents involving patients were minimized not least because the group home administration saw every patient's presence as a source of revenue. The cost per patient staying at the home was around $250,000 annually, equivalent to the annual salary of eight staff members. However, the needs of any given patient could easily prove more than a one-to-one ratio could bear. For example, one day a violent patient attacked a white, house manager and bit him on the shoulder, and the victim was taken away bleeding in an ambulance. Had he bitten a black staff member, the administration would have left the incident unreported and unresolved.

One night, a Ugandan male colleague was asked to leave the work premises after getting into an altercation with a frequently violent patient. There were three staff members on duty: my colleague was in the middle level (first floor); I was on the upper (second floor); and there was a Haitian male on the ground floor. At around three am, the student started screaming aloud, demanding to talk to his mom because he could not sleep. I could hear my colleague on the top floor trying to calm him, but far from relenting the patient would respond with ever louder screams. Protocol held that we were not supposed to leave our designated floors until the person attending the patient specifically asked for help, so I stayed on my floor. But the noise grew louder, to the extent that it was waking the patients on my floor.

I realized the house was about to go into meltdown, so I went downstairs briefly to consult my colleague at to what should be done. I found my Ugandan and the Haitian colleagues both trying to restrain the patient on the floor in the hope that he would eventually calm down, so I assisted them by restraining his legs by placing my weight on his knees. I noticed that the Ugandan's glasses were broken. Finally, the patient calmed down and the Haitian worker asked me to contact the overnight supervisor and report the incident while they continued restraining the student. After calling the supervisor, I returned to my own floor and the other patients returned to their beds.

The supervisor arrived after the patient had become calm. Both of my colleagues gave different accounts of the incident and the supervisor asked each to write his own report. The Haitian worker claimed he found my Ugandan colleague fighting with the patient in his room, away from the cameras, and had not bothered to even call for back up or staff support in restraining him, which would have been the normal procedure. Meanwhile, the Ugandan colleague in his report said the patient invited him to his room to fix a radio and suddenly started punching him, which caused his eyeglasses to shatter. He said that he did not fight back but only wanted to defend himself from being injured. The latter account was definitely inaccurate as I had clearly heard the patient demanding to see his mother *before* the altercation. Likely the patient attacked him in the face and broke his glasses and he retaliated. Also, the patient had some bruises on his face and the supervisor demanded to know what caused them.

As a result of the incident and the inconclusive following up, the supervisor called her bosses, read to them both reports and returned with orders for the Ugandan colleague to leave the group home immediately. I had stayed out of the crisis for most of the night, just observing more staff members arriving and calling for an ambulance to take the patient to the hospital. But in the morning, I started getting calls. The Ugandan colleague wanted to know what had transpired when he left at night and then instructed me about what I should say to investigators if they called me as a witness. He wanted me to tell them something like the following: "I was a witness. He did not beat the student; that the Haitian was confused, that he had called for backup, and the Haitian arrived earlier than me because I had a knee injury and could not be quick to arrive on the scene." The way he wanted me to account for the events was akin to "save me first and we shall see what to do for you if you are implicated with your tricky knee."

Instead of investigators from the school calling me, it was the police, so I knew that the incident was being taken seriously. I told the police how little I had been involved in the crisis; just coming onto the scene to help restrain the patient on his legs and call the supervisor. It seemed likely that the police called me at the same time as they spoke to my Ugandan colleague because a few minutes after their call, I saw his come up on my phone as an incoming call. Tired of the fiasco and desperate for sleep I ignored the call and switched my phone to silent mode. He called my brother and asked for our home address, telling him he wanted to tell me what to tell the police in case they called again and that he was coming with some Ugandan elders to counsel me to stick to the script. My brother later told me he gave him the address after noticing he was in a real panic. Eventually, the former staff member was taken to court.

Being understaffed at night was problematic. For example, most patients were assigned a one-to-one ratio with staff during the day but at night that would grow to four-to-one. The school management assumed that the violent patient would sleep at night but that was not always the case. He would stay up from two until dawn and almost all the staff on all the other floors would have to abandon their areas as we concentrated on taking care of him as he became more violent if he couldn't sleep. Sometimes it was because the day staff had put him to bed earlier—the rules were to let him sleep after nine pm, but on occasion they would let him go to bed as early as seven because they were relieved when he slept. But, on those days, he also was likely to be awake after midnight.

The floor on which the violent student stayed was one that everyone who worked at that group home always tried to avoid. The best ways to avoid it was always to come early and take the topmost floor. The ground floor was always reserved for the young woman who also worked at the house for overnight. Sometimes I would come in as much as an hour early in an effort to avoid the troubled "first floor," but still there were a couple of times when I was slated to work there and there was no getting out of it. On such nights I relied on prayers that the troubled man would sleep or at least remain calm if he did wake. If he woke, I would even give him my laptop so he could play games (which was not allowed) to keep him occupied and stop him from fighting. But there were times when he was really bad and nothing would occupy him. Those days I would call the other staff on the top floor and, if we needed to restrain him then insist that we do it on the floor in front of the surveillance cameras.

On one occasion we had to restrain him in the morning, because he was swinging at other patients and staff members. As usual, we were understaffed: only three workers and everyone was awake. Two of us restrained him and we asked the young woman who worked with us to keep calling school emergency numbers for backup and to oversee other students so they would not interfere in the restraining process. As we held him down, he somehow managed to move his right knee and hit my colleague, which opened a gash on his mouth that was bleeding. It was a chaotic scene, and my injured colleague wanted to withdraw but I begged him to hold on as it would have been dangerous to let him go at that moment. Another five minutes passed and the patient calmed down.

The senior support staff arrived an hour later, checking that we had not hurt him during the restraining procedure. After ensuring the student was safe, they turned to the injured staff member to get him an ambulance. As usual they consoled him that the school was going to pay his medical bills—as if this in itself was compensation. As we sat on the couch waiting for the ambulance, he said, "Yasin, this is not worth it. I need to get out of here before I lose an eye for 12 bucks." I corrected him that it was actually less than that after they deducted the taxes, but I added that instead of frowning at the low pay in the dangerous workplace he would be frowning at his country's dictator who has sold the nation to the lowest bidder and left its citizens wandering in the world. I told him the kind of jobs open for him as an immigrant were for the 3 D's (Dirty, Demanding and Dangerous) and this was the case wherever he would go.

I wanted him to be thankful that the support staff had not found any marks on the boy to investigate us or even take us to court for abusing him. But still they had blamed us for restraining the boy with only the two of us explaining it was not what they taught us. We realized they were trying to blame the young woman who had not joined in the restraint and we did stand up to say that we were at fault for asking her to stay away and take care of other students. The young woman in her early 20s, a daughter of immigrants from one of the neighboring U.S. islands, was in her first job while she pursued her college studies. A week earlier another patient had grabbed one of her breasts, squeezing it while she was administering his medications. She told him to stop and when we went to the ground floor level, we noticed the boy pleading to her for forgiveness. We asked her to write a report but she decided against it because they wouldn't punish him because of his mental health disabilities.

Not all the misfortune was dealt to my colleagues; I had my fair share. One incident that really hurt me happened one morning when a patient was in the restroom for longer than usual—more than 20 minutes—and it was causing problems. When another student wanted to use the restroom we had to redirect them either to the one in the basement or the one on the first floor. This situation continued until it was time to board the vans and go to school, but the patient still hadn't come out. I knocked on the door, asking if he needed help or more time and there was no answer. Then I decided to open the door and there he was standing holding his own filth in his hands. When he saw me he threw it in my face. We had to delay the trip to school for 30 minutes while we both cleaned up.

I considered myself lucky to have held onto this particular position for six months. I had seen many colleagues hired and fired. I had even started picking up hours at the school, accompanying students and staying in class as a teaching assistant, helping them complete their class assignments, maintaining order, restraining a student when they turned violent in class, and taking them to gym. I would accompany them to the canteen, feeding lunch to those who needed help eating, and escorting students to the restroom and giving them any help they required there. For the four days I didn't work at my PCA live-in job I was working at the school during the day and at the group home at night. In total, I was working for this company 18 hours every day. The longer work hours also strained on my effectiveness, especially at nights when I had to stay awake and work on this book's manuscript. I was starting to do less and sleeping more in the house sofas or chairs.

Like I said earlier, almost all the staff slept at some point during the night. But the night supervisors who came to check on that had once been residential staff members themselves, and so knew all the tricks. Most night supervisors were Ugandans and one in particular who was the Head of the Supervisor's Department was corrupt. He ran a racket in which he extorted money from the night staff in exchange for allowing them to sleep without being reported. I had heard about his racket but since he had not yet found me sleeping, he had not yet offered me a deal.

Inevitably on one of those busy days, he did indeed find me sleeping and demanded that I pay him $2,000 to keep the job. The amount was startling and I knew right away that I was not going to pay it but I sought to buy some time that day and I offered to pay him in four installments, starting from the next pay check which would come due in two days. I talked to some Ugandan people who also worked at the company and everyone told me his racket was an open secret but the amount he sought to extort from me was excessive. Some told me he was extorting a lot because he knew I was working at the school and house which meant a lot of hours and in his understanding, I was making good money. Others told me that it was because I did not bargain that he always asked for large sums but with a bargain he would even take $500. I myself didn't see any reason to negotiate because I knew I was not going to give him any money.

Pay day came and I ignored several of his calls. Then when I came back to work on Monday night, he found me sleeping on my computer laptop again and he said, "You don't want to pay but you want to sleep, I am not leaving until you pay the first installment here and now or you need to find another job." I told him I had not been to the bank as I was running from job to another, but I suggested that we connect during the day. When I received his first missed call during the day, I knew it was time to call it off by reporting myself to the school management and resigning effectively. I told the house manager in a text message that he did not need to fire me as I was resigning because I could not pay the $2,000 the Night Supervisor wanted from me to cover up for my sleeping on duty at night. My resignation was accepted and upon investigating the supervisor's conduct, he was also fired.

I had built my life and career on investigating and reporting on corruption. I also realized how vulnerable I could become in such a situation, afraid that being honest would cost me the livelihood that I worked so hard to obtain. Many migrant workers face the same predicament. The choice is particularly hard because doing the right thing offers little or no assurance of economic security. It is worth remembering that migrant workers make sacrifices that their critics would not countenance: there are reasons why few Americans take these jobs. Yet they ask for little more than a modicum of justice in wage, working conditions, and prospects. Yet, one should think in good conscience what this hypocrisy means: when people demonize migrant workers who are trying desperately to do the right thing. There is a broader lesson of humility in the act of changing a soiled diaper for an elderly patient or for helping to calm a patient who does not know or understand why he acts violently. It is the gateway to human dignity and respect for everyone.

Many migrant caregivers have upgraded their career by going to school to attain a certificate of Licensed Practical Nurse (LPN) or Registered Nurse (RN) because the health care sector was one that was more open to migrants, especially of color. But the vast majority of migrants have also taken on taxi driving jobs. The majority of the drivers at quasi-taxi companies Uber and Lyft are migrants. For migrants taxi driving, though tiring and dangerous, is a sought-after job, preferable to caregiving or working at fast food outlets and grocery stores. Those who have switched their first jobs to taxi driving brag frequently about how their incomes have more than tripled, earning in one week what caregivers bring home for a full month.

Chapter 32: Driving Uber/Lyft

"It's hard to teach children about our migration West when they're thinking, "Why didn't you just call an Uber?" Neil Leckman

After two years in the USA I contemplated driving rideshare taxis for the companies Uber and Lyft. I desperately wanted to stop working at homes for people with disabilities, so instead I planned to drive for a living. That said I decided to keep the PCA job with my quadriplegic client. The plan sounds simple enough, but it didn't prove so. It is not as easy to enter the professional driving sector as it is to access others in the U.S. There are good reasons—in the form of employment restrictions—that keep caregiving as the only realistic option for new migrants.

One such restriction is that in order to drive for Uber you have to have an American driving permit that has been in use for at least a year; a stipulation that alone has kept many aspirant taxi drivers out of action for some time. Another significant obstacle is that you have to have a new car: the taxi companies only accept a car within a decade of its manufacture and many migrants, including me, have vehicles that are at least several years older. By the time my license had been active for a year I had started saving for a new car that would help me to realize my plan, drive for Uber, and increase my income.

So, my first challenge was to actually get a new car. My savings were still not adequate to pay for a vehicle that meets the requirements. I was still driving a 1999 Toyota Corolla that I had bought for $500 a few months after I arrived in the U.S., and though the ignition was good the body was falling apart. Friends used to tease me that I should drive carefully so as not to fall out through the holes in the door caused by the rust.

I talked with Wahab about the difficulty of saving money in caregiving and his advice was to secure a car loan from the bank, but I was hesitant to start accumulating American debts before a decision about my asylum has been made. One day I told Wahab that I had found a good and affordable Honda Civic for sale—in a garage where I had my oil changed. My brother broke into laughter and said something to the effect that moving around garages and looking for a car to drive taxis on the road is like going to a hospital and asking nurses to hook somebody up with one of their longtime patients for marriage.

The large majority of Uber and Lyft drivers are immigrants. It's one of the easiest entry-level jobs to obtain in the U.S. and recruitment is handled online with minimal documentation required. I was surprised to learn that even the Employment Authorization Card—normally the first requirement for any job application, was not needed to apply to Uber or Lyft. Indeed, just four documents were: driver's license, car title, current inspection sticker, and vehicle insurance.

It came as a considerable relief to learn all this as not only was my employment authorization set to expire in a few months, but also the renewal process was taking as much time as for the asylum application. Without the authorization I would have lost the caregiving job—even if only temporarily—so I would at least be bringing in some income.

Rideshare companies have often been criticized for not being more vigilant and rigorous in their recruiting, but these lapses are not so much the product of circumstance than as that of the companies trying to meet the demand for driving services. Again, as with so many other jobs, many American citizens shy away from these opportunities while immigrants are willing to be on the road as long as the demand for rides is there.

I want to step out of my personal narrative for a moment in order to look at the ridesharing sector in general, which has become a target in public discourse on immigration, one of the core tenets of which is, as we have already seen, the (in my view) misguided belief that migrants are taking jobs from Americans. It is fair to say that Uber and Lyft may well qualify as emblematic of the wider gig economy, the benefits of which are not easy to discern, as any gig tends towards exploitation.

Uber drivers, who mostly work full time, are still classified legally as independent contractors, a status that doesn't obligate their employers to provide benefits, insurance coverage or holiday pay. Drivers have their own cars, purchase their own fuel, and keep up with car maintenance including oil changes, routine parts replacement and repairs for more serious problems and cover the capital depreciation of the vehicle. In short, the operational costs are passed to the owners of the cars and the profits to the owners of Uber. The only tool or material that Uber provides is the software and the digital infrastructure that facilitates ride transactions. In terms of actual pay: Uber decides what to pay drivers for each trip; a figure that fluctuates continuously depending on market and ride demands.

Furthermore, Uber claims it takes an average of 21 percent of earnings on each ride but in my personal experience it is—at least on occasion—the driver who ends up receiving the 21 percent. Every completed trip registers the driver's earned compensation immediately. They might be dissatisfied with that amount but would have virtually no recourse to complaint and as a result receive a revised amount. As drivers, we always call the feature of UberPool a big rip off. One time I took a pool from Boston to Peabody in Massachusetts and asked the passengers how much they had paid. Three paid Uber a total of $75 but Uber paid me just $26 for this trip. Another reason drivers dislike pools or shared rides is because most customers using that service either have limited budgets or just refuse to tip.

This issue is a about much more than this company. That a legally incorporated institution could get away with abuse on such a scale and still yield eye-watering profits sets a dangerous precedent within the corporate culture of the nation. In addition, Uber has competed against small, franchised taxi businesses, forcing them to close. Again, some would prefer to blame immigrants for this. Uber and Lyft are cheap and accessible in many cities and their convenience have lured customers into making the switch, as they no longer have to signal with their arms to catch a taxi or walk to a designated stand or station. Some people assumed that as taxi companies went out of business, their drivers would relent and join Uber or Lyft. It is akin to assuming that as legacy retailers have been forced out of the market, retail employees would take up jobs packing up boxes or delivering packages for e-tailer giants such as Amazon. Many Americans forget that as these monopolies have emerged rapidly on the scene, the resulting income disparities are not because of immigrants taking jobs from them, as some echo without a second thought the nativist sentiments of politicians they support. It is easy for politicians to escape realities and fix blame on immigrants, while protecting the vested interests of corporate donors and lobbyists who are happy to fund political campaigns for such willing mouthpieces.

In its early years, Uber grew rapidly, as potential drivers were tantalized by the company's promising advertisements. Drivers could make up to $25 per hour, maintain a schedule tailored to their flexibility and receive signing bonuses in the thousands of dollars. In a recent survey of more than 2,600 active drivers with calculations based on the Ridester's 2018 Independent Driver Earnings Survey,[172] Uber's claims ring closer to the truth in some cities and are far from it in others. Drivers in Honolulu, Long Island, and Seattle can earn the $25 per hour rate, as Uber claims. Meanwhile, in other major metropolitan areas around the country, drivers often earn an average of less than $10 per hour and below the federally mandated minimum hourly wage. This includes Akron, Ohio ($4.94 per hour) and Raleigh/Durham, North Carolina ($6.62 per hour). Some of the nation's largest cities fare just as poorly: Houston, for example, is just $8.72 per hour while Tampa-St. Petersburg in Florida is $8.95 per hour. Uber/Lyft spend more time on the road circling around and looking for riders and this time, fuel is not paid for or compensated. Uber does not even pay for fuel or time the driver takes to go and pick up a rider even though that may be some distance.

The drivers and their customers are separated by an economic divide that translates directly into geographical distance. They have to live in cheap neighborhoods, a long way from the affluent areas that will generate fares. For example, I would have to drive 15 miles from Acton to Boston before I started picking up fares. Later, the distance grew as I commuted from Boxborough, some 25 miles away. It's not uncommon for Uber drivers in my area to sleep in their cars so as to minimize the cost of doing business.

The scale of the *commute* is not the only problem faced by drivers. In order to make any money they have to work long hours, which makes staying awake and alert a challenge. Inevitably, some drivers push their limits. Uber has become aware of the problem, but it resolved it by automatically turning off the access to the mobile app once a driver has been online for 12 hours. However, most drivers will just switch over to Lyft. To stay awake, drivers use coffee or caffeinated cold beverages. Now I understand Dunkin' Donuts slogan: "America runs on Dunkin." It is an example of ironic truth in advertising.

But, even the caffeine solution is not fail-safe. After drinking Coffee bathroom breaks become so urgent that one has to give up a requested trip, to locate an available nearby restroom. If a destination was the airport, finding a restroom was easy enough. The challenge, though, was to rush in, use the facilities, and return to the car that was parked in the five-minute zone. Any delay would be costly, with a ticket issued by the airport police. Destinations at a mall or shopping center are much more amenable for a quick rest stop but the worst were destinations in residential areas or Boston's central business district. I discussed these dilemmas with other Uber drivers, in the hopes of discovering a clever solution. One driver recommended to be looking always for a port-a-potty near a construction site or park with playground structures. He said construction managers often would allow him to use one, if he asked politely enough.

The one aspect that perhaps is the most positive driving Uber is finding a passenger with an interesting background story to tell. Some passengers make small talk about the weather or the city while others discuss politics and yet others are of a more personal nature.

One memorable conversation was with a white female in her late twenties about her struggles to pay off her student loans. She told me the income from her teaching job could not sustain her financially and still make the debt obligations on a loan, so she had taken up a second job as a bartender for three days each week. She earned so much in tips from bartending that she wondered why the job that she went to college in order get, could not provide enough. "It's frustrating being there to serve and smile to happy people, when inside yourself you are not happy, but that smile is what brings the tips and from these tips I pay toward my student loan every month," she said.

I told her I shared her concerns and asked if she thought that immigrants were responsible for her financial problems. "No," she replied. She blamed the government for not providing free college education and for not paying teachers well enough to live decently. I asked her whom she believed benefited the most from the student loan debt and she answered the corporate bankers. I then told her of how the same corporate banks had devastated economies in Africa and Latin America, with them contributing to the desperation that has forced immigrants to venture to the U.S. I added that those banks escape blame because they control politicians in Washington and have the means to influence the mainstream media narrative. As the trip concluded we had formed a bond, convinced we are both just victims of the same corporate greed.

Another memorable instance was a black American in his mid-twenties with his four-year-old son. The man told me he had been released from prison a week earlier and he was getting to know his son who was born while he was incarcerated. He told me he was going to try as much as possible not to go back to prison because he wanted to stay with his son. He didn't want his son to grow up without a father's guidance because that could mean he might risk ending up in prison as he did. The man recalled that his own father had been arrested when he was young, and that his mother struggled to rear him and two siblings.

When they were teenagers, he recalled, they ended up on the streets to hustle and help their mother put food on the table. Having given up on school, he was arrested just before his 19th birthday. He didn't want to discuss his case, brushing aside my question with responses such as "usual stuff." But he told me that by the time he was arrested he had a girlfriend (whose father was also in jail) and that she was pregnant. When she visited him in jail, she promised him that she will not get an abortion but that she would hustle to earn enough money to take care of the baby. He added that few black families in America have grown up with fathers in the house; the white folks in police and courts have believed all black men belong in prisons and the cycle has been hard to break. I asked him if he was trying to find a job and start working, and he told me he still was not having luck finding one because of the background checks that uncover criminal history and deemed him unfit for employment. I could sense the strong bond between the son and father in their interactions in my car, even though they had just met. It was clear his son adored his father. Once they left, I only wondered how long the young man would be able to stay out of jail to be with his son.

Not all my interactions were positive. Some white clients did not hide their racist attitudes. One white man asked me for a favor before he sat in my car. He had locked his car keys inside, and he said if I could help him open his car and get his keys, he would pay me the Uber fare without needing me to take him to his destination. His explanation was unclear at first and I tried to repeat the details back to him. I asked if he wanted me to break into his car and retrieve his keys and he said that was the request. I understood that this was a favor he only would ask from a black driver. I told him I didn't know how to break into a car; that even if my own car was locked I would be unable to do so. He sat in my vehicle, visibly distraught because I had let him down.

Clients also bring their daily experiences and moods into an Uber trip. One day, a woman who appeared to be middle age, entered my car and announced as I started the engine that she was pregnant and if I hit any potholes with such force that she could have a miscarriage, she would sue me and Uber. After arriving at her destination, I asked her if she was fine and the baby was still intact, she said yes and I breathed a sigh of relief.

Once, I picked up an old couple in their mid-seventies at a Boston hospital and the wife told me they had had a bad day: her husband Jack had just been diagnosed with cancer. She told me the doctors were willing to help but they also asked for the husband's cooperation, which meant quitting his smoking habit—something he hesitated to do. "Imagine: when I went to do the paperwork after that bad news, I came back to where I left Jack and he was missing," the woman said. "I looked for him everywhere and couldn't find him. Then I went where people smoke and there he was, smoking again."

I decided to offer my own encouragement, telling Jack it was better for him to quit smoking and that the doctors had the ability to give him a longer life if he quit smoking. Jack had not said a word since he entered my car but then he blurted, "If you two don't stop picking on me, I am stopping this Uber right here and giving you a single-star rating with a nasty comment." I apologized and stayed

188

quiet for the remainder of the trip. It was his wife who continued talking: "Jack, you are threatening a poor Uber driver for telling you something that is good. Jack, that is not right. Please, Jack, say sorry to him." After we arrived at their destination, I checked my app and Jack had given me a $5 tip.

A few weeks after I started driving for Uber, the story of a Ugandan Uber driver, Mayanja Daudah, was circulated widely in the Boston media. He was charged with raping his client—a white woman. The allegations shocked what amounts to a community of Ugandan Uber drivers. Their immediate response was that every Ugandan driver for Uber and Lyft fitted cameras to their cars so they would have evidence in the event of an allegation of this kind. After the driver was arrested, some Massachusetts politicians called for legislation requiring all Uber and Lyft drivers be fingerprinted, a practice that both companies discourage and believe will never be a foolproof measure.

Chapter 33: Migrants vs. Citizens

"It says something about our country that people around the world are willing to leave their homes and leave their families and risk everything to come to America." George W. Bush

Politicians like President Donald Trump of the USA have convinced citizens that migrants are a competitive threat to their jobs. This virulently nativist message has been driven through mainstream media without addressing the question of whether experts in labor economics have found evidence to support or challenge this position. Politicians rushing to portray themselves as champions of worker's rights have proposed anti-immigrant policies as protectionist measures of citizens workers without considering if, indeed, the policy makes economic sense.

This deception is widespread and has been difficult to shake free of, but the real context of the debate is one that few people care to consider publicly. Take for example the *types* of jobs many migrants take in the U.S. Even people with advanced degrees (such as me), or those who have trained as doctors and lawyers have felt compelled to take jobs that are far beneath their education and experience. And, these are jobs that certainly no American with comparable training would dream take. Few people seem to wonder why highly educated and professionally trained migrants are passed over for jobs that require such skills and instead are directed toward lower-paying menial jobs that have traditionally been difficult to fill.

Here is a position that rarely enters the public debate: American-born and migrant workers have common concerns about employers who exploit them. Rather than frame the discussion in an adversarial perspective, it would be wise to consider the labor rights issue from the overlapping concerns of both groups of workers. Politicians consciously deploy rhetoric to manipulate lower-income and lower-middle class groups into blaming angry migrant workers for their troubles. It is a distractive ploy that undermines the pervasive and genuine concerns that American workers have held for a long time as they have seen their labor rights diminish while corporate protection rackets have led to record-setting profits and wages have stagnated, even during strong periods of economic recovery and growth (as in the case of the U.S. economy as it rebounded from the Great Recession of 2008).

Antagonism from native workers towards immigrants is nothing new of course. In the early 20th century in U.S., black and non-black workers opposed each other. The northern non-black working-class movement effectively excluded the freedmen, the slaves and the five million poor whites of the south.[173]

Today, in the U.S., many customer service companies have outsourced work to India, South Africa, the Philippines, and elsewhere. The incentive to pay lower wages is strong. For example, an entry-level IT worker in China might be paid $7,000 a year and $8,400 in India. India and the Philippines have attracted U.S. employers for locating their call centers because residents in those countries speak English. Every time my supervisor for personal care assistants has called Amazon, she has asked the person who answered the call from where they are based. She enjoys mocking their countries and often teases them about their heavily accented English, especially if they are from India or South Africa. Meanwhile, few Americans consider that many corporate enterprises also are buying millions of acres of land parcels in Africa, which displace homeland natives and turns them into migrants seeking labor abroad. Rarely, anyone traces the entire cycle of what is happening while leaving politicians' remarks about the issue unchallenged.

It is hard to make the case that migrants have made a negative impact on the job picture in the States. Immigration also has an economic impact that has managed to keep inflation in check even with low unemployment rates. In the early years of the 21st century, the large pool of low-skill immigrant workers, especially from Mexico, who came to California made it cheaper for citizens to have their houses cleaned and lawns mowed. Likewise, the demand for workers on farms to pick and process local produce was substantial.

But, while politicians have argued for anti-immigrant policies, the nature of migration has changed dramatically, effectively making the political messages moot and irrelevant. By 2016, the number of immigrants coming to California from Mexico, according to the Public Policy Institute of California, has declined significantly by more than 70 percent since 2000. This means that fewer than 150,000 Mexican citizens now come annually to California.

Indeed, California now received more migrants from China than it does from Mexico and, if current trends continue, then India, the Philippines, and Vietnam will all soon be above Mexico in that league table. Many of California's newer immigrants have much higher education levels, including a completed baccalaureate degree:

> The sharp increase in highly educated immigrants and the decline in less-educated immigrants reflect the changing labor market in California. Unemployment rates for workers with at least a bachelor's degree (3.3 percent) are about half those of less-educated workers (6.5 percent). With California expected to face a shortfall of 1.1 million college graduates by 2030, highly educated immigrants are a key component to helping the state address the workforce skills gap.[174]

Migrants are essential to keeping the U.S. economy competitive in rapidly evolving global markets, as they open firms, adopt innovative market practices, and create additional jobs. More than 40 percent of all Fortune 500 companies in U.S. were founded by immigrants. Three quarters of patents from top universities in 2011 had a foreign-born inventor. And immigrants account for a large share of Nobel Prizes: 33 percent in chemistry, 26 percent in economics, 34 percent in medicine, for example. While current U.S. politicians insist on short-sighted critiques of immigrant labor without considering the ramifications of changing a system that has not been revamped since 1965, a time when both the American and global economies were so different from their current renditions.

But the tightening restrictions on migrants coming into the U.S. have caused shortages in some areas of the health sector typically staffed by migrants. In the November 2018 U.S. mid-term elections there was a proposed ballot question in Massachusetts to mandate nurse staffing ratios in hospitals, depending upon a specific unit of services, and the bill pitted health care employers against nurses. The Massachusetts Nurses Association that initiated the bill argued that safe staffing ratios are necessary to ensure that nurses are able to care adequately for patients. They relied on reports from registered nurses who are assigned an excessive caseload of patients to care for within a single time, which can result in medication errors, longer hospital stays, or accidental patient injury. They cited studies that show higher rates of complications when nurses are caring for more patients than what can be managed satisfactorily.

However, the Massachusetts Health and Hospital Association opposed the bill and spent millions in ads, urging people to vote against the initiative. The group also commissioned a study, which found that mandating nurse staffing ratios would cost the Massachusetts health care system $1.3 billion in the first year and $900 million each year after that. The initiative failed at the polls, with 70 percent of voters rejecting it but the campaign also managed to push the question of the understaffed and overburdened nurses to the public's view. A critical component of this debate that was entirely absent from public discourse, concerned immigrants. The nursing profession employs many migrants, but with current restrictions there are growing concerns about leaving that demand unmet. While employers and hospitals fought successfully against this particular initiative, the problem of staffing is likely to worsen.

Americans have tended to use Japan as an example of a country that doesn't take in immigrants and has prospered. But, behind this prosperity is a façade rarely discussed. In Japan, many elderly people die alone in their homes without anyone knowing, with no families or visitors to speak of in the events. Local newspapers in Japan are full of reports of solitary death. This phenomenon is known as *kodokushi*. A *New York Times* report in late 2017 summarized the phenomenon:

> A single-minded focus on economic growth, followed by painful economic stagnation over the past generation, had frayed families and communities, leaving them trapped in a demographic crucible of

increasing age and declining births. The extreme isolation of elderly Japanese is so common that an entire industry has emerged around it, specializing in cleaning out apartments where decomposing remains are found.[175]

Every country has cases where elderly people die alone, but none experiences it quite like Japan, home to the world's fastest-aging population. More than a quarter of the population is over 65, a figure set to rise to 40 percent by 2050. Lonely-death statistics are hard to come by—the central government doesn't collect them—but regional figures show a sharp increase over the past decade. NLI Research Institute, a Tokyo think tank, estimates that about 30,000 people nationwide die this way each year.[176] They're discovered often months after they've died, after their mailboxes fill up or they fall behind on their rent, or when the smell draws attention to their home.

As the number of lonely deaths has grown, so too has the lonely-death-cleanup industry. Numerous firms offer this kind of service, and insurance companies have started selling policies to protect landlords if their tenants die inside their properties. The plans cover the cost of cleaning the apartment and compensate for loss of rent. Some will even pay for a purifying ritual in the apartment once the work is done.

Besides lonely deaths, the elders' loneliness in Japan where there are no migrants working as personal care assistants reaches such levels of desperation that it has forced some of them to commit minor crimes so they can spend the rest of their lives in prison with stability and a community. Japan is constructing special prison wards just for elderly inmates to address the record number of crimes committed by senior citizens—a growing problem sparked by poverty and an aging society. With the elderly crime rate nearly quadrupling over the past two decades, around 20 percent of women in prisons are now senior citizens.[177] In most instances, the crime they commit is generally minor and petty, usually shoplifting. For them, living the remainder of their lives behind bars is a better alternative to being alone in their homes. In 2017, a Japanese government survey revealed that over half of all elderly people caught shoplifting said they lived by themselves, while 40 percent claimed they did not have any close relatives.

The Japanese Government has already realized that it can no longer sustain the consequences of a policy of blocking migrants coming into their countries to handle jobs involving elderly care. The government has now signed agreements with Indonesia, Vietnam, and the Philippines under which applicants who complete job training and pass a language proficiency test can work at a Japanese nursing home. But if they want to stay beyond three years, they must pass a national caregiver's exam so difficult that 40 percent of Japanese applicants fail.

Many Japanese also express concern about the impact of cultural differences.[178] The Japanese policy that has hitherto been hostile towards migration is the latest iteration of a cultural phenomenon that goes back millennia: the Japanese prefer to remain culturally separate from the rest of the world.

The Japanese example should give cause for thought to those Americans and Europeans who have admired their anti-immigrant policies. This lesson of failure is not limited to Japan. Indeed, the U.S. as well as European countries that have embraced such stances will experience similar impacts sooner than later, especially as demographic trends increasingly mirror what has occurred in Japan over the last half-century.

Japan provides other compelling examples that demand the attention of the U.S. and Europe. Like other industries in a rapidly aging Japan, the construction business is desperate for labor. One-third of the country's construction workers are 55 or older, with those aged 29 or younger totaling just 11 percent of the industry workforce. As baby boomers retire, the labor shortage—in construction and in the wider Japanese economy—is bound to become more acute.[179] The scenario should sound familiar to Americans, especially where Hispanics, Latinos, and Chicanos have become essential to the U.S. construction industry.

Without fanfare, Prime Minister Shinzo Abe has steadily loosened Japan's once tightly controlled visa policy, resulting in a near doubling of the number of foreign workers in Japan to 1.28 million over the last five years. In its latest move on immigration, Abe's

Government is expected to create a new class of five-year work permits for unskilled workers in hopes of attracting more than 500,000 new overseas workers by 2025. At some point, Americans will have to address the realities much as Japanese leaders have in recent years. Currently, American discussions about immigration are dominated by anti-immigration arguments that do not reflect true motivations and the issue of immigration often emerges to be most salient after news events in which images dominate the social media channels. Most of the current discourse reflects a blatant disregard or at best a misunderstanding of immigration policy and enforcement. Ironically, the greatest losers are not just the immigrants but the many millions of others who benefit daily from the presence of migrant workers who do everything positive to avoid causing any undue burden upon American society.

Chapter 34: My Own Stifled Voice

"If liberty means anything at all, it means the right to tell people what they do not want to hear." George Orwell

In Dubai, I chronicled the injustices and inequalities experienced regularly by the migrant workers. My first book contained a good deal of this kind of material. After it was published but before it could reach aspirant migrants with their sights set on the wealthy Emirates, the Dubai Government was trying to stifle my voice. They blocked the recently published copies of my book from coming into Dubai, got me sacked, and then deported me to Uganda. Everything was done in complete silence, and had it not been me trying to post a few Twitter and Facebook posts no one would have known what had happened. I tried reaching out to some international human rights groups and media, but the response from most went something like: "You know exactly what you got yourself into; deal with it." Some told me simply that they were not focused on migrants in Dubai. A few journalists who tried to pursue my story as a gesture of solidarity, told me either that their editors were not interested in my deportation or that the story had been pulled after the editor noticed my deportation was to Uganda not the UK or the U.S.

It is intriguing to me that throughout my deportation ordeal, everyone thought I was being funded by an organization. Individual activists asked me to tell them in confidence who funded me to write the book. When I told them that no one did, they were surprised. One asked me how I could take such risks without a third-party funder? How could one accomplish all the work alone? God forbid if the dictators I exposed in the book had me arrested or killed then who would defend or speak for me? Did I not realize that I could be harmed in silence? But I didn't write the books in ignorance or without fear, but rather in the knowledge that the work of exposing injustice is more important than me.

I felt that someone among the migrants has to speak about the injustice that causes so many to leave our homes and families and loved ones in order to migrate. The story should not be left to privileged, Western writers to condescend to explain—to shape the narrative of—African migration. Like previous narratives on slavery and colonialism that were left to whites to document in the form of charity their African victims, the mass migration narratives of today inevitably will suffer the same fate, if we do not acknowledge the essential role for the victims to speak openly and freely.

For the two years I stayed in Uganda after being forced out of the Middle East, I became a regular at the office of the Anti-trafficking Unit office as well as that of Labor Export at the Ministry of Labor and Social Services. I escorted the parents of missing or murdered workers in the Gulf Arab countries to see how these offices would treat them. Sometimes I published their stories with the Thomson Reuters Foundation (TRF) or the Migrant Rights website. On occasion that publicity forced the authorities to take action and help the victims. After one such story—that of a young woman missing in Saudi Arabia—was published by TRF, authorities in Saudi Arabia searched for the victim and asked her employer, who had confiscated her passport and telephone for more than a year, to let her go back to Uganda. When the young woman arrived in Uganda she hadn't been paid for a year but she was free and her family was deeply grateful.

This work put me in conflict with Ugandan companies that were recruiting workers to go to Saudi Arabia, as they saw me as a threat to their business. Representatives of these companies denounced me on local radio stations as a selfish person who had made a "lot of money" as a journalist in Dubai and was trying to kick down the ladder. Sometimes I was invited to debate the issue with these representatives, and I tried to dismantle some of the accusations against me. I said in response to my being selfish that I had not gone to Dubai through a recruitment company that had no part in my success as a journalist. I explained that the people the companies took to Dubai to work as housemaids or security guards included those with college degrees and some with master's degrees. Many of those had been led to believe that the companies would find them professional jobs commensurate with their education and training. I accused them of defending their work in the same way that middlemen had defended slavery in Africa: because of the commission they received from white slave traders. On that radio program, it seemed like the recruiting spokesperson lost the debate, as callers, one by one, condemned them for their misinformation and for the exploitation of desperate Ugandans.

However, on another day, I lost. I was invited to a local television station to participate in a debate with a representative from the Ministry of Labor and a manager from an overseas recruiting company. As we introduced ourselves in the lobby of the television station, the manager was astonished to learn I was the Yasin Kakande he had heard about, and there was no way he was going on the same platform—let alone a live television show with me. He called the station's management and a woman from management showed up. She asked for Yasin Kakande, led me outside the building saying that my invitation was a mistake and that the station would pay for my travel; I refused. The journalist who was supposed to host us called me later to apologize, explaining that the recruitment companies had an advertising contract with the station and the management prioritized the interests of the station.

My family and friends often asked me why I continued working in a way that risked my family's livelihood. But whenever a parent of a worker stranded in Dubai called, it was hard to say no. I felt their pain and it was only natural that I would want to help. In every generation there are those who accommodate oppression and those who revolt against it. The former are always the majority, but the latter can leave a legacy that stands up to history's relentless scrutiny.

Once I called a contact in the Dubai Police to help in the search for the niece of a school friend of mine, Sharif Migadde, who was an attorney. He told me that the family had last heard from her one morning when she called them and complained that her sponsor had beaten her and that she was going to police to report it and then ask the police to return her to Uganda. When I called my contact at the Dubai Police, she was surprised to receive a call from Qatar, where I had relocated to work in a newspaper and furious that I was calling her, but she promised to investigate the case and try to find the missing young woman. She asked me not to call her again regarding other cases because she feared that she would be punished for associating with me, now that I was labeled a problematic activist in Dubai. A week later the young woman returned to Uganda and her family called to thank me. They told me that when she reported the case to police, the police summoned her sponsor who accused her at the police station of stealing 20,000 *dirham* in cash as well as gold bracelets. The case changed from being an abused housemaid to theft and prosecutors threatened the young woman to produce what she stole or she would rot in prison. This incident taught me that there were many people working for despotic governments who were willing to help, but they like everyone else were careful not to antagonize those in power for fear of the consequences. Help had to come from the system, not from individual people of good will. It is the only way that abused migrants will find justice.

Chapter 35: Humility and Conscience:
A Voice Gains Strength

"If we don't believe in free expression for the people we despise, we don't believe in it at all." Noam Chomsky

During a writer's workshop in Boston I had the opportunity to meet a popular black writer and after exchanging introductions he told me he was fascinated by my work. I asked him why he did not write similar pieces or books on similar topics. After all, he was more qualified and credible than me and his work would get more attention than mine, given his profile. He offered me two reasons. Firstly, there would be no advances or grants available for the subject matter. He told me he respected me for researching and writing these books without any funding. Secondly, he told me that even with his reputation and popularity, if he took on the kind of work I was doing it would never be well disseminated, because it involves criticizing the owners and managers of the very channels through which it would need to travel. He told me that any knowledge, however relevant it is, if it is not well disseminated it is useless.

My work is not well disseminated but in the bubble I live in I don't consider it useless. I always do my best to try and disseminate it but I also understand the many hurdles to achieving the level of distribution that is needed in order to have an impact. In the words of Hemingway's *For Whom the Bell Tolls*: "defending the dignity of others is never a lost cause whether you succeed or not." This work has not yet made the difference to the world that I hoped that it would but in the Gulf Arab region at least it has illuminated the plight of migrant workers to the extent that various governments are trying to reform some of their policies. On the one hand those governments have been keen to arrest activists, ban critical books from shelves, and sack and deport their critics, on the other they have definitely read my work and considered some of my recommendations. There have been pressures created by my works, even if some view it as being poorly disseminated. There have been very hard tradeoffs but sacrifices also have always been part of any struggle; this work is important even in its small outreach.

While still in Uganda I applied for the TED Fellowship Program, as my interest was more in giving a TED Talk that would put some spotlight on my activism work for the increasing numbers of African migrants being trapped, exploited, abused, and even murdered in the Gulf Arab countries. Unfortunately, by the time the TED Fellows team offered me a fellowship and a chance to give the talk I had migrated to the U.S. to apply for asylum, the only route I could see to stay in the country legally. The rules for asylum seekers are strict and the process is excruciatingly slow. If you leave before it is granted, then the application is null and void and you will never be able to come back to the U.S.

My TED Fellowship required me to travel to Arusha in Tanzania to give my talk. After being granted the fellowship I knew I was facing a dilemma. I didn't rush to let the TED Team know I was likely to be restricted in my ability to travel for fear that the opportunity could be withdrawn immediately. Instead I hired an immigration lawyer to help expedite my case and help me to obtain the necessary travel documents. The lawyer explained to me that the timing was not in my favor and though he could help expedite the asylum interview with immigration officials he strongly advised against seeking a travel document to leave the U.S. for any purpose whatsoever before my asylum status was decided. For about a month, I was torn between working my "3 D's" immigration jobs, preparing my asylum papers with the lawyer to help expedite the process, and writing the TED Talk that I realized I might never deliver.

Finally, I felt I had to tell the TED team about the travel restrictions. They offered me the counsel of one of their immigration lawyers who also advised me against seeking a travel permit. The team promised to put me back on the roster of future TED Talks, once my asylum process was concluded, and in December 2017 my name appeared again on another list for the April 2018 TED Talks. I panicked and tried to fast track everything to be able to travel to Vancouver and speak. I had completed my asylum interview in September of 2017 and expected a decision any time soon but it had yet to arrive and around the end of January 2018 I had to ask the TED Team to allow me to give my talk virtually.

I had changed the theme of my talk from advocating for rights of migrants in the Middle East to "Why Africans were migrating to Europe, the Middle East and the USA." I was already attending preparatory sessions with the TED team that involved how to deliver an effective talk and then promote it. The hardest part was cutting the talk to four minutes. Whenever we met online, they would time me as I read the draft and advised me to cut. It was evident the team liked both thematic talks that I had proposed.

Finally, they offered to record the talk in their offices in New York, a month before the conference was scheduled to be aired in Vancouver. I watched it on my laptop livestream during the conference. I noticed that more cuts had been made in the edits of the video. The overall video, even as concise and tight as it was, amplified the message I wanted to articulate. However, I also recognized that with such a few minutes, where every word counts for impact, I still believed that I did not have enough time to explain the extent of how African countries have been exploited to the extent that they cannot achieve economic independence. Nonetheless, I was excited and I deeply appreciated the TED Talks team for its efforts and for recognizing the significance, breadth and depth of this issue of why African migrants search so desperately for their own economic reward and for justice. The TED Talk was a good start. Hopefully, this book will ignite and expand the serious discussions needed as a prelude to changing our collective mindset regarding how the continent can achieve economic independence.

Chapter 36: My Struggle for Asylum

"Give me your tired and your poor who can stand on their own two feet and who will not become a public charge." Ken Cuccinelli

There is no question that the times of the Trump Administration is the worst imaginable time for new immigrants. Determined to stifle and paralyze asylum the process, Trump has sought to implement his signature policies of building a wall along the country's southern border and reducing the number of asylum applications from migrants and refugees to an unprecedented low. At the end of 2018, he stubbornly refused to compromise, in effect shutting many key sectors of the Federal Government. While budget and policy battles have led to shutdowns in the past, they have often been resolved within a day or two. But this shutdown extended well into January, with federal employees working without pay and the effects beginning to take a toll on an otherwise healthy economy.

The idea of President Trump's wall has generated a flurry of debate and analysis concerning the significance of walls and boundaries in the American cultural psyche.

While some reporters have covered the story of contemporary immigration responsibly, many others have covered the arrival of migrants within the metaphorical frame of a dangerous hurricane ready to make landfall—a disconcerting parallel to how European media chronicled the sea journeys of African migrants seeking to come to their continent for a new life. Reading through the President's tweets, one could be forgiven for believing that the constituents of the infamous migrant caravan had walked 2,000 miles carrying drugs in their pockets to sell to Americans.

Many Americans seem frustrated if not exasperated by the President's callous tone and gross stereotyping, and they ask how this could be happening in a country established upon the premise of fairness and justice for all. They are shocked by the scenes of migrant children torn from their parents and kept in camps where some succumb to treatable illnesses because they are not given proper medical attention. Problems like dehydration have been observed but often these images of illness and death are broadcast not to sway minds for policy particularly as much as to signal that for those who desire to come to the U.S. should reconsider. Many Americans wonder how things got this bad and how much worse they will get before sanity and humanity return to politics. But a significant number of others agree with the President and look to justify the ways in which migrants are treated partly by dehumanizing them. It is worth noting that the migrant crisis and the American response to it is entirely consistent with a history of racist violence: towards the indigenous population, towards slaves and towards immigrants.

Why people—mostly women and children—take this dangerous and desperate journey is not a question that is examined in detail in the mainstream media. Some journalists sometimes forget that they are tasked with writing the rough draft of history, many are simply overwhelmed by the number of beats they are asked to cover, and few media outlets have journalists dedicated to covering immigration. Perhaps, in an industry with scarce resources the decision has been taken at an editorial level to let future generations figure out the underlying reasons for the migrant crisis.

Likewise, the global markets and economy also affect the nature and tone of such coverage. If the media focused more extensively on the economic and structural reasons that have led to widespread migration, that visibility might reverberate with impacts compromising the stability of domestic trading markets in agricultural products (e.g., bananas, tropical fruits, and coffee) and natural resources and minerals from the countries in question. In these affected countries, the demand for such products has consolidated the enormous concentration of land in the hands of a few oligarchic families, thereby leaving the largest population share of these countries with no economic prospects while the U.S. keeps a military presence to maintain that arrangement on behalf of a country's government that is beholden to the oligarchic status quo.[180]

Similarly, there has been a casual attitude and lack of urgency with regard to innocent Latinos—again, mostly children and women—who are fleeing from drug-related violence in their countries where cartels wield substantial power, politically and economically. In strange ways, the U.S. government also wants to maintain a peculiar status quo to sustain its drug enforcement industry and infrastructure. The drug wars have made money for many, especially those in the private prison industry.

Some might wonder why I decided to apply for asylum during this period of hostility towards immigrants, but my attorney was convinced that my journey would be easier than most. After all, much of the evidence I presented had been published and was available online. I compiled that material and within a few weeks my attorney assured me that I was prepared for the interview. We sought to expedite the process, hoping for a three-week turnaround, as opposed to the possible years it might take. Several months after the interview and with no decision from the immigration authorities in sight, reality hit home and we acknowledged how wrong we had been to think both that we could rush the process and that my case would be a straightforward one. In truth there were no easy asylum cases in the U.S. Normally, the asylum process for a candidate like me would have been resolved within a few months but now I was facing years in limbo.

The delay in the process affected the disabled woman I was working for as a PCA as well. Almost every day she would ask me if the immigration officials had responded to my asylum interview and the answer was always no. I had been working for her for almost a year and we had formed a strong bond. She was not only worried about losing a worker who could lift her up and put her in the wheelchair—a freedom she cherished—but also worried that the Government might soon block all asylum applications and there would be no one to help her. She mentioned that she could help get me a Green Card on the understanding that I wouldn't leave her after obtaining it. However, I was not certain I was willing to be her caregiver for the rest of my life.

My position changed after ten months of waiting for a decision. I started seriously considering her proposal and asked her what she could do for me. She told me to contact my lawyer for an update, as she believed he was handling my case badly. But I felt that these problems were not particular to me or to my lawyer, given the political climate. Nonetheless, I wrote an email to the lawyer who agreed to check with immigration officials but explained that delays of this length had become common and the wait could be up to a year. The immigration officials replied that my case was still under investigation and that they would let us know as soon as possible.

After a year without a decision I became worried. What troubled me most was the fact that I wasn't allowed to travel outside the U.S. I had missed opportunities to attend conferences where I was a speaker, including TED Global and Q Berlin. Moreover, I felt imprisoned and I was missing my family terribly. My daughter Hadija with whom I share a birthday told me on the occasion of her sixth birthday that she was furious this was the second birthday she would not be celebrating with me. She said to me carefully, as only a child can explain a concept that's difficult for adults to understand, that she wanted me at home so we could sing birthday greetings to one another like we used to. The truth was my children were missing me as much as I missed them. It looked increasingly likely that they were going to miss me for many more years to come. There was no chance that I would be going to Uganda anytime soon or that I would be allowed to bring my family to the U.S.

My PCA employer suggested that she could contact Massachusetts U.S. Senator Edward J. Markey on my behalf and that he would be able to get me a Green Card. The process required a senator to initiate a private bill on my behalf. Such an option is extremely rare. Fewer than 100 immigrants receive such consideration annually. I told her that there was no chance, but she insisted that there was no harm in trying. She called Markey's office and I signed papers authorizing the Senator to make an inquiry regarding my case. After the inquiry, the immigration officers called my lawyer and scheduled a second interview with me. I remained in contact with the senator's staff and believed their actions had re-animated my dormant asylum file. The lawyer called me into her office to prepare for the interview. My employer worked concurrently, asking her friends and contacts how best she might help. She even offered to attend the interview, but I knew that that would not be allowed. In the end she settled for convincing the mayor to write a testimonial about the quality of my work in caring for her.

My lawyer said that while she appreciated my employer's endeavors, she would not be presenting the testimonial or my employer's recommendation because it was irrelevant: being a good caregiver was not among the eligibility requirements for asylum. But she photocopied them and suggested that we kept the copies in case I was referred to an immigration court, where these documents could be presented meaningfully. By way of preparation she simply wanted me to be answer in a way that was consistent with the first iteration. After all, we had a strong case.

The second interview was much shorter than the first, lasting only 20 minutes. My lawyer asked when the immigration officer expected a response and he promised it would come within three months. However, that time elapsed and the decision had not yet arrived. I was surprised. I could understand the Administration's aggressive policy of limiting the number of refugees, but I couldn't understand why even a rejection was not forthcoming.

My employer was equally unsettled with the delay. The first question when I arrived: "Did they write to you?" She had wrongly assumed that by involving her Senator a decision would be made quickly. She called the Senator's office almost every week to ask them to intervene but as one of the senator's staff had told me there were limits on their powers of intervention. The subject of my immigration status was always on her lips and she told her friends how she worried that losing me would mean that she would be thrown into a nursing home.

When I had started working for her, she had just spent two months at a rehabilitation center (similar to a nursing home) and she feared returning to that environment. She would tell her friends in my presence that she was fighting my battle so that they would not have to consider putting her in a nursing home. Her friends would caution her, explaining that there were no guarantees: there was every chance that I would leave as soon as I got a Green Card and that, in fact, she would *have* to go to a nursing home. She would reply: "if he disappears after my helping him to get a green card then that would be World War III." These conversations were often carried out in my presence and that embarrassed me, but my pleas for her to stop fell on deaf ears. Her friends always wanted updates and once she started, she would never stop. Her church started including my name on their weekly newsletters as someone everyone should pray for to get a Green Card.

Her doctor wrote a letter of support that I could present to immigration court if that's how it ended up. It was clear that she had started preparing for the court referrals. One of her friends suggested that my being a Muslim was the cause of my delays, but I was not from any of the six Muslim countries which President Trump had elected for a travel ban (that was later replaced with stricter vetting). It is true that the general acceptance rate of Muslim asylum applications had gone down from 40,000 in 2016 to only 8,000 in 2018, a cut of 80 percent but I didn't believe that my religion was slowing the process.[181] The delay was simply an indication of the contradiction inherent in the U.S. immigration policy: politicians want migrants to "get legal" but then prevent them from so doing.

Little wonder then that many immigrants see phony marriage as the only viable route. And no surprise that the cost of such a marriage has shot up from $10,000 during President Obama's Administration to almost $30,000 in the Trump Era. But, as mentioned above, that route is also fraught with challenges including the risk of abuse and the ordeal of scrutiny. Women are especially vulnerable.

A Ugandan co-worker at a group home for people with developmental disabilities told me how her arranged marriage turned sour. It involved a Haitian man and cost $25,000, $10,000 of which she paid in cash to start the process, with the balance to be paid in monthly installments. The man proposed they rent a house so as to look more convincing. After a few days the man demanded sex and, because she owed him a lot of money, she consented. When she became pregnant he demanded that she get an abortion but she refused, hoping the baby would be good evidence to immigration officers. Unfortunately, a few months after they had the baby the man had and successfully brought a young bride from Haiti. My colleague was looking for solidarity as well advice. One colleague advised her to go back to her immigration lawyer and continue pursuing her asylum process.

Achieving the American Dream through fake marriage is an expensive exercise that costs not only a lot of money but also a person's dignity. Migrants sell everything they have in order to get to the U.S., only to realize that will have to make more sacrifices; to work day and night for years to pay to have the opportunity for a legal stay in this country. But none of that will stop them from coming.

As I close this book, I want to mention that the problem is not actually immigration, as the politicians and corporate moguls of the West have brainwashed every Western citizen into believing through their corporatized media. President Trump has himself pointed out that he would be glad to welcome migrants from Norway. The problem is largely individualism, as Europeans and their American cousins become more protective of the global wealth that has for centuries been collected across all the continents on the planet and has accumulated in their countries.

It is not possible for the West to open its borders and welcome everyone from poor, persistently underdeveloped countries, but it is possible for the West to control the corporate plunder of the wealth and natural resources of those countries. Most people would be reluctant to become migrants if only their economies could offer them a reasonable standard of living, but the economies of the undeveloped world are being exploited by the West to the point of being dysfunctional. Left to their own devices they would survive and maybe even thrive. As the West calls for the migrants to stop coming so the migrants shout back that the West should stop the pillage and leave us with what is ours so we can live decently.

The only problem is that our screams are muted or ignored. But as long as poor economies are plundered by richer (with the help of local despots) migrants will come. The nature of human beings everywhere is to struggle to survive and live decently at all costs. There are no restrictions that could stop this. The solution will be complex and no one can claim a monopoly of the right ideas, but what is missing from the debate is honesty. Solutions that are nationalist such as "America First" are no longer viable. We can no longer thrive by trampling on other people. At some point, the migration crisis will become an existential one for human civilization. The solution to it should be human based on the principle that everyone—regardless of their country of origin—should be treated fairly. It seems simple but hitherto has proved politically elusive, but it remains possible.

To my African and Latin American brothers now is the time to understand that fleeing our homes to the USA or Europe is not sustainable. We have to start looking for solutions in our own countries. This starts with rethinking the fake independence our countries are so proud of.

At the time of writing, like millions of others, I am still waiting for a decision.

ENDNOTES

1   See http://www.cnn.com/videos/world/2017/11/13/libya-migrant-slave-victory-lon-orig-md-ejk.cnn.

2   See https://www.theguardian.com/world/2017/nov/28/libya-slave-trade-cnn-report-trump-fake-news.

3   Mannix, Daniel *"Black Cargoes." The Viking Press 1962.*

4   Hochschild, Adam 'King Leopold's Ghost: A Story of Greed, Terror, and Heroism in Colonial Africa' 1999 Houghton Mifflin Company, New York.

5   See   http://ngm.nationalgeographic.com/ngm/data/2001/10/01/html/ft_20011001.6.html.

6   Miller, Joseph. "West Central Africa." The Way of Death. University of Wisconsin. 1988.

7   Adam Hochschild, *Bury the Chains, The British Struggle to Abolish Slavery* (2005).

8   Ibid.

9   http://www.bbc.co.uk/history/british/empire_seapower/barbados_01.shtml.

10   Ibid.

11   Herman Merivale, Lectures on colonization and colonies, Longman and Roberts, London 1861 (reprinted by Augustus Kelley, New York, 1967).

12   Ana Lucia Araujo. *African Heritage and Memories of Slavery in Brazil and the South Atlantic World,* Cambria Press February 2015.

13   Morgan, E. S. (1975, 2003). *American Slavery, American Freedom: The Ordeal of Colonial Virginia.* WW Norton & Company. 129.

14   Frantz Fanon, "The Wretched of The Earth" Grove Press New York 2004.

15   Adam Hochschild, *Bury the Chains, The British Struggle to Abolish Slavery* (2005).

16   Qutb Muhammad, Islam The Misunderstood Religion, Kanz Publications 1980.

17   Rhoden William, Forty Million Dollar Slaves: The Rise, Fall and Redemption of the Black Athlete, 2006, New York.

18   Sims-Alvarado, FalechiondroKarcheik. "The African-American Emigration Movement in Georgia during Reconstruction." (2011).

19   Brockey, Liam Matthew (2008). Portuguese Colonial Cities in the Early Modern World. Ashgate Publishing, Ltd.

20   Bolt, J.; van Zanden, J.L. (2014). "Maddison Project Database, version 2013" It can be retrieved on this link; https://www.rug.nl/ggdc/historicaldevelopment/maddison/data/mpd_2013-01.xlsx.

21   See http://memory.loc.gov/cgi-bin/ampage?collId=llsl&fileName=002/llsl002.db&recNum=0463.

22   Sanchez Manning (24 February 2013). "Britain's colonial shame: Slave-owners given huge payouts after" *See https://www.independent.co.uk/news/uk/home-news/britains-colonial-shame-slave-owners-given-huge-payouts-after-abolition-8508358.html.*

23   Qutb Muhammad, Islam The Misunderstood Religion, Kanz Publications 1980.

24   See http://www.catholicity.com/commentary/curp/05378.html.

25   Adam Hochschild, *Bury the Chains, The British Struggle to Abolish Slavery* (2005).

26   Ibn Khaldun, Franz Rosenthal and N.J Dawood, The Muqaddimah: An Introduction to history, Bolligen Series, Princeton University Press 1969.

27   Qutb Muhammad, Islam The Misunderstood Religion, Kanz Publications 1980.

28   *BBC News.* 9 August 2007.

29   See http://www.bbc.co.uk/worldservice/specials/1458_abolition/page4.shtml.

30   The Middle East Quarterly *December 1999.*

31   See http://www.telegraph.co.uk/news/worldnews/africaandindianocean/sudan/3795607/Darfur-civilians-seized-as-slaves-by-Sudan-military.html.

32   El-Tom, Abdullahi. "Darfur People: Too Black for the Arab-Islamic Project of Sudan, Part I." *Irish Journal of anthropology*9.1 (2006): 5–11.

33   Ibid.

34   Ibid.

35   Burawoy, Michael. "The functions and reproduction of migrant labor: comparative material from Southern Africa and the United States." *American journal of Sociology* 81.5 (1976): 1050–1087.

36   Ibid.

37   Ibid.

38   Claudio, Luz. "Waste couture: Environmental impact of the clothing industry." *Environmental health perspectives* 115.9 (2007): A449.

39   Ibid.

40   *Walter Rodney. How Europe Underdeveloped Africa.* Howard University Press; Revised edition 1981.

41   *Freedman, Estelle. No Turning Back: The History of Feminism and The Future of Women.2002. Random House Publishing.*

42   Frantz Fanon, "The Wretched of The Earth" Grove Press New York 2004.

43   Hochschild, Adam 'King Leopold's Ghost; A story of Greed, Terror, and Herroism in Colonial Africa' 1998 Houghton Mifflin Company, New York.

44   Hochschild, Adam. *King Leopold's Ghost: A Story of Greed, Terror, and Heroism in Colonial Africa.* Houghton Mifflin Harcourt, 1999.

45   Ibid.

46   Ibid.

47   Sundaram ,Anjan.*Stringer; A reporters journey in the Congo*, New York 2014.

48   *Maylam, Paul (2005). The Cult of Rhodes: Remembering an Imperialist in Africa. New Africa Books.*

49   Frantz Fanon, "The Wretched of The Earth" Grove Press New York 2004.

50   Mkandawire, Thandika. "The terrible toll of post-colonial 'rebel movements' in Africa: towards an explanation of the violence against the peasantry." *The Journal of Modern African Studies*40.2 (2002): 181–215.

51   See https://www.bloomberg.com/news/articles/2014-04-17/african-monetary-union-stirs-criticism-of-france.

52   See http://www.bbc.com/news/world-africa-41094094.

53   See   https://twitter.com/UKinKenya/status/984320658099396608.

54   Hochschild, Adam 'King Leopold's Ghost; A story of Greed, Terror, and Herroism in Colonial Africa' 1998. Houghton Mifflin Company, New York.

55   Ibid.

56   Tharoor, Ishaan (20 October 2011). "Mobutu SeseSeko". *Top 15 Toppled Dictators*. Time Magazine.

57   Kuperman, Alan J. *How the media missed the Rwanda genocide.* na, 2000.

58   Ibid.

59   See https://www.foreignpolicyjournal.com/2018/01/10/shadow-armies-the-unseen-but-real-us-war-in-africa/.

60   See https://dod.defense.gov/portals/1/features/2018/0418_niger/img/Oct-2017-Niger-Ambush-Summary-of-Investigation.pdf.

61   See http://allafrica.com/stories/201702160232.html.

62   Ibid.

63   See https://www.bbc.com/news/world-asia-18901656.

64   French Howard, China's second continent: How a million migrants are building a new Empire in Africa, 2014.

65   See https://www.news24.com/Africa/News/african-union-head-calls-china-spying-report-lies-20180208.

66   See   https://www.whitehouse.gov/briefings-statements/re-marks-president-trump-working-lunch-african-leaders/.

67   See http://africanarguments.org/2017/02/01/trumps-africa-pol-icy-unclear-and-uncertain/.

68   See https://www.nytimes.com/2018/03/20/world/europe/nico-las-sarkozy-custody.html.

69   See https://www.mediapart.fr/en/journal/international/280412/gaddafi-funding-sarkozy-election-campaign-proof.

70   See   http://www.lemonde.fr/societe/article/2011/09/11/domi-nique-de-villepin-et-jacques-chirac-mis-en-cause-dans-des-operations-de-financement-occulte_1570662_3224.html.

71   See http://www.bbc.com/news/world-europe-43879251.

72   See   https://pmepmimagazine.info/conseil-de-ministre-sene-gal-sest-tenu-france-lautorite-ministres-francais/.

73   See http://www.faridanabourema.org/2018/01/making-togo-rel-evant.html.

74   See   https://www.npr.org/2017/07/21/538608486/rwanda-works-to-ban-sale-of-second-hand-clothes-within-2-years.

75   See   https://www.npr.org/2017/07/21/538608486/rwanda-works-to-ban-sale-of-second-hand-clothes-within-2-years.

76   See   https://www.nytimes.com/2017/10/12/world/africa/east-africa-rwanda-used-clothing.html.

77   See   https://www.theguardian.com/global-development/2017/may/24/world-is-plundering-africa-wealth-billions-of-dollars-a-year.

78   See http://www.gfintegrity.org/press-release/new-report-on-un-recorded-capital-flight-finds-developing-countries-are-net-creditors-to-the-rest-of-the-world/.

79   See   https://twitter.com/CelestinMonga/sta-tus/1015572447251369984.

80   See   https://www.ladepeche.fr/article/2012/03/10/1308713-pieds-noirs-ceux-qui-ont-choisi-de-rester.html.

81   Dennis D. Cordell, African Population and Capitalism: Historical Perspectives, University of Wisconsin Press; 2nd ed. edition 1994.

82   Mau, Steffen, et al. "The global mobility divide: How visa policies have evolved over time." *Journal of Ethnic and Migration Studies* 41.8 (2015): 1192–1213.

83   Andreas, Peter, and Timothy Snyder, eds. 2000. *The Wall around the West: State Borders and Immigration Controls in North America and Europe.* Lanham: Rowman& Littlefield.

84   Mau, Steffen, et al.

85   Yoweri Kaguta Museveni, Sowing The Mustard Seed; The struggle for Freedom and Democracy in Uganda, Revised edition 2007, Moran Publishers, Kampala Uganda.

86   Yoweri Kaguta Museveni, Sowing The Mustard Seed; The struggle for Freedom and Democracy in Uganda, Revised edition 2007, Moran Publishers, Kampala Uganda.

87   Ibid.

88   See https://www.youtube.com/watch?v=dBlKq0fATeU.

89   *Ofcansky, Thomas P., (1999). Uganda: Tarnished pearl of Africa. Boulder, Colo.: Westview Press.*

90   See http://www.bbc.com/news/world-africa-12421747.

91   See https://truthout.org/articles/us-funding-of-ugandan-military-aids-in-citizens-repression/.

92   See http://www.nytimes.com/1994/03/26/world/last-us-troops-leave-somalia-what-began-mission-mercy-closes-with-little.html?pagewanted=1.

93   See http://www.monitor.co.ug/News/National/Museveni-blames-Juba-war-on-sectarianism-/688334-2307298-3rgk2u/index.html.

94   Mahmood Mamdani (2002) *When Victims Become Killers: Colonialism, Nativism, and the Genocide in Rwanda*, Princeton University Press.

95   Himbara, D. (2017, December 26). Kagame-American Romance Is Over – How Trump Administration's 2018 Budget Will Sharply Reduce Aid To... Retrieved from https://medium.com/@david.himbara_27884/kagame-american-romance-is-over-how-trump-administrations-2018-budget-will-sharply-reduce-aid-to-86bf20d0e857.

96   Ibid.

97   See "The Looting of Congo." 2001 May 29. The New York Times. https://www.nytimes.com/2001/05/29/opinion/the-looting-of-congo.html.

98   Ibid.

99   See https://www.law.cornell.edu/uscode/text/22/8422.

100   See https://www.csmonitor.com/World/Africa/Africa-Monitor/2014/0203/Why-is-Uganda-s-Army-in-South-Sudan.

101   See http://africanarguments.org/2014/03/04/is-yoweri-museveni-still-the-wests-man-in-africa-by-angelo-izama/.

102   See https://foreignpolicy.com/2016/02/18/is-the-us-military-propping-up-ugandas-elected-autocrat-museveni-elections/.

103   Ibid.

104   Smith, David. February 22, 2014. "Uganda's Yoweri Museveni puts anti-gay legislation on hold." *The Guardian*. https://www.theguardian.com/world/2014/feb/23/uganda-museveni-anti-gay-bill-hold.

105   See http://www.aljazeera.com/news/2018/01/yoweri-museveni-loves-trump-frankness-africans-180124060449997.html.

106   See http://africanarguments.org/2017/04/10/uganda-stella-nyanzi-charged-calling-president-museveni-pair-buttocks/.

107   https://twitter.com/PaulWilliamsMP/status/986646857836310533.

108   Ogbimi, F. E. "Structural Adjustment is the Wrong Policy." *African Technology Forum*. Vol. 8, No. 1. http://web.mit.edu/africantech/www/articles/PlanningAdjust.htm.

109   See https://www.voanews.com/a/us-arrests-chinese-national-former-foreign-minister-of-senegal-in-bibery-scheme/4127399.html.

110   Goldstein, Matthew. September 15, 2018. "U.S. drops charges against ex-Senegal official in Chinese energy bribery case." *The New York Times*. https://www.nytimes.com/2018/09/15/business/cheikh-gadio-china-bribery-case.html.

111   See https://offshoreleaks.icij.org/stories/sam-kahamba-kutesa.

112   Burgis, Tom, The Looting Machine: War Lords, Oligarchs,Corporations, smugglers, and the theft of Africa's wealth 2015, New York.

113   See https://www.theguardian.com/commentisfree/2018/aug/25/uganda-torture-bobi-wine-human-rights-museveni-magnitsky-act.

114   See https://www.observer.ug/news/headlines/58601-museveni-i-can-do-away-with-parliament.

115   See http://observer.ug/viewpoint/56434-paying-the-price-for-the-life-presidency.html.

116   See https://www.publicintegrity.org/2015/12/17/19051/us-lobbying-pr-firms-give-human-rights-abusers-friendly-face.

117   Crabtree, Justina. "Here's how Cambridge Analytica played a dominant role in Kenya's chaotic 2017 elections." March 23, 2018. *CNBC*. https://www.cnbc.com/2018/03/23/cambridge-analytica-and-its-role-in-kenya-2017-elections.html.

118   See http://www.thelondoneveningpost.com/exclusive-museveni-ordered-murder-of-kayiira-kazini-and-many-others/.

119   See http://eagle.co.ug/2015/09/15/uganda-and-its-unexplained-deaths.html.

120   See https://www.hrw.org/news/2018/09/11/history-violence-repeat-uganda.

121   Ibid.

122   See https://www.economist.com/middle-east-and-africa/2017/12/19/one-year-after-a-massacre-in-uganda-a-king-faces-trial

123   Balikuddembe, J. K., Ardalan, A., Khorasani-Zavareh, D., Nejati, A., &Munanura, K. S. (2017). Road traffic incidents in Uganda: a systematic

review of a five-year trend. *Journal of injury and violence research*, *9*(1), 17.

124   See   http://www.independent.co.uk/news/world/africa/ ugandas-masaka-kampala-highway-is-this-the-worlds-most-dangerous-road-a7331391.html.

125   Ibid.

126   Ibid.

127   See   https://twitter.com/KagutaMuseveni/status/958951105878220800.

128   Mayiga Charles Peter, Uganda: 7 Key Transformational ideas, Prime Time Communications Kampala Uganda 2016.

129   Walk the Talk: A call to action to restore coffee farmers livelihood. 2002. Oxfam.

130   Nkandu, Joseph. May 31, 2018. "Why Coffee Farmers are Poor – And How an Innovative Ownership Model Can Help." Next Billion: An Initiative of the William Davidson Institute at The University of Michigan. https://nextbillion.net/why-coffee-farmers-are-poor-and-how-an-innovative-ownership-model-can-help/.

131   See https://www.newvision.co.ug/new_vision/news/1309963/ challenges-agriculture-oil-economy.

132   See http://news.trust.org/item/20160922085317-710ha.

133   See http://news.trust.org/item/20160921130225-mrjja.

134   Mittal, A. April 2015. WeSay The Land Is Not Yours:Breakingthe-SilenceagainstForced DisplacementinEthiopia. The Oakland Institute. http://www. oaklandinstitute.org/sites/oaklandinstitute.org/files/Breaking%20the%20 Silence.pdf.

135   See http://news.bbc.co.uk/2/hi/africa/7952628.stm.

136   See https://opinion.premiumtimesng.com/2018/09/12/africa-china-romance-and-crocodile-tears-from-the-west-by-simbo-olorunfemi/.

137   See Financial Times January 9 2009 "US investor buys Sudanese warlord's land".

138   See *Financial Times* January 9 2009 "US investor buys Sudanese warlord's land".

139   https://www.vice.com/en_us/article/znw83a/cowboy-capitalists-0000296-v21n4.

140   Ibid.

141   http://rightsandresources.org/wp-content/uploads/FactSheet_ WhoOwnstheWorldsLand_web2.pdf.

142   https://www.washingtonpost.com/business/why-land-seizure-is-back-in-news-in-south-africa/2018/08/01/7a0712f8-9585-11e8-818b-e9b7348cd87d_story.html?utm_term=.58017d48d02a.

143   Walter Rodney, 1981. *How Europe Under Developed Africa*. Howard University Press.

144   See https://www.migrant-rights.org/2017/10/35-ugandans-committed-suicide-in-the-uae-this-year/.

145   Is South Africa home to more than a million asylum seekers? (February 2, 2018). Retrieved from https://africacheck.org/reports/south-africa-home-million-refugees-numbers-dont-add/.

146   Ibid.

147   Crush, J., Tawodzera, G., Chikanda, A., Ramachandran, S., &Tevera, D. S. (2018). Migrants in Countries in Crisis: South Africa Case Study: The Double Crisis—Mass Migration From Zimbabwe And Xenophobic Violence in South Africa.

148   Ibid.

149   Ibid.

150   Ibid.

151   See www.un.org/en/ development/desa/population/migration/data/estimates2/ estimates15.shtml.

152   See http://www.pewglobal.org/2018/03/22/at-least-a-million-sub-saharan-africans-moved-to-europe-since-2010.

153   Lind, D. (2018). Birthright citizenship explained. Vox.com. https://www.vox.com/2018/7/23/17595754/birthright-citizenship-trump-14th-amendment-executive-order.

154   See https://www.nytimes.com/2018/01/11/us/politics/trump-shithole-countries.html.

155   See https://au.int/en/pressreleases/20180112/african-union-mission-washington-dc-reacts-president-trumps-shithole.

156   See https://www.washingtonpost.com/news/post-nation/wp/2018/06/16/america-is-better-than-this-what-a-doctor-saw-in-a-texas-shelter-for-migrant-children/?utm_term=.33e6d64233fe.

157   Lopez, M. H., Gonzalez-Barrera, A., and Krogstad, J. M. (October 22, 2018). More Latinos have serious concerns about their place in America under Trump. Pew Research Center. http://www.pewhispanic.org/2018/10/25/more-latinos-have-serious-concerns-about-their-place-in-america-under-trump/.

158   See https://www.usatoday.com/story/news/world/2018/02/23/america-no-longer-nation-immigrants-uscis-says/366207002/.

159   See https://www.nytimes.com/2018/01/12/world/europe/trump-immigration-outrage.html.

160   Silver, L. (October 22, 2018). Immigration concerns fall in Western Europe, but most see need for newcomers to integrate into society. Factank: News in The Numbers. Pew Research. http://www.pewresearch.org/fact-tank/2018/10/22/immigration-concerns-fall-in-western-europe-but-most-see-need-for-newcomers-to-integrate-into-society/.

161   Ibid.

162   Ibid.

163   Borjas J George, Friends or Strangers: The Impact of immigrants on the US Economy, New York 1990.

164   DeSilver, D. (2017, March 16). No U.S. industry employs mostly immigrant workers. Retrieved from http://www.pewresearch.org/fact-tank/2017/03/16/immigrants-dont-make-up-a-majority-of-workers-in-any-u-s-industry/.

165   Passel, J. S. (2017, March 8). Immigration projected to drive potential U.S. labor force growth through 2035. Retrieved from http://www.pewresearch.org/fact-tank/2017/03/08/immigration-projected-to-drive-growth-in-u-s-working-age-population-through-at-least-2035/.

166   See https://60caregiverissues.org/facts-and-trends-issue-10.html.

167   See https://www.migrationpolicy.org/news/raise-act-dramatic-change-family-immigration-less-so-employment-based-system.

168   See https://phinational.org/news/new-data-u-s-home-care-workers-earn-10-49hour-despite-surging-demand/.

169   See https://www.bostonglobe.com/metro/2018/09/16/pipeline-from-africa-recent-immigrants-much-success-paying-back-breaking-work-caring-stories-frail-americans-home-back-home-they-seen/kosI4rn-pckOHnAUDBLfhcO/story.html.

170   Osterman Paul, Who will Care For Us? New York, 2017.

171   See https://www.bostonglobe.com/metro/2018/09/15/stranger-worse-house-frail-seem-elderly-people-scarcely-know-many-aides-they-invite-into-their-homes-leaving-them-vulnerable-theft/XJOMrm-v46Ruu94B2ZbTZgK/story.html?p1=Article_Related_Box_Article.

172   See https://www.ridester.com/how-much-do-uber-drivers-make/.

173   Robinson J Cedric. *Black Marxism; The Making of the Black Radical Tradition*, The University of North Carolina Press 2000.

174   Public Policy Institute of California. (2018, June 18). See https://www.ppic.org/blog/how-changes-in-immigration-affect-californias-workforce/.

175   Onishi, Norimitsu (2017, November 30). A Generation in Japan faces a lonely death. *The New York Times.* https://www.nytimes.com/2017/11/30/world/asia/japan-lonely-deaths-the-end.html.

176   See https://www.washingtonpost.com/news/world/wp/2018/01/24/feature/so-many-japanese-people-die-alone-theres-a-whole-industry-devoted-to-cleaning-up-after-them/?utm_term=.419da8e3c2a6.

177   See http://www.newsweek.com/senior-citizens-japan-are-committing-crimes-because-they-want-go-jail-854842.

178   See https://www.washingtonpost.com/world/asia_pacific/meet-the-youngsters-helping-solve-japans-caregiving-crisis-like-kunio-odaira-72/2017/01/28.

179   See https://asia.nikkei.com/Spotlight/Cover-Story/Famous-for-its-resistance-to-immigration-Japan-opens-its-doors.

180   LaFaber Walter, Innevitable Revolutions: The United States in Central America 1983 New York.

181   See   https://www.cato.org/blog/trump-cut-muslim-refu-gees-91-immigrants-30-visitors-18.

Made in United States
North Haven, CT
17 March 2023

34211143R00146